CAMBRIDGE MONETARY THOUGHT

Cambridge Monetary Thought

Development of Saving–Investment Analysis from Marshall to Keynes

Pascal Bridel
Professor of Economics
University of Lausanne

St. Martin's Press   New York

© Pascal Bridel, 1987

First published in the United States of America in 1987

Printed in Hong Kong

ISBN 0–312–11441–9

Library of Congress Cataloging-in-Publication Data
Bridel, Pascal, 1948–
Cambridge monetary thought.
Revision of thesis (Ph. D.)—University of Cambridge,
1981.
Bibliography: p.
Includes index.
1. Saving and investment.   2. Neoclassical school
of economics.   I. Title.
HB843.B75   1987   332'.0415   86–17792
ISBN 0–312–11441–9

Contents

v

Foreword

The revival of the analytical principles of classical political economy that has gathered pace since the mid-1960s has been based on the firm foundation of a logically coherent theory of value and distribution. It was the failure to provide this foundation which for many years confined the classical approach to being, at best, a repository of useful ideas on growth and technological progress (Smith's discussion of the division of labour and Marx's dissection of the labour process being good examples), or, at worst, identified with simple-minded devotion to the labour theory of value as the 'qualitative' expression of capitalist exploitation – the position to which Hilferding retreated in the face of Böhm-Bawerk's critique of Marx, so depriving the surplus approach of any quantitative significance as a theory of value and distribution. The publication of Piero Sraffa's *Production of Commodities by Means of Commodities* changed all that. Sraffa not only generalised the mathematical solutions to the surplus approach which had been advanced by Dmitriev and Bortkeiwicz, but also presented the analytical *structure* of the surplus approach with stark clarity. Moreover, Sraffa provided a critique of the neo-classical theory of the rate of profit and so of the entire neo-classical explanation of value, distribution and output – hence clearing the ground for the redevelopment of classical theory.

With the analytical core now secure, attention can be turned to the development of other facets of classical and Marxian theory and to the empirical insights which this theory provides. In stark contrast to the neo-classical approach, which reduces all economic activity to a single principle – the competitive resolution of individual attempts to maximise utility subject to the constraints of technology and endowment – classical theory is constructed from a number of analytically separable components. The core of the theory, the surplus approach to value and distribution, takes as data the size and composition of output, the technology in use (the conditions of reproduction) and the real wage (or, in some cases, the rate of profit). These data do not, however, lie outside the realm of economics (as, for example, the neo-classical economists' utility functions do). We need to provide theoretical explanations of their determination. Hence Smith, Ricardo and Marx advanced theories of the real wage and of the level of output (Say's law in the case of Ricardo), and Smith and Marx presented detailed analyses of technological change. Assembled around the core, these theories are the building-blocks of a general theory of the operations of the capitalist economy. There is in all this a clear danger of constructing a disjointed *ad hoc* collage of theories and empirical generalisations. This is avoided by enveloping the entire edifice in a general characterisation of the economic system: the clear specification, that is, of the capitalist mode of production. This serves both to cement the elements of the theory together and to eliminate propositions that do not fit.

Broadly, there are two jobs to be done in developing and extending the classical framework.

First, the classical theory itself must be developed and generalised. All the elements surrounding the core analysis of value and distribution – theories of output and employment, of accumulation, of technology, of the wage, of competition and so on – require reassessment and 'modernisation' in the light both of Sraffa's results and of the many changing facets of the modern capitalist system. This will involve both theoretical development *and* empirical analysis, for one of the important characteristics of classical theorising is the manner in which theory is grounded in the socio-economic data of the system under consideration – the institutional environment is an essential part of the theory.

Second, the rejection of the now discredited neoclassical theory throws open a wide range of problems in international trade, development economics, fiscal and monetary policy and so forth, into which the classical approach can provide new insights. In part these will lead to the refreshing task of debunking the policy prescriptions of orthodox theory which revolve primarily around the fundamental theorem of welfare economics and the supposed 'efficiency' of competitive markets. But there is also a positive job to be done. The reconstruction of economic theory will inevitably precipitate a reinterpretation of economic policy and problems.

Pascal Bridel uses the ideas that have grown out of Sraffa's critique of the neoclassical theory of value and distribution and the subsequent clarification of the relationship between long run and short run to dissect the interdependence of the Marshallian theory of value and distribution and Cambridge monetary theory. The interdependence of the orthodox analysis of value and distribution and its theory of money and output is little noticed, yet it is the key to a clear understanding of the true structure of the theory. Although Pascal Bridel is dealing with the history of economic ideas, the confusions which he exposes are all too present in modern monetary thought.

Trinity College, Cambridge JOHN EATWELL

Preface

This book is a revised version of a Ph.D. thesis written for the University of Cambridge over the period 1977 to 1981. It would be difficult to do credit to all the discussions I have had which have helped me to develop the ideas presented here. However, I should like to mention the names of my supervisors. Dr Richard M. Goodwin (Peterhouse) and Dr James Trevithick (King's College), who gave me aid and advice over these years. Above all, I owe a great debt to both my then fellow research students, Murray Milgate (Harvard University) and Björn Hansson (Lund University). Were it not for the countless weekly meetings of our informal study group, their incisive criticisms and their invaluable help in reading drafts at various stages of my research, this book would never have taken its present form. It goes without saying that all errors and misinterpretations are entirely my own responsibility.

There would not have been any book at all without the generous financial assistance from the Fonds national suisse de la recherche scientifique.

Finally, my gratitude to Claude, and to my daughters Cécile and Claire, extends far beyond the making of this book.

Lausanne   PASCAL BRIDEL

'Disputes about the meanings of Saving and Investment may appear to be arid, but they are in reality of immense importance, because they involve decisions about definitions which determine the whole course upon which theory will subsequently proceed.'

(Hicks, 1942, p. 54)

'the saving–investment problem . . . [is] the likely place to start in looking for the key to macroeconomic instability'.

(Leijonhufvud, 1981, p. 201)

1 Introduction

The primary aim of this book is to provide an analysis and a critical evaluation of the origin and development of the *saving-investment technique of analysis* undertaken by various members of the Cambridge School in the first part of this century. This analysis, which involves analysing the impact of changes in the market-rate of interest on the economy through its effect on the supply of savings and the volume of investment rather than through changes in the money-supply and price-level, is the line of reasoning which ultimately led to Keynes's principle of effective demand in 1936. Thus, on the one hand, the discussion is centred on the progressive refinement, in the realm of monetary theory, of Marshall's basic theory of interest. By concentrating on the role played in the economic theory of that period by the theory of interest as the adjusting mechanism between planned investment and decisions to save it is possible to shed light on some neglected aspects and contributions to this technique of analysis. In particular Hawtrey's income approach (1913), Robertson's 'forced-saving' doctrine (1926) and Keynes's pre-1936 analysis of the speculative demand for money (1930) clearly stand apart as the main original building-blocks of this technique of analysis. On the other hand, it will also be possible to put in a slightly new perspective Keynes's insights into the pathologies of decentralised economies as expressed in his principle of effective demand. Building on Keynes's own assertion (e.g. JMK, xiv, p. 212) this interpretation[1] suggests that the crucial source of the difference between Keynes and the post-Marshallian Cambridge economists is to be sought in the theory of the rate of interest. A detailed examination of the evolution of the analysis of the interrelation between saving, investment and the rate of interest before the *General Theory* will provide material to test the solidity of Keynes's attempt to depart from the traditional saving-investment relationship. Furthermore, after half a century of controversy on 'Mr Keynes and the "classics"', the time seems ripe to re-examine the twenty-five-year build-up in terms of the saving-investment technique of analysis which led to the principle of effective demand. By doing so, besides filling a rather surprising gap in the literature,[2] it will be possible to put Keynes's contribution to economic theory in its proper historical perspective.

A central theme is that the notion of liquidity preference and the basic elements of an optimum portfolio analysis ('threefold margin') were already part and parcel of a dominant loanable-funds interest theory before 1936. This fact will strengthen one of the prominent conclusions of the present study: the primary contribution of the *General Theory* is not to be sought in the formal analysis of incentives to liquidity, the notion of liquidity premium or the concept of uncertainty usually linked with monetary factors as the phenomena which inhibit the tendency of investment to settle at the full employment level (see, e.g., Hicks, 1937, p. 133, and Eshag, 1963, p. 66). In fact, Keynes's basic contribution consists in his attempts at introducing changes in the level of income (and not the interest rate) as the long-run adjusting mechanism between saving and investment; that is, the principle of effective demand. Even if, within the theoretical framework of the *General Theory*, a long-run interpretation of this principle raises very serious problems of consistency, it is clear that Keynes visualised the replacement of the Marshallian interest theory by his own adjustment process between saving and investment as central to his thesis according to which the economic system, if left to its own devices, would not tend towards the full employment of labour.

To sustain and consolidate conclusions such as these, it is essential to draw the clearest possible picture of the theoretical apparatus underpinning the various contributions to the development of the saving-investment technique of analysis *prior* to 1936. Not surprisingly, since the central contributions from this period emanated from Cambridge, the common analytical foundation was that established by Alfred Marshall. This is made up of two basic (though familiar) propositions: on the one hand, that there is an inverse relation between the volume of planned investment and the rate of interest (i.e. a downward-sloping investment-demand curve) and, on the other, that, despite short-run 'frictions', the interest-rate is assumed to be sensitive enough to divergences between investment decisions and full-employment saving to ensure, in the long run, its equilibrating role. To put the same argument in a slightly different way, the central theme is that the market-rate of interest oscillates *in the short run* around a 'natural' rate of interest determined *in the long run* by the supply and demand for capital as a stock, which, in turn, guarantees the equality between planned investment and full-employment saving.[3]

Once the logic of Marshall's theory of interest is understood, it then emerges with great clarity that, starting from Marshall's own contributions (written as early as the 1870s and 1880s), the entire development of the saving-investment technique of analysis took place *within* the limits imposed by the second proposition outlined above: namely that, in the long run, the interest-rate is assumed to be sensitive enough to divergences between investment decisions and full-employment saving. In other words, the concepts of an interest-elastic demand curve for investment and 'natural' rate of interest were never called into question. The whole debate took place in terms of the analysis of various short-run forces which temporarily keep at bay the long-run forces behind saving and investment.

The core of the present work (Chapters 3–8) demonstrates that the development of the saving-investment technique of analysis by Hawtrey, Robertson, Pigou, Lavington and Keynes (up to the early 1930s) can be seen as a progressive attempt to integrate monetary and trade-cycle theory with Marshall's long-run analysis. As Robertson put it, what Marshall's pupils did at Cambridge until 1936 was 'to elucidate – by means of a step-by-step analysis . . . – the inter-relations between credit creation, capital formation [i.e. investment] and "abstinence" [i.e. saving]' (1926, p. ix; see also Hayek, 1933, p. 33 n., and Hicks, 1935, pp. 62–3). Building up (at first independently and later in a more co-ordinated way) a kind of 'immanent criticism' (to use Myrdal's aphorism apropos Wicksell's pupils) of both Marshall's interest and quantity theories, these various authors reached by the early 1930s a fully fledged analysis in terms of saving and investment, including a well-reasoned loanable-funds theory of interest. It is only with the introduction in the *General Theory* of the principle of effective demand that an attempt was made by Keynes to escape from the traditional logic of this technique of analysis. By devising the principle of effective demand as more than another short-run explanation of how and why the rate of interest might not temporarily adjust planned investment to full-employment saving, Keynes tried to offer a more radical explanation of the failure of the economic system to generate sufficient investment to guarantee the full employment of labour.

Unfortunately, Keynes's theory is not capable of bearing the weight he clearly assigned to it. His adoption of Marshall's investment theory in the *General Theory*, together with a weak critique of the orthodox theory, paved the way for a rehabilitation of the traditional approach. The principle of effective demand has thus come to be visualised by the neo-classical synthesis as an interesting addition to the stock of short-run explanations of economic fluctuations.

Hence, the whole pre-1936 loanable-funds theory of interest in particular and the long-run self-adjusting capacity of the economic system in general were left intact. At the end of this study it should be clear that the long-run validity of Keynes's principle could only be secured by forging his insights into a coherent theory of effective demand – a task that is still in its infancy some forty years after the publication of the *General Theory*.

The argument commences (Chapter 1) with an examination of Marshall's analytical framework which underlies the interest-elastic investment-demand and saving-supply curves and the determination of the 'equilibrium' rate of interest. This requires a detailed discussion of the stock–flow issue which shows that the sequence of investment-demand functions for 'free' capital (flow of investment) reflects (on average and in the long run) a demand function for 'specialised' capital (capital as a stock expressed in value terms) elastic with respect to the rate of interest. It is then argued that this argument implies the (subsequently) crucial hypothesis that the level of investment is determined by decisions to save.

Building on this typical piece of Marshallian long-run theory, the argument then concentrates in Chapter 2 on Marshall's primitive version of the 'cumulative process' resulting from his analysis of the relation between money, interest and prices. The failure to provide a proper stability analysis in the realm of monetary theory does not bar Marshall from laying down in a still unsystematic way some of the main stepping-stones on which the saving-investment technique of analysis was eventually to be built: a basic loanable-funds interest theory, the idea of speculative demand for money and an early version of the 'threefold margin' argument. However, Marshall failed to overcome the dichotomy between equilibrium analysis and trade-cycle theory and was thus unable to explore the influence of monetary changes on equilibrium magnitudes, and in particular, the concept of 'forced saving'.

Moving then to the central part of this essay, Chapter 3 marks the beginning of the step-by-step analysis of the progressive development of the saving-investment technique of analysis. After Keynes's (1911) and Pigou's (1912) pre-war contributions along Marshallian lines, Hawtrey's crucial novelty in terms of an 'income-approach' to the quantity theory brings for the first time to the forefront an analysis of saving and investment in monetary terms (1913). Then, Robertson's over-investment theory (1915) linked to his first sketchy formulation of the 'forced-saving' doctrine (1922), Keynes's switch from an 'over-investment' (1913) to an 'under-investment' theory of the cycle (1923), Lavington's analysis of the speculative demand for money (1921) and Pigou's attempt at a synthetic formulation (1924) illustrate the various and still unco-ordinated directions in which Marshall's monetary framework was extended until 1925 (Chapters 4 and 5).

In Chapters 6 and 7 the systematic co-ordination and extension of these scattered contributions by Robertson (1926) and Keynes (1930) are examined in detail. This study of the apogee of the saving–investment technique of analysis is built around the rise and fall of the 'forced-saving' doctrine between 1925 and 1930. Robertson (with the help of Keynes) managed to give the first formal set-up, by means of a step-by-step analysis of the interrelation between credit creation, saving and investment, to this century-old doctrine. In the *Treatise* Keynes brought to its peak this technique of analysis by showing (by means of his liquidity-preference analysis) that the gap between saving and investment can no longer be directly connected with changes in the volume of bank credit and/or hoarding. If this analysis reduced to very little the scope of validity of the 'forced-saving' doctrine it eventually brought to fruition a fully fledged loanable-funds theory of interest including the 'threefold margin' portfolio analysis. Robertson's (1934) and Hicks's (1935) extension of this central contribution of the *Treatise* (Chapter 8) eventually brings home the argument that, in opposition to the traditional interpretations, the 'fundamentals' of the standard modern loanable-funds theory of interest were actually worked out *before* the publication of the *General Theory* . However, despite this substantial difference of opinion between Keynes and Robertson about how gaps between saving and investment come into existence, there was no disagreement whatsoever about the meaning of such gaps. For both of them a 'divergence between saving and investment' is a coefficient of tension in the economic system which can only be corrected by a suitable interest-rate policy.

Moving then to the *General Theory* itself, the argument examines in Chapter 9 the crucial 'separability' of Keynes's principle of effective demand from any theory of interest. Besides a demonstration of how this new adjustment mechanism between saving and investment is offered by Keynes as a *direct* challenge to the theoretical foundations of the 'forced-saving' doctrine, an attempt is made to assert its solidity as a long-period theory of production. The next step involves testing the robustness of Keynes's 'alternative' theory of interest, i.e. his concept of liquidity preference. It is shown that Keynes's argument, according to which the traditional interest theory ignored the effects of the speculative demand for money on the interest-rate, does not hold water in so far as this discovery was the main novelty of the *Treatise*. Furthermore, an appreciation of Keynes's poor showing in the liquidity preference versus loanable-funds debate strengthens the widely shared contention that Keynes's 'alternative' theory cannot be turned into a long-run theory of interest without pegging it in a way or another to productivity and thrift. The final step of the discussion is to examine how the adoption of an investment theory based on Marshall's investment-demand curve further barred Keynes from giving any strong theoretical basis to a long-run interpretation of his principle of effective demand. In fact, since the marginal-efficiency-of-capital schedule does imply that there is an inverse relation between investment and the rate of interest (leaving thus intact the possibility of the establishment of a full-employment interest-rate) Keynes was ultimately forced into defending his principle of effective demand on the weak grounds that the elements of uncertainty linked with monetary phenomena would inhibit the tendency of investment to full employment. All this leads to the conclusion that a more radical departure from the traditional Marshallian analytical framework would have been the only way for Keynes to give his principle of effective demand the long-run validity he so obviously wanted it to bear.

2 Supply and Demand for 'Free' Capital and the Rate of Interest: Marshall's 'Real' Analysis

Despite Keynes's claim that 'no consecutive discussion of the rate of interest [is to be found] in the works of Marshall' (JMK, vii, p. 186) it is nevertheless possible to get a fairly clear picture of Marshall's theory by collecting and piecing together various passages, elements and hints scattered in the *Economics of Industry*, the *Principles*, the *Official Papers* and *Money, Credit and Commerce*.

This chapter is devoted to the study of the determination of the long-run 'normal', 'natural', 'equilibrium' or 'real' rate of interest. No temporary monetary (or other) influence is allowed to disturb the reader's attention from the logic of Marshall's application of the supply and demand apparatus to determine the ultimate tendency towards a uniform rate of profit on capital:

> The rate of interest is determined in the long run by the two sets of forces supply and demand respectively, . . . interest being the price paid for the use of capital in any market, tends towards an equilibrium level such that aggregate demand for capital in that market, at that rate of interest, is equal to the aggregate stock forthcoming there at that rate. (1961, p. 534; see also p. 521)

To use Ricardo's celebrated expression Marshall fixes his 'whole attention on the permanent state of things' (1951–73, vii, p. 120) by using the time-honoured long-period method of analysis. As Marshall puts it himself at the end of his chapter on 'The interest of capital', 'we are supposing . . . that all values are expressed in terms of money of fixed purchasing power, just as astronomers have taught us to determine the beginning or the ending of the day with reference not to the actual sun but to a *mean sun* which is supposed to move uniformly through the heavens' (1961, p. 593).

This chapter is structured as follows. First of all (Section 2.1) the question of capital as a 'factor of production' is discussed in connection with the all-important distinction Marshall draws between the rate of interest on 'free capital' and the quasi-rent on 'specialised capital' (namely, a stock-flow distinction). It is then possible to provide a more detailed analysis (Section 2.2) of the various determinants of respectively the schedule of demand for 'free' capital (i.e. the investment-demand function) and the schedule of supply for 'free' capital (i.e. the saving-supply function). Finally (Section 2.3) we discuss the rate of interest as the adjusting mechanism between planned savings and planned investment to show how, for Marshall, the decisions to save determine the level of investment, or alternatively that savings pre-exist investment.

2.1 CAPITAL AS A FACTOR OF PRODUCTION

The premises which underly Marshall's theory of interest are a particular application to the market for capital of a more general conception of the social process of production first developed by the marginalist school around the twin concepts of marginal utility and marginal productivity. As is well known, the various elements needed for production are treated as 'factors of production' which can be used in proportions which vary as the relative prices of their services vary. This crucial property stems from a decisive characteristic attributed by the marginalist school to both production and consumption processes: *the principle of substitution* (Marshall, 1961, pp. xvi, 169–72, 341, 351–4, 404–6, 418–21, 434–7, 662–3, 665–6). On the one hand, there is 'substitutability' between consumption goods which generally require different proportions of the factors of production to be manufactured; on the other hand, for any given technology there are alternative methods of producing the same commodity, each of these methods requiring a different combination of the various factors of production. Under the assumption of continuous variability of factor proportions (arising from substitution between consumption goods and/or between techniques of production) the usual profit maximisation condition in terms of 'marginal products' is the logical outcome of this analysis.

Hence, whatever route we take we end up with an inverse relation between the price of the service of any factor and the quantity in which this factor is used in equilibrium (of course, it implies that the quantity of other factors is given).

If that crucial hypothesis is sufficiently demonstrated, and adopted as *the* cornerstone of the whole system, the way is paved for the introduction in the marginalist model of a rationale for a self-adjusting economic system tending, in the long run, to a full utilisation of productive capacity.[1] If there exists on each and every market an inverse relation between the price of the service and the quantity employed of the corresponding factor of production, competition among owners of each and every factor will modify each and every price until the available supply of each and every factor is fully employed.

This relation is none other than a demand function for the service of any factor of production which, in conjunction with the supply function of the same factor (direct functional relation between price and quantity supplied according to the marginal utility principle), will make the price vary until the quantity demanded is equal to the available supply; or, put in other words, until excess demand is zero.

Capital goods have obviously to take their place among these factors of production and are no exception to the principle of substitution or to the general rule about prices (i.e. interest-elastic demand function). However, and as it has become well known since the early 1950s, capital goods as a factor of production raise some special problems which were never squarely faced by early marginalist economists, in particular by Marshall. According to their general framework, competition among owners of capital goods give rise to a tendency to a *uniform* rate of return on all kinds of different capital goods, over what is strictly necessary for their replacement.[2] From these premises, it follows that, if this uniform rate of profit is the price paid for the service of capital goods, these goods have ultimately to be quantified *in value terms* in order to get an homogenised magnitude – namely the 'factor of production capital' on which this very uniform rate of return (interest) will be determined. It is none other but the now well-known 'circular argument' at the root of the capital controversy of the 1960s: the principle that the proportions in which the various factors of production are employed vary with the prices of their services *cannot* be deduced from the conditions of equilibrium in production because the quantities of the factor capital cannot be defined independently of the system of prices.

Marshall was imperfectly aware of that problem. For example, in an oft-quoted passage, he clearly points out that the maximising process which makes an entrepreneur invest up to a point where the 'marginal product' is equal to the current rate of interest is an allocation mechanism and *not* a theory of distribution: 'But illustrations of this kind . . . cannot be made into a theory of interest, any more than into a theory of wages, without reasoning in a circle' (1961, p. 519).[3]

In fact, all his analytical efforts in the field of capital theory are an attempt to by-pass this main obstacle and to reassert, by means of a so-called short-run theory avoiding the notion of 'quantity of capital', the marginalist theory of distribution based on the crucial fact that 'the general theory of the equilibrium of demand and supply is a Fundamental Idea running through the frames of all the various parts of the central problem of Distribution and Exchange' (1961, p. viii).[4]

So far, we have discussed a factor of production 'capital' defined in value terms and supposed to take the physical form of capital goods appropriate to a given equilibrium situation. However, it still remains to provide a meaning to the concept of the value of that capital. Marshall's solution to this problem is very much in line with the rather vague hints given by the other leading marginalist economists. In his chapter on 'The Growth of Wealth' (Book IV, vii), Marshall assimilates the existing quantity of capital resulting from past investment to the original savings from which all the growth process stems. In other words, capital accumulation through investment is the outcome of an original 'postponment of enjoyment' (1961, p. 233), i.e. savings: the factor of production 'capital' is thus homogeneous with savings measured in some composite unit of non-consumed consumption goods. Using Marshall's own terminology (on which more later) we can conclude that 'free' capital, namely savings, is transformed through a process of investment into 'specialised' capital which will periodically – at the end of each period of production – re-emerge in a 'free' form to be either reinvested in capital goods of a same or different form, or, alternatively, turned back into consumption.

Despite numerous and various attempts to provide a general solution to the problem of distribution by contemporary economists,[5] Marshall never formulated explicitly his long run equilibrium version characterised by a uniform rate of profit. As late as 1920, when he published the 8th edition of the *Principles*, he remained faithful to his short-run approach to the variability of the proportions between factors of production. Such a theoretical device seems to allow him to by-pass the notion of an available 'quantity of capital' as a given magnitude measured in *value* terms (e.g. Clark's 'pure capital'). In fact, this short-run approach to the substitution theorem allows him to take as given the existing production equipment in *physical* terms. This 'specialised' capital yields a quasi-rent depending on the level of wages (if there are only two factors of production, capital and labour) and the demand for the products. The real wage is itself determined by the supply and demand apparatus applied to the labour market, the demand for labour depending itself on the demand for goods.

The rate of interest proper is eventually determined on a *separate* market for 'free' capital by the intersection of the demand curve for current investible resources (i.e. the investment-demand function) and a supply curve for currently available savings. This analytical technique, which splits the capital market into a market for capital as a stock and a market for capital as a flow, is similar to Walras's distinction between a market for capital goods proper and a market for new capital goods produced (1954, part v). Thus, so far as the conditions of static equilibrium are concerned, 'specialised' capital goods are assumed to be present in given quantities as part of the data of the historical situation; the respective income of productive services (Walras, 1954, pp. 269–70) or quasi-rent (Marshall, 1961, pp. 416–17) are valued in the usual way, in conjunction with the technical coefficients and the prices of products. 'Durable' (Walras) or 'specialised' capital goods derived then their value by a process of capitalisation of the market value of their respective services (quasi-rent) per time-period.[6]

Obviously a general solution to the problem of distribution cannot arise from such theory of interest (or profit): there is no reason why the valuation of a particular 'specialised' capital good should bear any close relation to its reproduction-cost. In other words, if the assumption is made that what is given are the various capital goods as specified elements of a given productive equipment, it is then clearly impossible either to obtain a uniform rate of profit on the supply prices of capital goods or to draw a demand function for capital elastic with respect to the rate of interest. One ends up at most with a value for each 'specialised' capital good derived from a quasi-rent (capitalised at the *current* rate of interest!) based on entrepreneurs' expectations about what the future is likely to be for every specific piece of capital equipment (with respect to relative prices, demand for goods, rate of interest, wage-rates, price-level, etc.).

It is clearly impossible to derive from such a short-run method of estimating the 'value' of 'specialised' capital goods any systematic relationship showing how this given productive equipment can be modified by current investments. In particular, in such a framework, the crucial inverse relation between investment and the rate of interest is simply a *non sequitur*. The investment-demand function can take any possible shape and can have no definite relationship with an equally indeterminate demand function for capital as a stock.

So, Marshall seems to end up in an awkward and paradoxical situation. On the one hand, he argues constantly in favour of a long-run normal rate of interest determined – like any other long-run normal price – by the twin forces of demand and supply for capital which reflect productivity and thrift (see, e.g., pp. 520, 534). On the other hand, aware of the logical circularity involved in an equilibrium situation characterised by a uniform rate of profit on the supply price of capital, he takes as given the existing equipment the value of which is determined by capitalising the various quasi-rents estimated by entrepreneurs on each physically specified capital good by means of a '"general rate of interest" [which] applies in strictness only to the anticipated net earnings from new investments of free capital' (Marshall, 1961, p. 533). The only possible way to save the logic of Marshall's apparatus implies a 'synthesis' or a 'homogenisation' of some sort between the market for 'specialised' capital and the market for free investible resources.

Hence, the only escape route out of that apparently insoluble dichotomy is the one Marshall actually takes implicitly himself. He reintroduces what he has tried to by-pass by splitting the capital market into two components: *the notion of capital as an amount of value*. A close examination of the market for 'free' investible resources reveals in fact that an analysis in terms of saving and investment to determine the rate of interest is bound to be conducted in terms of 'capital' expressed in value terms. On the one hand, such an approach is the only way to compare heterogenous investment goods when it comes to take a decision to invest; an investment-demand function cannot be expressed in anything else but value terms (at both individual and aggregate levels).

On the other hand, as already argued (see Marshall's express analogy with Clark's 'pure' capital, 1961, p. 73), the supply of capital as a flow (namely, saving) is measured in some composite unit of consumption goods; it can only be a value magnitude.

For once Marshall is very clear about this issue: 'the rate of interest is a ratio: and the two things which it connects are both sums of money' (1961, p. 412; see also p. 73). Once it has been realised that capital as a flow is treated as a factor of production in value terms on the market for 'free' capital it is relatively easy to show that an investment-demand function can be connected with a long-run demand for capital as a stock, *the latter being a time sequence of the former* (see below Section 2.3 for a formal demonstration of this link). As a matter of fact, as investment in 'free' capital is only made to adjust the (given) stock of capital goods, it is only in the light of the long-run forces acting on the market for 'specialised' capital (namely, productivity and thrift) that investment and saving decisions can be taken. At any point in time 'capital' is incorporated in a given set of physical goods; it is not a 'fluid' taking instantly the 'right' physical form appropriate to an equilibrium situation in which the condition of a uniform rate of profit on the various capital goods is realised. It is only through time that the stock of capital goods in existence can be brought closer to the appropriate physical form via an investment process of the portion of it set 'free' by savings (namely, a reincorporation in capital goods of different kinds of past savings re-emerging periodically in a free form from 'specialised' capital).

Hence, such an approach must be based – to be coherent – on a conception of a demand for capital (as a value magnitude) inversely related to the rate of interest. In the last analysis the sequence of investment demand functions for 'free' capital reflects (on average and in the long run) a demand function for 'specialised' capital elastic with respect to the rate of interest (see Kaldor, 1955–6, pp. 221–2, and Garegnani, 1978, pp. 347–8).

Despite his repeated warnings that 'the phrase "the rate of interest" is applicable to old investment of capital in only a very limited sense' (1961, p. 593). Marshall provides also several indications that, after all, the rate of interest and quasi-rent have much in common being 'different species of a large genus': 'Our central doctrine is that interest on free capital and quasi-rent on old investment of capital shade into one another gradually' (1961, p. 421). This subtle distinction between the rate of interest and quasi-rent is not, however, as clear cut as Marshall wishes to see it.

On the whole Marshall's capital theory is rather unsatisfactory. Its lack of clarity stems not so much from the conceptual weakness of the analytical framework but from Marshall's well-known predilection for 'realistic' analyses (Schumpeter, 1954, p. 1046). He clearly saw – and much better than most of the other marginalist theorists of the time – the difficulties connected with capital as a factor of production;

he tried to escape that contradiction ('it cannot be made into a theory of interest') and confused the whole subject with his dubious rate-of-interest v. quasi-rent dichotomy. He did see the crucial difficulties involved in capital theory but did not want to, or more probably could not draw all the logical conclusions which would have been so damaging for the core of the marginalist analysis he had done so much to promote.

The best example of this seemingly 'dual' approach is given by two quotations extracted from two *consecutive* pages of the *Principles*:

> the income derived from capital already invested in particular things . . . is properly a quasi-rent and can be regarded as interest only on the assumption that the capital value of the investment remained unaltered. Leaving this difficulty on one side for the present; and recollecting that the phrase 'the general rate of interest' applies in strictness only to the anticipated net earnings from new investments of free capital, we may resume briefly the results of our earlier studies . . . [as follows]: [t]he rate of interest is determined in the long run by the two sets of forces of supply and demand [for capital] respectively. (1961, pp. 533–4; see also 1879, pp. 123 and 126)

In their *Economics of Industry* Marshall and Mary Paley suggest in a crude form a solution to the stock-flow problem anticipating very much the interest/quasi-rent doctrine of the *Principles*. As a matter of fact they expose very bluntly what Marshall later tries to conceal in the *Principles*, i.e. that the long-run normal rate of interest is nothing else but an 'average' of short-run rates fixed on the market for investible resources:

> Of course there are some years of depression of trade in which the Net Return [i.e. quasi-rent] of a good deal of machinery is nothing at all; and again some machinery is made which never gives any Net Return [quasi-rent]. But if we look at average results, we find the Net annual Return of the machinery and other capital in use in a country just affords interest on its value *at the rate current there* [i.e. the rate of interest]. (1879, p. 123, emphasis added)

In other places Marshall defines the 'normal' rate of interest as the rate 'to be obtained for permanent investments' (1926, p. 272), or as 'governed by the relation between the supply of capital and the need for services of capital' (1926, p. 270); or, still in another way, as the rate 'which can be got for the investment of capital' (1926, p. 49).

From all the above, it is clear that Marshall did not consistently adhere to a precise definition of the 'normal' rate of interest. Yet, despite his lack of clarity at the 'operational' level between 'free' and 'specialised' capital, Marshall provides here the fundamental theoretical framework in which all the controversies of the 1920s and 1930s were to take place. On to the permanent forces of productivity and thrift, expressed in the long run on the market for 'specialised'capital, are grafted temporary forces and short-lived factors which make the actual rate of interest determined on the market for 'free' capital fluctuate around the 'equilibrium', 'normal' rate of interest. Savings and investment (and thus the market or actual rate of interest) *are* influenced by these short-run disturbances but, in the long run and on average, they are ultimately and only undertaken to adapt the structure of the existing 'specialised' capital along the lines laid down by the dominant forces of productivity and thrift.

2.2 THE DETERMINANTS OF THE SCHEDULES OF SUPPLY AND DEMAND FOR 'FREE' CAPITAL

An examination of Marshall's analysis of the determining factors behind the saving and investment functions is called for, now, for two main reasons. On the one hand, it will back our interpretation of the market for 'free' capital as being heavily influenced by 'permanent forces' despite the 'flow' flavour attached to it. On the other, it will allow us to prepare the grounds for further discussions (Section 2.3) of the logical consequences of the inverse relationship between the rate of interest and the volume of planned investment.

The schedule of supply for 'free' capital, or saving–supply function

As already argued, the supply of 'free' capital (saving) is homogeneous with the factor of production 'specialised' capital expressed in value terms; both are measured in some composite unit of consumption goods and it is through a process of investment that 'free' capital is turned into 'specialised' capital from which it will re-emerge periodically to be either reinvested or turned back into consumption. For Marshall, the volume of saving depends on two sets of factors:

the former are not primarily economic in character (exogenous factors), the latter are strictly linked with economic magnitudes (endogenous factors). The exogenous factors are rather similar to and anticipate Keynes's 'subjective factors' of the *General Theory* (JMK, vii, pp. 107–8). In the *Principles* Marshall devotes a whole rather moralising chapter (Book IV, chap. vii, 1961, pp. 220–36) to a detailed discussion of these motives. Suffice it here to reproduce the 'provisional conclusions' Marshall eventually ends up with to get all what we really need to know: 'The accumulation of wealth [i.e. saving] is governed by a great variety of causes: by custom, by habits of self-control and realizing the future, and above all by the power of family affection' (1961, p. 236).

A few pages earlier Marshall discusses the idea of 'security as a condition of saving' (p. 226) meaning by this the present and future states of the social and political conditions. Eventually he concludes this review of these exogenous motives by discussing the psychological elements behind the 'willingness to wait'; it is at that stage that Marshall introduces his celebrated concept of the rate of interest as the 'reward of waiting' (1961, p. 232). He later connects it with 'man's *prospectiveness*' or what he calls the 'faculty of realizing the future' (1961, p. 233).

In that same chapter Marshall discusses only *en passant* two important and strictly endogenous factors which affect saving, namely the level of income and the rate of interest.

Even if it may come as a surprise to some modern economists,[7] practically all the great marginalist theorists had already drawn a clear, if somewhat incomplete, functional relation between the level of income and the volume of saving. Marshall is no exception. Savings depend on the 'surplus of production over the necessaries of life' (1961, p. 224) and 'the power to save depends on an excess of income over necessary expenditure; and this is greatest among the wealthy' (1961, p. 229). This straightforward piece of marginalist analysis has been seen to anticipate in some respects Keynes's saving function. However, it is obvious that Marshall did nothing with such a critical relationship. It is only well after the *Treatise on Money* that, giving up the assumption of a marginal propensity to spend equal to unity implicit in Marshall's analysis (i.e. by stating his 'fundamental psychological law'), that Keynes began to understand the crucial part played by variations of income as the adjusting mechanism between saving and investment.

It is clear that Marshall was exclusively interested in the connection between the volume of saving and what is for him the only long-run adjusting mechanism between saving and investment – namely, the rate of interest.[8]

However, Marshall is unable to draw a saving-supply curve relating directly, and under all circumstances, the volume of savings to the rate of interest. As a matter of fact it is quite possible for Marshall that in some cases the rule 'the higher the rate of interest the greater the saving' (1961, p. 234) is not verified. Indeed, Marshall discusses at length two important exceptions to that 'general tendency'. In one case he admits that saving can take place even at a negative rate of interest (1961, pp. 231–2); in the other the volume of saving may even vary inversely with respect to the rate of interest (backward-bending saving curve; see 1961, p. 235).

However, Marshall did not regard these special short-lived cases as a major hindrance to the general applicability (in the long run) of a supply-for-saving curve elastic with respect to the rate of interest:

> But though saving in general is affected by many causes other than the rate of interest: and though the saving of many people is but little affected by the rate of interest; while a few, who have determined to secure an income of a certain fixed amount for themselves or their family [the Sargent effect], will save less with a high rate than with a low rate of interest: yet a strong balance of evidence seems to rest with the opinion that a rise in the rate of interest, or demand-price for saving, tends to increase the volume of saving. (1961, pp. 533–4; see also pp. 232–6)

Despite this profession of faith, the income–saving link and this weakness on the supply side of the market for 'free' capital or two points which, according to Keynes, 'might . . . have warned the classical [i.e. marginalist] school that something was wrong' (JMK, vii, p. 182) with the idea of the rate of interest as the reward of waiting. As a matter of fact Keynes refers to Cassel and not to Marshall, who shared the same doubts about the validity of the functional relationship between saving and the rate of interest (Cassel, 1903, pp. 155–6, and the opposite view on p. 147). Keynes introduces his discussion of that problem with a sentence which summarises very aptly how marginalist economists viewed their theory of interest and where they thought its main weakness lay:

it has been agreed [e.g. by Marshall and Cassel] . . . that it is not certain that the sum saved out of a given income necessarily increases when the rate of interest is increased; whereas no one doubts that the investment demand-schedule falls with a rising rate of interest. (JMK, vii, p. 182)

If Keynes's affirmation is to be taken at its face value it is very revealing of the priority given by marginalist economists to the investment-demand function over the saving function. If they are quite prepared to give ground on the direct functional relationship between saving and the rate of interest they are adamant on the strict application of a downward-sloping investment curve. As will be largely confirmed later in this chapter, they rightly saw the investment-rate of interest relation as *the* crucial element in the adjustment process between saving and investment. However inelastic or oddly shaped the saving function may be with respect to the rate of interest, it has no decisive influence on the tendency towards full employment of the volume of investible resources made available through this very saving process. As Cassel puts it:

> The real cause which . . . actually governs the rate of interest is the demand for the use of capital . . . It is therefore reasonable to assume that [the rate of interest] has . . . no very considerable effect on the actual accumulation of capital. (1903, pp. 155–6, see also Marshall, 1961, p. 534)

The schedule of demand for 'free' capital, or investment-demand function

As argued in Section 2.1 there are difficulties about whether Marshall's determination of the investment-demand function is based on short- or long-run considerations. We have seen that Marshall's solution relies eventually on the traditional 'market' v. 'natural' price distinction applied to the rate of interest. Short-lived forces expressed on the market for investible resources make the actual rate of interest oscillate around the 'normal' or 'equilibrium' rate, determined in the long run by the dominant forces of productivity and thrift. It seems hardly necessary to add that this equilibrium rate of interest need not be either a constant or an actual observable variable.[9] Such a magnitude is only an abstraction, a centre of gravity free from temporary influences which allows an analysis of the long-run dominant forces at work in an economy.

In fact, Marshall's investment-demand function is based on long-period conditions, and the short-run determinants grafted on to these long-run forces can be easily disposed of, to reveal the essence of the argument; namely, the inverse relation between the demand for 'free' capital and the rate of interest.

Marshall's analysis can be substantially clarified with the help of Lerner's (1937, 1944, 1953b) and Robertson's (1958) contributions to the stock-flow problem arising in the *Principles*. Figure 2.1, borrowed from Lerner, simply aims at giving a more formal expression to the theoretical relation between an investment-demand curve and the schedule of demand for fixed capital.

One surface of Figure 2.1 is made up of the schedule of the marginal productivity of capital *MPC* (*AE*) inversely related to the rate of interest measured on the *Ab* axis. If – for example – the quantity of capital is *bM*, the marginal productivity of this particular amount of capital is shown by the vertical measure *MC*.

The second surface is made up of the investment-demand curves, one such schedule for each quantity of capital.[10] All these curves (like *AB* or *CD*) are inversely related to the rate of interest. Each of them shows how high the rate of investment must be at various rates of interest, given the quantity of capital, if the marginal efficiency of investment (*MEI*) is to be equal to the rate of interest.

The set of all investment-demand curves forms the third surface, *ABFE*, each of them corresponding to a given quantity of capital spreading from *b* to *N*. In accordance with the general principles of marginal analysis the greater the quantity of capital the lower the *MEI*, and the smaller the rate of investment.

If the rate of interest (resulting from the ruling conditions expressed by productivity and thrift) is measured by the height *GH*, the rate of net investment will be equal to *MG* and the *MEI* equal to the rate of interest. Since the *MPC* is higher than the rate of interest, investment will take place at a decreasing rate from *H* to *L* until the diminishing *MPC* is equal to the *MEI*, itself already equal to the rate of interest. At point *L* we will have reached a long-period equilibrium where the rate of interest is equal to both the *MPC* and the *MEI*; the rate of interest is just enough to induce the owners of capital goods to keep their stock constant. At that point, and at that

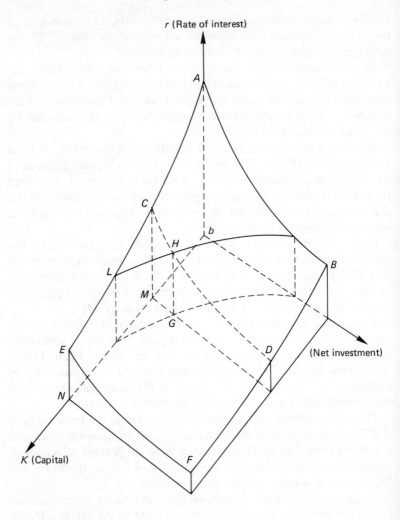

Figure 2.1

point only, the quasi-rent on 'specialised' capital will be equal to the
rate of interest on 'free' capital devoted to the replacement of
worn-out 'fixed' capital. In all other intermediate positions – keeping,
of course, at bay all passing and short-lived influences linked with
trade- or credit-cycle theories – the quasi-rent on 'specialised' capital
will be higher than the rate of interest.

The basic idea underlying Figure 2.1 is of great consequence, however simple it may seem at first sight. Robertson states it in the following way:

> so long as the growth of capital is continuing, we see the rate of interest at any time continually standing *below* the marginal productivity of the existing stock of capital, – more strictly, standing below what the rate of return would be on the cost of replacement of the machines falling out of service, *if* only just enough machines to replace those falling out of service were being built. (1958, pp. 67–8)

For his part, Lerner offers an even more concise statement of the whole question:

> The difference between the marginal productivity of capital and the rate of interest is the force tending to make the capital stock grow or decline. The rate at which this change proceeds is given by that rate of net investment or disinvestment which makes the marginal efficiency of investment equal to the rate of interest. (1937, p. 351)

In other words it is only because the *MPC* is greater than the rate of interest that the rate of investment is not equal to zero; or, alternatively, if the exact amount of investment is determined in the short run by the difference between the *MEI* and the rate of interest, the fact that there is any investment at all depends on the difference between the *MPC* and this *very* interest rate. Whatever may be the short-run fluctuations of the rate of interest it cannot but oscillate around the *MEI*, and hence the *MPC*, given our assumption on the behaviour of the supply side of the market.

Hence, in the long run, and under the influence of dominant forces, capital goods will have acquired the physical composition compatible with the equilibrium conditions, namely a uniform rate of return on these various (old and new) capital goods. This very solution is none other but Böhm-Bawerk's, Wicksell's or Clark's: the amount of capital is a single homogeneous magnitude ('pure' capital for Clark and 'real' capital for Wicksell), which can alter easily and costlessly its 'form' – though not its quantity – in order to acquire the physical composition required by the equilibrium conditions. It must be by now abundantly clear that the investment-demand function, as a flow version of the capital-demand function, is inversely related to the rate of interest.[11]

From this inverse relation it seems possible to infer that any gap between investment decision and full employment savings will be closed by a variation of the volume of investment induced by a change of the interest rate. It is to what we now turn.

2.3 THE RATE OF INTEREST AS 'THE FACTOR WHICH BRINGS THE DEMAND FOR INVESTMENT AND THE WILLINGNESS TO SAVE INTO EQUILIBRIUM WITH ONE/ANOTHER'[12]

In Chapter 14 of the *General Theory* Keynes accurately summarises the main consequence we are now in a position to infer from Marshall's theory of interest: 'Marshall . . . surely believed, although he did not expressly say so, that aggregate saving and aggregate investments are necessarily equal.' (JMK, vii, pp. 177–8) As a matter of fact we have to amplify the main conclusions which logically stem from Marshall's theory of interest. In Marshall's analysis the factor of production 'capital', like any other factor, follows the rule of the supply-and-demand apparatus built on the marginalist approach to the theory of value: in the long run, and under the influence of the more persistent forces at work in an economy, there is an inverse relation between the rate of interest and the quantity in which 'capital' would be employed in equilibrium. In the short run the investment-demand curve is downward-sloping and elastic with respect to the rate of interest. In Marshall's own words:

> The rate of interest . . . rises with a diminution and falls with an increase of . . . the amount of [free] capital offered for loan. Conversely, the amount of [free] capital . . . increases with a fall and diminishes with a rise in the rate of interest at which [free] capital is offered on loan. (1879, p. 124)

On the supply side of this market for free capital it has been shown that, given the level of income, the dependence of decisions to save (even in the long run) on the rate of interest is uncertain in direction and intensity. However, as Marshall concludes himself, 'a strong balance of evidence seems to rest with the opinion that a rise in the rate of interest, or demand-price for saving, tends to increase the volume of saving' (1961, p. 534).

This uncertainty on the supply side of the market for 'free' capital weakens the ideal symmetry which should exist between the respective influence of saving and investment on the rate of interest. As the saving-supply function may not always be well-behaved (i.e. upward-sloping) a greater share in the stability analysis falls on the investment-demand function.

However, regardless of the way in which the supply of available investible resources is determined, it is essential for the validity of Marshall's analysis that the demand for savings is sufficiently interest elastic; it is in fact the only possibility left to foster a competitive tendency towards an equilibrium between saving and investment. In other words, however oddly shaped the savings-supply function might be, the interest elastic investment-demand function will always secure, in the long run, a full employment of the available volume of saving. Any divergence between decisions to invest and full-employment saving will be met by a decrease in the rate of interest to bring about an increase in the volume of investment equal to the gap between the supply and the demand for 'free' capital. Hence, allowance being made for frictions, temporary disequilibrium and rigidities linked with credit or trade-cycle theories, the system will always tend towards an equilibrium, or 'natural', or 'normal' or 'real' rate of interest at which decisions to invest are equal to full-employment saving. In Marshall's own words, at that rate of interest, 'the whole supply of capital can find employment' (1879, p. 126).

From these premises follows the conclusion that, if the same forces leading to a downward-sloping demand curve for saving can be applied to all other factors of production (and in particular labour), the economic system would tend in the long run towards full employment of all factors. In particular, and in anticipation of Keynes's later criticisms, it appears clearly from Marshall's argument that in a situation of temporary unemployment a fall of money wages would lead to the full employment of labour on the premises that market forces ensure the equality between saving and investment. As a matter of fact, for Marshall, a decrease in the money wage-rate is synonymous with a reduction of the real wage-rate *because* investments adjust to changes in savings consequent on changes in the level of employment and income.

It is crucial to make this point very clear. It is because – and only because – the level of investment always adjusts to the community's decision to save that a reduction in money wages will lead to a proportional drop in real wages and hence will foster a tendency towards full employment. Put in another way it is only because the extra-saving arising from the increased level of income due to the rise in employment following a drop in wages always tends to be invested thanks to the inverse relation between the rate of interest and the volume of investment, that there is no problem of effective demand in Marshall's model.

Ultimately the condition on which the entire self-adjusting capacity of the economic system, as seen by Marshall relies, is nothing more than the crucial hypothesis that the level of investment is determined by the decisions to save. This idea that saving pre-exists investment, or more precisely that, in the long run, the rate of capital accumulation is function of the rate of saving, underlies the entire debate in terms of saving and investment which was to take place at Cambridge between the end of the First World War and the publication of the *General Theory*.

As a matter of fact Marshall's determination of the 'real' rate of interest was never called into question during that period. Instead a tremendous amount of energy was devoted to refining its monetary superstructure. Put in more familiar terminology the inverse relation between the amount of investment and the rate of interest was taken for granted, leaving thus the entire theoretical argument of the 1920s and 1930s to be conducted in terms of the relative insensitivity of the rate of interest to a divergence between planned investment and planned saving.

It is to Marshall's own and prior treatment of this second step in terms of a rudimentary 'cumulative process' that we now turn.

3 Marshall's Monetary Theory

One of the central motivations of Marshall and his pupils in Cambridge (including Keynes up to the *Treatise*) was the desire to integrate monetary and value theory by means of the cash-balance equation. For Marshall the value of money is determined by the use of ordinary supply-and-demand curves in perfect accord with the same laws on which his general theory of value is based. In his own words 'the value of [money] is determined by the relation in which the supply of it stands to the demand for it' (1926, p. 177). Pigou later organised his famous essay on the 'Value of Money' (1917) under the successive subtitles 'The Demand for Legal-Tender Money', 'The Supply for Legal-Tender Money' and 'Demand and Supply'. In his textbook on *Money* Robertson stresses the fact that 'the theory of money [is] a special case of the general theory of value' (1922, p. vii). Eventually Keynes emphasises approvingly in his 1924 Obituary Memoir that Marshall always taught 'the quantity theory of money as a part of the general theory of value' (JMK, x, p. 191, italics removed).[1]

Twenty-five years before Wicksell's 1898 masterly defence and illustration of the quantity theory (1936, p. 50), Marshall already declared himself as one of its whole-hearted supporters (1871, p. 173). However, and along the same line as Wicksell's,[2] he stressed vigorously the limits of such an approach to the determination of the price-level. In his own words:

> While accepting the doctrine that, '*other things being equal*, prices rise or fall proportionately to every increase or diminution in the metal or metals which are used as the standard of value', I consider that the conditioning clause, 'other things being equal' is of overwhelming importance and requires careful attention'. (1926, p. 21)

Unfortunately while admitting the 'overwhelming importance' of what Keynes later called 'the mode by which through transitional stages an influx of new money affects prices' (1911, p. 394), Marshall did very little to improve the very poor stability analysis[3] he suggested in his 1888 and 1899 evidence. As a matter of fact, thirty-six years after the statement just quoted, Marshall did nothing more in *Money, Credit and Commerce* than to repeat the same argument, his original claim for an improved stability analysis having remained wishful thinking: 'if everything else remains the same, then there is this direct relation between the volume of currency and the level of prices'. (1923, p. 45) He added three pages later:

> This 'Quantity doctrine' is helpful as far as it goes: but it does not indicate what are the 'other things' which must be assumed to be equal in order to justify the proposition: and it does not explain the causes which govern 'rapidity of circulation'. It is almost a truism. . . . (1923, p. 48)

The failure to provide a proper stability analysis is not only a feature of Marshall's own treatment of the 'dynamic of the price level', but is shared by all his pupils until the mid-1920s. The asymmetry between Marshall's well-known discussion of stability conditions in his standard theory-of-value chapters (1961, pp. 345–6 and 806–8) and his failure to carry over that analysis to his monetary theory is at the centre of the origin of the Cambridge tradition in monetary theory. However, this absence of a detailed dynamic analysis of the determination of the equilibrium level of money prices does not imply that the real-balance effect is neglected altogether. On the contrary it can be found in several places in Marshall's and in his pupils' works. Unfortunately this crucial piece of analysis is not co-ordinated with, and does not find its proper place in, a general dynamic theory of the stability of the entire system.

To get the picture as clear as possible, and not only of Marshall's cash-balance equation, but also of his aborted dynamic analysis, this chapter is divided into four sections. Following the logic of Marshall's monetary theory, we will deal successively with the supply of money (Section 3.1), the demand for money and the interaction of the supply and demand for money (Section 3.2). We will then investigate at length Marshall's attempts to build a stability analysis, i.e. to study the connection he tried to establish between money, interest and prices (Section 3.3). Eventually a few remarks will connect Marshall's monetary and trade-cycle theories (Section 3.4).

3.1 THE SUPPLY OF MONEY

Perfectly in line with the logic of the then dominant gold-standard tradition Marshall's analysis of the supply of money gives the upper hand to gold, convertible notes and coins. Of course it does not mean that Marshall ignores banking instruments like the rate of discount and open-market operations for regulating the volume of credit. On the contrary we will see later that the part played by credit and banking instruments for credit regulation is crucial in Marshall's attempts to build a Wicksell-like cumulative process. However, the entire analysis of his well-known 'Appendix C' (1923, pp. 282–4) is conducted in terms of supply and demand for gold only. For the time being it is sufficient to add two remarks which will allow us to proceed smoothly to Marshall's demand for money analysis.

First, the analysis of the value of money can take place with any definition of money provided the same definition is used on the demand side (Pigou, 1917, p. 189). Second, Marshall stresses very clearly that all instruments of credit circulating freely (and perfectly secure) have the same influence on prices as gold and/or silver. In other words, the quantity of money available at any time is equal to the stock of gold (currency use) plus banknotes (convertible paper) plus credit. Moreover there is a strict proportionality between the volume of gold and the convertible notes issued by the Central Bank (currency principle), and between these banknotes and the volume of credit offered by banks (bank reserves principle). Thus, in the monetary system known to Marshall the analysis of the value of money could be conducted in terms of gold only without doing too much violence to everyday realities.

From these remarks eventually emerges the fact that the supply of money is purely an institutional (exogenous) problem. Hence, in Marshall's own words, its 'supply is therefore shown by a vertical straight line representing a given aggregate stock of gold' (1923, p. 283).[4] One element may be added here for the sake of completeness. In sharp contrast with the ordinary supply-and-demand apparatus the supply-and-demand curves for gold represent, in the Marshallian diagram, stocks and not flows. This indicates clearly that the problem of the determination of the value of money – or, in other words, the working of the quantity theory of money – is a long-run problem. The diagrammatic illustration implies indeed that the demand curve represents 'the stocks of gold which would probably be

appropriated . . . at various values . . . , *sufficient time having been
allowed for the necessary adjustments to be made*' (1923, pp. 282–3,
italic added). There is no room left to analyse how the system
behaves in the transition between two positions of equilibrium. Once
again, and as in all departments of economic theory, Marshall concentrates the thrust of his analytical effort in monetary theory on the
determination of long-run normal positions. From the beginning his
diagrammatical analysis of the value of money is a simple exercise in
comparative statics. When he comes to grip with these adjustments it is
almost incidentally and certainly not in a rigorous analytical framework.

3.2   THE DEMAND FOR MONEY AND THE
DETERMINATION OF THE VALUE OF MONEY

Marshall's analysis of the laws governing the demand for money is of
the utmost importance given the decisive influence it was to have on
later works on monetary theory at Cambridge. Until Keynes's *Treatise* the very core of this analysis was taken over successively by Pigou,
Keynes, Robertson and Hawtrey without substantial alteration. Despite Pigou's and Lavington's early hints at a possible speculative
demand for money, it is not until the *Treatise* that a thorough analysis
of a liquidity-preference-type demand for money was introduced
alongside the traditional determinants of the 'Cambridge *k*' (income
deposits) as outlined by Marshall. However, Marshall was already
aware of the direct relationship between the quantity of money
demanded and the rate of interest earned on securities.

To these two interconnected headings (motives for demanding
money and balancing at the margin the advantages from holding
money and other assets) must be added a study of the *volume* of real
resources which are held in cash form. Eventually an analysis of
Marshall's graphical representation of the demand curve for money
will provide us with all the necessary elements to appreciate the
demand-side of the cash-balance equation under long-run normal
conditions.

Let us first examine what nowadays would be referred to as
incentives to liquidity. According to Marshall the two chief motives
for holding cash are *transaction* and *precaution.*

The *transaction motive* includes in fact Keynes's income and business reasons for holding money (JMK, vii, pp. 195–5). In Marshall's
own words, 'a large command of resources in the form of currency

renders [people's] business easy and smooth and puts them at an advantage in bargaining' (1926, p. 268 also reprinted in 1923, p. 45; see also 1923, p. 38 and 1926, pp. 36 and 43–4).

The *precautionary motive* corresponds more or less to Keynes's similar category. However, without fully incorporating Keynes's speculative motive Marshall's precautionary motive embraces some elements of speculation, especially in connection with the so-called *law of hoarding* (1926, p. 6).

According to that early statement of what Keynes later dubbed 'real balances' (JMK, x, p. 192 n. 2) – and which was taken over by Pigou and Robertson and subsequently systematically developed in a general equilibrium framework by Patinkin under the name of real-balance effect – expectations of a rise or a fall in prices (and not only actual changes) lead people to reduce or increase their cash balances. Marshall's own statement of this law undoubtedly anticipates some fundamental ideas behind the two-view (bull v. bear) approach to liquidity preference as it was to appear forty-four years later in the *Treatise*:

> the demand for a metal for the purposes of hoarding is increased by a continuous rise in its value [i.e. a continuous increase in the purchasing power of money, namely deflation] and diminished by a continued fall [i.e. inflation], because those people who hoard believe that what has been rising in value for some time is likely to go on rising and *vice versa*. (1926, p. 6)

Second, the related question of the balance of advantages derived from holding money and other assets. As a matter of fact, and long before Pigou's seemingly original contribution (1917, p. 181), Lavington's refinements (1921, p. 30), Keynes's apparent rediscovery (JMK, v, pp. 127–9) and Hicks's surprising rediscovery of Keynes's rediscovery (1935, pp. 63–4), Marshall already suggested a very clear analysis of the determination at the margin of advantages derived from holding cash instead of other assets. According to the most basic principle of marginalism each individual balances the advantages derived from holding his resources in cash balances (demand for money) against the benefits which could be derived by alternative uses to which such resources could be put; it obviously includes the case (later emphasised by Keynes) where the substitution at the margin between bank-deposits and securities depends, *inter alia*, upon the rate of interest allowed on securities. Thus, even if tenuous and not developed at length, the idea of a speculative demand for money (in Keynes's *General Theory* sense) could easily be fitted into Marshall's theory;[5] and a link is even actually drawn by Marshall between the rate of interest on securities and the demand for money. Marshall is surprisingly explicit in this respect when he says:

> But currency held in the hand yields no income: therefore everyone balances (more or less automatically and instinctively) the benefits, which he would get by enlarging his stock of currency in the hand, against those which he would get by investing some of it either in a commodity – say a coat or a piano – from which he would derive a direct benefit; or in some business or plant or *stock exchange security which would yield him a money income.* (1923, pp. 38–9, italic added; see also his early 'Essay on Money', 'about 1871', pp. 166–7)

It is all the more surprising, given the clarity of the last sentence of this quotation, that his idea began to be developed in the early 1920s only, and then considered as something of a novelty.

The logical result of this piece of analysis is straightforward: the sum total of cash balances held by individuals, which are determined by balancing at the margin the different advantages derived form holding money rather than other assets, will equal the given supply of money currently available. As Keynes put it in his essay on Marshall: '[Marshall] went on to explain how each individual decides how much to keep in a ready form as the result of a *balance* of advantage between this and alternative forms of wealth' (JMK, x, p. 191).

Before examining the 'general relations' between the demand for money the stock of it and its current value, we have still to consider how Marshall explains the proportion of real resources which individuals are prepared to hold in cash form at any time. This amounts to giving a value to k in the cash-balance Cambridge equation; or, at least, to draw some general principles of how it is determined.

As has been the case till now, we are going to deal with a normal long-run situation – free from all temporary short-lived disequilibrium – in which the level of real income and wealth is slowly changing, if not constant. This implies that the behavioural determinants of the fraction of income and wealth held in cash will be kept unchanged and, thus, easier to define.[6]

For Marshall three elements have to be considered in order to determine the fraction of their resources people will hold in cash form at any time: wealth, income and the prevailing habits of business. In view of the 'cumulative process' to be discussed in Section 3.3, it is interesting to note that wealth – and not only the usual income and business habits – is a determinant of the Cambridge k.[7] Given the habits of business, which depend upon the general 'commercial environment' [i.e. the state of the credit market], 'the methods of transport, production and business generally' (1926, p. 268), 'the inhabitants of a country . . . keep by them on the average ready purchasing power to the extent of *a tenth of their annual income*, together with *a fiftieth part of their property*' (1923, p. 44). This wealth-effect is in fact a logical complement to the link between the speculative demand for money and the rate of interest on securities, and, like this one, remained only a potential instrument of analysis of the demand for money.

Even if the various foregoing passages provide a clear anticipation of an optimum-portfolio approach to the theory of money Marshall did not make any use of it due to his inability to distinguish formally between stocks and flows; namely, between income and wealth. It is only in the *Treatise* that full use will be made by Keynes of that connection between the demand for money and 'not only . . . the current increment to the wealth of individuals, but also to the whole block of their existing capital' (JMK, v, p. 127). Furthermore, when there is a wealth-effect there is usually a concomitant real-balance effect (if the change in all prices is equiproportionate), a mechanism to which Marshall is also alluding in a very loose manner (see 1923, p. 43). Of course, all this is very vague and will be dealt with in greater details in Section 3.3.

A detailed analysis of Marshall's diagrammatic representation of the cash-balance approach is eventually necessary to provide a more precise account of all its implications, especially in relation with the shape of the demand curve for money and the connected lack of stability analysis.

In the celebrated Appendix C to Book I, chap. iv of his *Money, Credit and Commerce*,[8] Marshall suggests a three-page-long diagrammatic note which enlightens greatly the basic assumptions on which the entire debate was to be conducted up to the late 1920s.

In Figure 3.1 the demand curve for gold as currency (or in its monetary use) is represented by the rectangular hyperbola dd', i.e. by a 'curve that presents demand of elasticity uniformly equal to one; which may be called the *Constant Outlay* curve' (1923, p. 283).

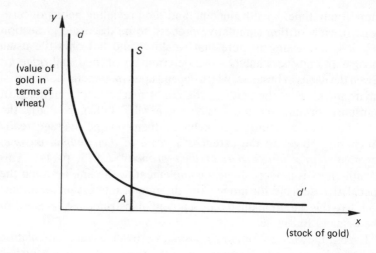

Figure 3.1

Similarly the 'supply [curve] is . . . shown by a vertical straight line representing a given aggregate stock of gold'. (1923, p. 283)

Marshall concentrates the first part of his analysis on a strictly monetary-type of demand and makes perfectly clear that *dd'* is a rectangular hyperbola without offering, however, any proof of it.[9] For him the whole exercise involved in that diagrammatic note 'does not claim to add anything to the reasonings . . . advanced' in the chapter to which this figure is appended (1923, p. 282). For the substance of his argument, Marshall sends the reader back to his straightforward long-run normal equilibrium statement according to which, other things being equal, prices rise or fall proportionately to increase or diminution of the money supply.

The absence of any stability analysis for the value of money and the unitary elasticity of the demand curve for money seem to be the two sides of the same coin; namely, the confusion made by Marshall between a demand curve and a market-equilibrium curve. Or, put in another way, Marshall's (and later Pigou's) claim that the value of money is determined by the use of ordinary demand-and-supply curves is – to say the least – not demonstrated. As a matter of fact the basic element which would allow such a claim is precisely missing: there is no trace whatsoever of any analysis of the disturbances brought in by a variation of the supply of money on the optimum relations between the level of money balances and individuals' expenditures (namely, the real-balance effect); or, put in other words, in his diagrammatic illustration Marshall implies (like in his previous demonstration) that an increase in money prices following an increase of the money supply, is always accompanied by an equiproportionate increase in nominal money-holdings. All that amounts to saying that the unitary elasticity curve is not a demand curve in the ordinary Marshallian sense, but an *(ex-post)* market-equilibrium curve. It simply seems that Marshall (and Pigou) coined this successful catch-expression as a complicated way of stating that an increase in the quantity of money ultimately causes a proportionate increase in prices – but without explaining how this result is reached.

Let us allow now increases in money prices *not* to be accompanied by an equiproportionate increase in nominal money holdings. Such an approach implies that during the adjustment process money prices do not change in an equiproportionate manner, even if *at the end of the process*, when the new equilibrium is reached, the general price-level will have risen proportionately to the increase in the quantity of money. In that case the price increase generates a real-balance effect which affects the demand for real-balances, and, hence, that for nominal holdings. Since agents' initial balances are increased above the level which they consider necessary, by way of the increased supply of money, they will seek to remedy this situation by increasing their amounts demanded of the various commodities, thereby increasing their planned expenditures, and thereby diminishing their balances. It appears clearly that – in order to estimate the adequacy of their money balances and hence to determine their influence on their demand for commodities – agents can only be guided by the *real* value of these balances. In the language Marshall and his successors would have used, it is with the extent of their liquid command over real resources that individual are concerned; namely, that the effective magnitude of these cash reserves can only be determined in relation with the price-level. The negative real-balance effect generated by the price increase causes the amount of real-balances demanded to diminish. Correspondingly the amount demanded of nominal balances will increase *less* than in proportion to the price increase. It means that the demand curve for nominal amounts is no longer a rectangular hyperbola and has a different elasticity at each point.

To restate the argument in a different way: it is only by neglecting the negative real-balance effect – namely, by postulating equiproportionate changes in nominal money-holdings *and* money-prices or, alternatively, by neglecting all distributional effects connected with the increased supply of money – that one gets a vertical demand curve for real-balances and a rectangular hyperbola as the demand curve for nominal balances. But as soon as this textbook case is dropped, the demand curve for real-balances reflects the real-balance effect and shows an elasticity greater than zero; the demand curve for nominal balances, for its part, is no longer a rectangular hyperbola, its shape being simply a reflection of the fact that this demand is also assumed to depend on wealth, inclusive of initial financial assets.

This confusion between demand curve and market-equilibrium curve was brought to its peak by Pigou, who argues quite bluntly that 'an increase in the supply of legal tender ought always, since the elasticity of demand [for legal tender] is equal to unity, to raise price in the proportion in which supply has increased' (1917, p. 196; see also p. 177).

However, it should be clear, as Patinkin puts it, that 'if properly interpreted, the Cambridge function does *not* imply uniform unitary elasticity' (1965, p. 170). Put in other words, the addition of a stability analysis to the Marshallian comparative-static analysis does not alter in any way its ultimate conclusion. In terms of the Cambridge equation, if kPT is the demand for money and M its supply, the excess-demand for money ($kPT - M$) reflects the property that an equiproportionate change in prices *and* initial money holdings causes a proportionate change in the money demanded. However, a change in prices *only*, generates a real-balance effect, and, hence, a change in the planned volume of transaction T and simultaneously a *non*-proportionate change in the demand for money (kPT). Incidentally this formulation shows very clearly that the quantity theory, properly interpreted, does not imply a constant volume of T and even more than that: as soon as there is a real-balance effect there *must* be variations in the volume of the demand for commodities.

Last but not least, an important issue must be briefly dealt with in order to connect what has just been discussed with Marshall's aborted stability analysis and his pupils' extensive research on the saving-investment technique of analysis, including the idea of 'forced saving'.

The validity of the conclusions concerning the demand-curve for money as well as those concerning the market-equilibrium curve clearly depends on the crucial assumption that individuals' initial money holdings are all increased in the same proportion. Let us, however, consider, for example, a doubling of the money-supply which is *not* distributed proportionately to the initial money balances.

In such a case, as Cantillon clearly saw it as early as 1755 (1952, pp. 98–9), the economy need not be restored to equilibrium by a doubling of all prices. On the money market the real value of the increased money holdings of each individual is not going to be the same as in the original equilibrium (his real wealth will be altered as well). Consequently the various excess demands for goods will not be the same either (i.e. the system of relative prices is no longer homogeneous of degree zero in money-prices). Patinkin puts in a more modern terminology this very idea expressed by Cantillon more than two centuries ago:

> In general, the new equilibrium position in this case [nonproportional increase of initial money-holdings] will involve higher relative prices for those goods favoured by individuals whose money holdings have more than doubled and lower relative prices for those goods favoured by individuals whose holdings have less than doubled. (1965. p. 45)

This fundamental issue is not discussed at all in Marshall's monetary theory, at least as far as his analysis of the value of money is concerned (see, however, a vague hint: 1926, p. 307, Qs . 11802–3). It is only when Marshall discusses the relations between interest and prices by means of a rudimentary Wicksell-like cumulative process that he suggests some very general considerations on the 'evil' influences of any increase of money on income distribution. But apart from wishful thinking about 'greedy speculators' and 'incompetent businessmen' (1926, p. 98) no analytical suggestion is offered to alter and to refine the crude theory expressed by the rectangular hyperbola demand curve for money. In particular it prevents Marshall from analysing the influence of money on the 'real' magnitudes saving and investment. The then already time-honoured 'forced-saving' doctrine is not even mentioned by Marshall. (It is all the more astonishing when this crucial gap is compared with the fully fledged chapter devoted by J. S. Mill to that very question; see 1909, Book III, chap. xxiii, pp. 637–50.) In this context it is not surprising that, in strong contrast with Wicksell's pupils, Marshall's successors had first to struggle with this distributional effect before moving to the novel issue of monetary equilibrium raised much earlier by Swedish and Austrian economists.

3.3 MONEY, INTEREST AND PRICES: MARSHALL'S PRIMITIVE VERSION OF THE 'CUMULATIVE PROCESS'

The absence of stability analysis brings once again in Marshall's story the basic confusion between stocks and flows. Instead of connecting people's increased *flow* of expenditures with their feeling that *their* stock of money is too large for their needs, a more-or-less direct link is drawn between an increased *outflow* of money expenditures with an increased *inflow* of money receipts. People spend more money because they receive more money, not because the value of their real balances has increased beyond the amount determined by what Marshall calls 'the habits of business' (1926, p. 268).

However, and it is absolutely crucial to keep this point very clear, this lack of all proper theoretical analysis of the real-balance effect does *not* imply that the relationship between money and prices is a mechanical one, i.e. that the effects of an increase in the quantity of money on prices is 'neutral', or equiproportionate. In that respect Marshall's approach is very similar to the classical quantity theory of Cantillon (1755), Hume (1742), Ricardo (1810) and especially Mill (1848):[10] the lack of stability-analysis through the real-balance effect does not prevent the recognition that a change in the quantity of money may generate 'distributional effects' of the 'forced saving' type.[11]

Bearing in mind that crucial weakness in Marshall's monetary theory we now turn to his own version of the cumulative process; namely, the interrelation between money, interest and prices.

Three main topics must be successively dealt with in order to gain a clear idea of the theoretical apparatus Marshall handed over to the protagonists in the inter-war saving-investment debates at Cambridge. First of all, keeping in mind how the 'real' rate of interest is determined, we investigate how the market rate (what Marshall calls discount rate) is fixed (Section I). Second, a detailed study of the dynamic relation between these two rates[12] demonstrates the weakness of Marshall's stability analysis (Section II). Third, we provide a general restatement of Marshall's theory of interest by integrating his 'real' and monetary analysis. It will be shown that, barring a clear understanding of the adjustment process through which the rate of discount tends towards the 'real' rate of interest, Marshall's theory contains all the elements put forward in the late 1930s by Robertson and Hicks in their loanable-funds theory (Section III).

I

Marshall was, of course, fully aware that the actual rate of interest on the loan market is determined by the supply and demand for loans: 'The supply of loans on the one hand and the desire of people to obtain loans on the other [determine] the rates of discount' (1926, p. 130; see also p. 273). As expected Marshall's theory is mainly devoted to a study of the supply side of the loan market. On the demand side the upper limit over which the rate of discount is higher than the estimated rate of return over costs is very much in line with the current long-run rate of interest, what Marshall calls the 'profitableness of business'. Of course, 'a rise in the rate of discount [may be] caused by an increase in the desire of some of those who use capital to borrow' (1923, pp. 256–7), but it cannot be analysed in terms of an excess demand for loans only. The ultimate cause of this increased demand for 'command over capital' is nothing other than increased demand for 'free' capital proper, due to a rise in the real rate of interest (or alternatively to a relative stickiness of the discount rate) which, in turn, 'indicates increased confidence, and perhaps increased prosperity' (1923, p. 257).[13] Thus, one must at least admit that the demand side of the loan market cannot be analysed in purely monetary terms.

On the contrary the supply side of the loan market, even if it is closely connected with the supply of 'free' capital proper, enjoys a far greater autonomy with respect to the market for investible resources. This relative independence simply arises from the fact that the banking system is able (within broad institutionally set limits) to alter (or fail to alter) the supply of 'command over capital' offered on the loan market. Put more generally, the variations of the money-supply are not connected in any proportional way with the supply for 'free' capital proper. As a matter of fact this is probably the most crucial issue in the traditional monetary theory, particularly in its Cambridge version. In 1928 Robertson rightly pointed out that this problem is at the heart of the saving-investment debate: 'the operations of lending and saving are shrouded behind a monetary veil, and . . . what really happens behind the veil is sometimes quite different from what appears to take place upon the surface' (1928b, p. 9).

Along similar lines Pigou rehearsed the same argument as late as 1949:

[Monetary facts and happenings] differ from 'real' facts and happenings in that, unlike these, they have no *direct* significance for economic welfare. Take the real facts and happenings away, and the monetary facts and happenings necessarily vanish with them; but take money away and, whatever else might follow, economic life would *not* become meaningless. (1949b, pp. 24–5; for the same idea indirectly expressed by Marshall himself see 1926, p. 115, Q. 9893)

In other words, and it is one of the favourite leitmotiv of the traditional marginalist school, the very intervention of money in any exchange operation is the root of all troubles. It is because *money is lent*, and the 'commodity'-free capital then *sold* in exchange for this money, that *temporary* gaps are open between the market-rate of discount and the 'rate which would be determined by supply and demand if real capital were lent in kind without the intervention of money' (Wicksell, 1936, p. xxv). However, even if 'the modifications which are called by the appearance of money are . . . fundamental in nature' (Wicksell, 1936, p. xxvi) one cannot escape the feeling that the very inner logic of Marshall's theory is relevant to a barter economy only. The very dichotomy between a 'real' rate of interest determined in the long run by supply and demand for 'real' capital around which oscillates a rate of discount fixed in the short run by the supply and demand for loans, shows unequivocally that, for Marshall, money is not an essential feature of a decentralised market-economy.[14] However crucial a part money may play in the short run, the long-run relations between real magnitudes remain unaltered by its presence.

Let us now examine the four main determinants of the rate of discount outlined by Marshall: variations of the supply (or demand) for 'free' capital; variations of the volume of metallic currency (what would be called today 'outside money'); changes of the volume of 'loanable money' in the banking system; influence of 'bulls' and 'bears' on the price of the stock exchange securities.

This first case directly links variations of the real rate of interest with the supply and demand for loans and hence with the rate of discount. The amount of real saving the public wish to make always takes eventually a monetary form (savings deposits with the banking system); equally, the amount of investible resources which industry requires always implies a transitory use of the loan market (line of credit). Thus, any fluctuation of the real rate of interest is bound to alter the discount rate. Indeed, this case is self-evident if one bears in mind Marshall's dictum according to which the rate of discount oscillates around the real rate of interest:

> It is obvious that the mean rate of discount must be much under the influence of the mean rate of interest for long loans; which is determined by the extent and the richness of the field for the investment for capital on the one hand, and on the other by the amount of capital seeking investment [i.e. by the 'real' rate of interest]. (1923, p. 255; see also pp. 41, 45, 130 and 257 and 1926, pp. 51 and 128)

However, and we come back to it later, variations in the rate of discount caused by variations in the same direction of the 'real' rate of interest have widely different consequences – once the adjustment process has been carried out – than cases 2, 3 and 4 in which variations in the rate of discount have the initiating part to play. It is in these latter cases that the supply side of the loan market (i.e. the banking system in general and the Central Bank in particular) have the upper hand on the regulation of the rate of discount.

The second and most obvious case is the variation of the volume of gold. It is easy to carry out this time-honoured piece of analysis in which, for example, an increase in the volume of gold is linked with an increased supply of loans and hence a drop of the discount rate (1926 pp. 130 and 274). This straightforward case need no further elaboration to show how, through the traditional mechanisms of reserve ratio and credit multiplier, an 'increase of currency . . . increases the willingness of lender to lend in the first instance, and lowers [the rate of] discount' (1926, p. 274). The opposite case – a rise of the discount rate following a contraction of the monetary base due to, for example, an export of gold in payment of trade deficit – is also fully worked out by Marshall.

The third case sees Marshall interested in various technical niceties on the loan market. His central idea is to show how various elements on the demand side of this market would alter the discount rate if unchecked by the banking system. Marshall first discusses *expected* variations of prices on the behaviour of borrowers. For instance, 'a temporary stringency caused by the withdrawal of money from the city to the country in harvest time' (1923, p. 259) could be given 'undue significance' by would-be amateur borrowers; this small initial rise of the discount rate would make them believe that the markets are all on the brink of a permanent increase of prices inducing them to borrow *en masse*. The result would be an obvious increase of the discount rate as long as this speculative mood dominates the market.

Bearing in mind the crucial part it was to play in later development in monetary theory, the fourth and most interesting case is the one in which Marshall analyses the influence of 'bulls' and 'bears' on the market for loans, and hence, on the rate of discount (1923, pp. 258–9). As a matter of fact this piece of analysis is nothing else but a hint at a central element of Keynes's liquidity-preference theory; more precisely this problem was to be thoroughly reworked in the *Treatise* (JMK, v, pp. 127–9) in connection with the determination of the price-level of investment goods.

Even if – in this analysis of the influence of the 'two views' on the rate of discount – Marshall is not aware of the stock-flow distinction as Keynes is in the *Treatise* (JMK, v, p. 127) the crucial point of a speculative demand for money or loans linked with 'bulls' and 'bears' expectations is stated quite clearly. In other words, if for example the rate of discount is expected to increase, or to keep increasing, or, alternatively, if stock exchange securities are expected to fall, or to keep falling, and if this 'bearish' attitude dominates the market, a 'small [initial] rise in the rate of discount may initiate a stock exchange avalanche' (1923, p. 259) and a further sharp rise in the discount rate. Conversely a market dominated by 'bulls' would obviously ease the tension on the money market and induce a fall in the rate of discount.

This led Marshall to advocate 'prompt action by the Bank of England in regard to the rate of discount [to check] unreasonable expansions of credit' (1923, p. 258).

II

Let us now turn to the core of the analysis: Marshall's explanation of the adjusting mechanism which makes the short-run discount rate oscillate around the long-run 'real' rate of interest.

The best way to render Marshall's analysis seems to be in his own words. By piecing together various passages scattered in no less than four books it is possible to give a fairly clear picture of Marshall's approach. It will then be possible to comment on the various steps of the reasoning, including the missing ones.

Starting from a position of equilibrium in which the rate of discount is equal to the real rate of interest, Marshall assumes that the supply of gold is increased by an influx of gold into the banking system (1926, pp. 49 and 51). Such an increase on the supply side of the loan market induces a fall in the rate of discount (1926, pp. 130–1). However, and this point is crucial, Marshall completely fails to understand the distribution effect of 'forced saving' which is the logical consequence of such an increased volume of 'command over capital':

> [A lower rate of discount] *does not increase the amount of capital in the strictest sense of the word*; it does not increase the amount of building materials, machinery, etc . . . . but it does increase the amount of command over capital which is in the hands of those whose business it is to lend to *speculative* enterprise. Having this extra supply, lenders lower still more the rate, which they charge for loans, and they keep on lowering it till a point is reached at which the demand will carry off the larger supply. When this has been done, there is more capital in the hands of speculative investors, who come on the markets for goods as buyers, and so raise prices. (1926, pp. 51–2, italic added)

If Marshall fails to draw *all* the consequences of an increased amount of 'command over capital', or, alternatively, of a drop of the discount rate, on the rate of investment and the rate of capital accumulation, his use of the price-level as the adjusting mechanism is much more satisfactory: 'and whatever form [people's] speculation may take, it is almost sure, directly or indirectly, to raise prices. This is the main issue' (1926, p. 131).

This increase in prices is then stimulated by the expectation of further price rises in the future (1926, p. 131).[15] This, in turn, causes additional demand for loans, setting in motion a *cumulative process* (the very word *is* after all in Marshall's evidence) of growth in demand for loans and rise in prices until a new position of equilibrium is reached again:

> the cycle . . . seems to be this. The new currency, or the increase of currency, goes . . . to the banking centres; and, therefore, it increases the willingness of lenders to lend *in the first instance*, and lowers discount; but it *afterwards* raises prices, and, therefore, tends to increase discount. This latter movement is *cumulative*. (1926, p. 274)

Clearly, like Ricardo (1951, iii, p. 91), Mill (1874, p. 118), Wicksell (1935, pp. 198–9), but unlike Tooke (1844, p. 123 n.) Marshall perfectly understood as early as 1887 what Keynes later dubbed 'Gibson's paradox' (JMK, vi, pp. 177–86 and 346), which throws into sharp relief the latter's claim to originality.[16]

Even if the purely logical succession of the theoretical argument is not as detailed as Wicksell's, Marshall got the message through. His use of 'the confident spirit in the business world' as a device to explain reversals of tendency is simply a weak non-analytical substitute for the real theoretical idea:[17] the price increase following the fall of the rate of discount due to an increased supply for loans due in turn to an influx of gold, generates *itself* an internal drain which draws bank reserves down, and hence, forces them to raise their discount rates again – or, what is the same thing, to decrease again their supply of loans.

Thus, while variations in the supply of money induce changes in the rate of discount (and by extension in the rate of interest on long loans) and open a gap between the actual market-rate and the 'real' equilibrium rate of interest, such changes will only be relevant to a short-run analysis; a cumulative movement in prices and demand for loans brings the discount rate back to an unaffected long-run natural rate of interest. Keeping in the strict and narrow limits of monetary theory, two remarks on Marshall's cumulative process may be suitable here. First, as argued earlier, the initial disturbance does not arise from the influence of an influx of gold on the discount rate only, but from any factor influencing the supply and/or the demand for credit. However, even if Marshall is aware of the influence, in the long run, of the 'real' rate on the discount rate, he fails to point out that the failure of the banking system to adapt the discount rate to the new 'real' rate is probably the most common happening. (What Wicksell calls 'routine' (1935, p. 204) and later writers the 'trailing bank rate doctrine' (e.g. Ellis, 1934, p. 300). Put in other words, the initial shock usually comes from the money or credit market. Without referring specifically to the real-balance effect, Marshall however clearly shows that he has grasped why, once the initial increase in money-supply has been allowed to work out all its influences, the new level of prices will be sustained. However, it is probably the nearest he comes to understanding the part played in the cumulative process by people's intention to keep their real-balances constant:

the higher prices are sustained by the fact that the amount of cash which a person cares to keep depends upon the habits of business . . . together with his individual peculiarities; if they are not changed, any increase in the amount of currency which falls to his share will raise proportionately prices so far as he is concerned. (1926, p. 25)

Second, it is clear that Marshall only saw half of the influence of the distribution effect which follows an increase in the volume of credit. Numerous passages could be quoted to show that he is aware of the 'evils of inflation' for those with fixed income,[18] but none can be provided to show how a fall of the rate of discount under the real rate fosters – for a given level of output – an increase in the level of investment in *real* terms, and, consequently, a contraction of the volume of consumption (i.e. 'forced saving') and a reduction of the marginal productivity of capital and, hence a drop of the 'real' rate of interest. In 1930 Keynes had already clearly pinpointed this weakness of Marshall's analysis (JMK, v, p. 172).

Furthermore, in a very revealing sentence Keynes clearly shows how Marshall's successors at Cambridge understood the master's monetary theory that was to be their common starting-point in the early 1920s:

This seems to me to be the doctrine on which I was brought up, and which certainly did not bring home to my mind any clear idea of the relationship between the volume of earnings at any time, the volume of savings, and the volume of goods coming forward available for consumption, or of *the connection of these things with the equilibrium between savings and investment*. (JMK, v, pp. 172–3, italic added).

We come back in Section 3.4 to Marshall's mythical 'greedy specula-tors' and 'incompetent businessmen'. However, it must be by now evident that Marshall completely failed to carry out this piece of short-run analysis to its logical end, and to connect it properly with his long-run theory of investment. The only way the real rate of interest can be altered is through long-run variations of the rate of capital accumulation; and this rate of investment is insensitive to short-run variations of the rate of discount: '. . . the [real] rate of interest which can be got for the investment of capital . . . is being lowered by the rapid and steady growth of capital – I do not mean the growth of credit, I mean the growth of things, the actual excess of production over consumption' (1926, p.49).

Ultimately, money is neutral with respect to productivity and thrift, or, alternatively stated, with respect to the supply and demand for investible resources (flow); or, in the last analysis, with respect to the supply and demand for capital as a stock.

III

It remains to be shown that Marshall's interest theory already exhibits all the characteristics of what became later to be known as the loanable-funds theory of interest.

As a matter of fact, and given the assumptions on which it is based, this theory does not show in any way what Keynes calls the 'unabridged conflict' between the 'real' and 'monetary' theories of interest (JMK, vii, pp. 182–3). Quite the contrary. Within the marginalist framework, and even if Marshall's particular version is weak and incomplete in many respects, the crucial idea that a rising price-level in the commodity markets affects the rate of interest on the loan market is undoubtedly present.[19]

This schematic outline of Marshall's theory of interest should not only summarise the argument discussed in Chapters 1 and 2, but also provide a standard framework of reference against which further developments in Cambridge will be compared.

For Marshall the actual rate of interest is determined on the market for 'command over capital', expressing in terms of supply and demand for loanable funds, temporary deviations from the basic underlying dominant forces of supply and demand for 'specialised capital' (or more precisely, through the flow proxies of supply and demand for 'free' capital determined by the intersection of an investment-demand and a saving-supply curve). In diagrammatic terms the ruling rate of interest is determined by a supply and a demand curve for 'free' capital which can be, and in fact most of the time are, shifted in one direction or another by the influence of the supply-and-demand curves for various instruments of 'command over capital' (money, credit, overdrafts, etc.). Alternatively the locus of actual market rates of interest through time can be seen as fluctuating under temporary short-lived forces arising on the various markets making up together the supply and demand for 'command over capital', around a locus of 'real' rates of interest fixed on the market for 'specialised capital'. Our task, in summarising Marshall's theory, is simply to list the main forces at work on both sides of the market for 'loans'[20] or 'investible funds' on which the only *actual*, or effective rate of interest is ultimately determined.

The amount of investible funds which people – according to Marshall – are willing to put on the market at any price consists of the following elements (they all may, of course, be either positive, negative or equal to zero):

— supply of 'free' capital (i.e. current available savings) function of the income received in the previous period (i.e. the expression of the long-run thrift factor);
— savings made in the past and released from 'worn out' 'specialised' capital goods and so becoming available for reinvestment in the same or in different forms;
— money, or purchasing power previously saved and put in store for one reason or another and now being released and placed on the market, less, of course, money currently saved and withheld from the market; in other words it is nothing other than Marshall's embryonic portfolio analysis according to which people balance advantages derived from holding money (transaction and precaution motives) and other assets (loans);
— net additional bank loans due to an increase of the banks' gold reserves.

The amount of investible funds people are ready to demand on the loan market may be conveniently classified according to the various purposes for which they are borrowed:

— funds necessary to undertake current net investment (namely the flow of 'free' capital required in the process of adapting the stock of 'specialised' capital; or still in other words, the expression of the long-run 'productivity' factor);
— funds necessary to maintain or replace existing 'specialised' capital;
— funds destined to be put in store (this in fact is the counterpart of the third element on the supply side of the market); namely, funds borrowed in expectations of higher prices/interest-rates or expectations of a fall of stock securities;[21]
— funds borrowed by 'speculative' people destined for consumption and/or 'irrational' investments over their current income.

The market-rate of interest (Marshall's rate of discount) which emerges from the interaction of these schedules of supply and demand on the market for investible funds, shows the amount of 'command over capital' people are respectively willing to put on and to take off this market in any given short period. The supply-and-demand mechanism at work on the market for saving and investment proper (capital as a flow) is also adjusting the supply and demand of all financial assets (including money) on the various markets for money, securities, bonds, etc., grafted on to these real forces of productivity and thrift. Hence, the market-rate of interest always brings in line decisions to demand loanable funds with the supply of loanable funds. However, it is only in the long run that the market-rate of interest *tends* to be equal to the 'real', notional, equilibrium rate fixed by the marginal productivity of capital and the reward for waiting.

As already argued, the lack of a precise analysis – or even empirical description – of the adjusting process through which the rate of discount oscillates around the 'equilibrium' rate of interest is the main weakness of Marshall's approach. Even if many pregnant hints are offered in various places, no systematic and organised accounts of their working can be found in any of Marshall's contributions to the subject. Worse still, Marshall assumes a perfect neutrality of money and other financial assets on the 'real' side of the economy during the short-run adjustment process as well as in the long run, despite numerous remarks on unemployment, variations of output, 'overinvestment', etc., described in his trade-cycle theory. This lack of a systematic short-run monetary theory prevented Marshall from building an integrated monetary theory of the trade cycle in which the saving-investment method of analysis would have had a leading part to play. It was left to his pupils to fill that obvious gap. Thus, the way was open to a systematic sequential disequilibrium study of Marshall's market for 'free' capital by means of an extensive and integrated use of a refined version of his basic 'investible funds' theory of interest. However, the highly sophisticated state the monetary theory of the trade cycle in terms of saving and investment reached in the early 1930s, still *followed exactly the same pattern* of logic than Marshall's: the market-rate of interest equalises in the short run the demand to the supply of loanable funds and oscillates in the long run around the 'real' rate of interest which bring the level of investment in line with full-employment saving.

In the last analysis, however weak Marshall's short-run analysis of short-lived forces is, the crucial inverse relation between the rate of interest and the volume of investment holds in the long run. Accordingly the main thrust of the economic policy argument, from Marshall to Keynes, relies on manipulations of the market-rate as the corrective *par excellence* to the trade/credit cycle. Marshall's timid suggestion in favour of a counter-cyclical rate of discount policy by the Bank of England to 'check unreasonable [speculative] expansions of credit' (1923, p. 258) proceeds from exactly the same logic and anticipates Keynes's celebrated chapter on 'The modus operandi of the Bank-Rate' (JMK, v, chap. 13). A quote from the first page of that chapter bears testimony of that unbroken continuity in the analytical argument: '[The bank-rate] is the instrument by which a disturbance is set up or equilibrium restored between the rates of saving and investment; for to raise it stimulates the one and retards the other, and conversely if it is reduced' (JMK, v, p. 166).

3.4 SOME REMARKS ON MARSHALL'S TRADE-CYCLE THEORY

Keynes's assertion that marginalist economists always *assumed* full-employment (JMK, vii, pp. 12 and 191) does not hold water. The countless trade-cycle theories suggested by these authors as explanations of short-run deviations from the long-run full-employment centre of gravity are here to testify of the acute awareness of these economists to variations of output and employment. However, what is perfectly true is that the link between the apparatus used to determine long-run equilibrium values and actual short-run market values is very tenuous indeed, if not non-existent.

Marshall is no exception to that general tendency. His trade-cycle theory, and his well-known lifelong ambition to contribute to a solution to the problem of unemployment, are dealt with in an entirely different set-up than his theory of long-run 'normal' prices. Even a cursory reading of Marshall's version of the trade cycle (1961, pp. 709–12, as from 1879, pp. 154–5) would reveal its lack of integration with the 'Relations of Demand, Supply and Value' stated in Book V of the *Principles*.

Undoubtedly there always existed a clear-cut dichotomy in Marshall's mind between the 'general laws of value and distribution' and the causes of the trade (or credit) cycle. The 'mutual relations of the disorganization of credit, production and consumption' (1961, p. 711) have nothing in common at all with the basic marginalist theorems. Trade cycle forms a separate subject of 'supreme importance' (1961, p. 712 n.), but, 'the main study needed [to bring remedy to it] is that of the organization of production and credit' (ibid.) and not an integration of these 'complex social and economic forces of the world in which we live' (1879, p. 148) into the determination of 'normal values'.

A passage taken from Book II, chap. xiii of the *Economics of Industry* gives a fairly accurate statement of the 'relation of normal to market value', namely, the relation between value and trade-cycle theory:

> [The theory of normal value] does not tell us what will be . . . the price of a certain thing at any particular time. We cannot discover the Market value of a thing without allowing for the fluctuations of supply and demand, and for the resistance which local obstacles oppose to the free movement of the stream of competition. But on the other hand we can make no progress in explaining the movements of wages and prices, unless we first understand which of them are due to local and transitional causes, and which to the Normal action of free competition. (1879, p. 149)

However, while dominant forces are the only object on which a systematic analytical inquiry can be focused (normal value), transitory and arbitrary phenomena (market value), even if they cannot by definition be made into a systematic theory, are always defined by their relation to the market-clearing, full-employment level of output implicit within Marshall's theory of value.

Once this has been clearly understood it logically follows that Marshall's trade-cycle theory is a mere descriptive list of particular imperfections which limit in the short run the tendency towards a full-employment competitive equilibrium. But, the crucial element to keep in mind is the total independence of the 'normal theory of value' from the trade-cycle theory.

The analytical description of the trade cycle given by Marshall is closely related to Overstone's (1837, p. 44, actually quoted by Marshall in 1879, p. 153) and Bagehot's (1888, chap. vi, pp. 122–59): the main emphasis is laid on 'rising credit' – following good harvests (p. 152) – as the main amplifying element which upsets businessmen's anticipations, ruins their carefully planned expectations by bringing in uncertainty as to the value of money (p. 150) and future prices (p. 158); moreover, various other 'sources of error on the side of supply and demand' interact and reinforce this main disrupting cause which make 'market values oscillate up and down on either side of normal values' (p. 158). In the chapter on 'Changes in the value of money', after a brief repetition of his basic argument on the evil of credit inflation, Marshall reasserts the validity of Say's law and the impossibility of a general overproduction by means of Mill's well-known passage (1909, pp. 557–8, later used and misquoted by Keynes in the *General Theory*, JMK, vii, p. 18). However, Marshall makes amply clear – and it is the logical counterpart of his 'want of confidence' argument – that 'though men have the power to purchase, they may not choose to use it' (1879, p. 154; 1961, p. 710). In other words the normal long-run equilibrium situation is defined by market-clearing prices on each and every market; however, for various short-run reasons – 'the chief cause of the evil [being] a want of confidence' (p. 154) – actual market prices only tend towards equilibrium positions during the trade cycle. However, even if 'there may easily be an excessive supply of some particular commodities this state of things is nothing but a state of commercial disorganisation' (p. 154), i.e. is not a state of general overproduction. Accordingly the rationale for a trade-cycle theory is not to be found in some flaws in the price-system, but exclusively in temporary market fluctuations.

Three points (which were to become very important in the 1920s and 1930s) can be dealt with here. First, it is obvious that hoarding has to take place if people 'have the power to purchase but choose not to use it'. This central element will be subsequently taken over by Robertson and systematically discussed in his various papers on 'saving and hoarding'. *Second*, variations in output and employment are equally obviously part and parcel of Marshall's trade-cycle theory – even if agents react to price-signals only (1879, p. 154; 1961, p. 687). *Third*, Marshall deals fairly accurately with the part played by rigid money wages in the credit cycle, or, in his own words, 'with gradual changes in the purchasing power of money, and fluctuations of commercial credit' (1961, p. 709). The lack of elasticity of money wages during the depression prevents the variations of real wages necessary to keep the work-force fully employed: 'The more such a policy [rigid money wages] is persisted in by trade unions generally, the deeper and the more sustained is the injury caused to the national dividend; *and the less is the aggregate employment at good wages throughout the country*' (1961, pp. 709–10, italic added).

These three main disrupting elements linked with money, and hence with 'changes in the purchasing power of money' are only special cases of a larger genus; namely the 'errors of anticipation' made by economic agents. If money, or credit, are the most obvious examples which influence 'the state of confidence', expectations and uncertainty about the future, Marshall suggests a wealth of explanations independent of variations of the purchasing power of money which may temporarily make market prices oscillate 'up and down on either side of normal value[s]'.

On the supply side Marshall lists 'uncertainty of nature's return to man's efforts' (1879, p. 158) 'imperfect knowledge' of the future (1923, p. 260), 'Temporary action of dealers' (as opposed to producers, 1879, p. 160), the action of speculators, and various temporary and cyclical influences on costs of production (p. 161) as the main general elements disrupting entrepreneurs' expectations; and, hence, making market prices diverge from 'normal equilibrium' prices.

On the demand side Marshall analyses 'some fluctuations of prices that arise from the failure to forecast changes in demand' (p. 161), 'change of fashion' (p. 161), short-run non-substitutability between capital and labour, trailing wages ('wages almost always follow . . . movements in prices', p. 165) and other non-specified rigidities in the process of poduction. An allusion is even clearly made to an accelerator-principle-like argument (p. 163).

However complex and disorderly the actual courses of the markets might be, they undoubtedly express some regularities not only relevant for the economist, but also for the economic agent. As a matter of fact any agent can learn from past experience which particular value tend to prevail on such or such market. Moreover, as 'normal' values change very slowly, they can be seen as prevailing for long periods of time, and, hence, as providing a point of reference to economic agents in the formation of their expectations of the future. For instance, investment decisions are taken by entrepreneurs on the basis of their expectations of the future returns. These expectations are based on the more persistent forces existing in the economy as expressed by the 'normal' equilibrium rate of interest determined by the twin forces of productivity and thrift. Those entrepreneurs who have temporary false anticipations – following, for example, a 'credit inflation' due to a drop in the discount rate – will revise them in the face of disappointed expectations resulting from the downswing of the cycle which, according to Marshall, must necessarily results from the growing desire of lenders to decrease their loans as the boom progresses since they are 'among the first to read the signs of the times' (1923, p. 250). This process of revision is all the more effective in the presence of uncertainty which makes agents more ready to change their plans in accordance with actual results; namely, market prices. So agents' action, 'when they are competing freely with one another, is the same as it would be if their object were to restrain the oscillations of the market value on either side of the normal value' (1879, p. 158).

In the last analysis it appears clearly that expectations, plans and the non-realisation of plans under uncertainty play no part in the determination of normal values, i.e. that the equilibrium conditions are defined without reference to these short-run passing fluctuations. It is equivalent to saying that, in the determination of his 'centre of gravity', Marshall assumes that expectations are always fulfilled, or better, that anticipations, uncertainty and disappointed expectations are not part of the data determining the equilibrium position.

Marshall's pupils, while keeping intact the idea that the theory which explains the equilibrium position is not altered by transitory oscillations, progressively incorporated in the body of the master's theoretical apparatus the idea that short-lived forces can actually alter the equilibrium position determined by dominant forces. The progressive development of the saving-investment technique of analysis appears clearly as an attempt to integrate in an articulate framework the influence of short-lived (mainly monetary) forces on the traditional long-run forces by means of a rudimentary sequence analysis.[22]

4 Early Contributions I: Hawtrey and Robertson (1911–24)

4.1 THE FIRST SCATTERED HINTS ALONG MARSHALLIAN LINES (1911–13)

It is generally recognised that the economic and financial problems Britain faced during and after the First World War were instrumental in stimulating Cambridge economists to revise and improve Marshall's monetary theory (see, e.g., Eshag, 1963, p. 97; Kahn, 1984, p. 17). Yet if it is undoubtedly true that the 1920s and 1930s were two decades of 'high theory', particularly in Cambridge, it would be wrong to ignore the refinement already brought before the First World War to Marshall's standard framework. The decisive progress towards a systematic analysis in terms of saving and investment which began to appear in the mid-1920s is the result of an interest already clearly expressed in the three or four years immediately preceeding the First World War.

Barring the all-important contributions by Hawtrey and Robertson (which will be dealt with separately in Sections 4.2 and 4.3), various hints scattered in pre-1914 contributions by Keynes (1911) and Pigou (1912) reflect a keen interest in the 'transitional stages' through which an increase of the money supply affects prices.

In that respect Keynes's 'Review of Fisher's *Purchasing Power of Money*' (1911) is undoubtedly a very revealing testimony of the state of monetary theory in pre-war Cambridge. As a matter of fact Keynes's critical comments on Fisher's fourth chapter (1911, pp. 55–73) are merely a concise statement of 'the general outlines of the theory . . . indicated by Dr. Marshall' (1911, p. 395); but, they are just that and nothing more.

The core of the relevant sections of Keynes's review is entirely devoted to a study of the 'most serious defect in Professor Fisher's doctrine . . . [namely] . . . his account of the mode by which through transitional stages an influx of new money [i.e. gold] affects prices' (1911, p. 394). Then follows an 'abbreviated account' of Fisher's theory meant to show that, compared with Marshall's, it is 'incomplete and inadequate' (1911, p. 394).

What immediately strikes the reader is the fact that Keynes critical remarks aim at minimising the part the banking system is playing in Fisher's version of the cumulative process. In other words, Keynes – following Marshall to the letter – stresses the importance of the so-called 'direct mechanism' (increased stock of money) at the expense of the so-called 'indirect mechanism' (increase of bank credits). As a matter of fact Keynes criticises Fisher on three points: for failing to explain 'clearly *how* new gold raises prices *in the first instance*' (1911, p. 395); for neglecting the influence of 'the flow of gold *out* of the banks[1] . . . thus reducing their willingness to lend' (1911, p. 395); and for expounding his theory 'too emphatically from the standpoint of interest' (1911, p. 395). This line of attack is perfectly in accord with Marshall's approach: the initial reason for the bankers to expand their loans is an increase of their gold reserves; neither Wicksell's 'trailing market rate of interest' doctrine (Ellis, 1934, p. 300) nor his hypothesis that banks emerge from a slump in a liquid state prompting them to expand their loans are even hinted at by Marshall or Keynes. Actually Keynes appears even more 'conservative' than Marshall when he argues that, despite his agreeing with Fisher that gold is the single most important cause of any price rise, the rate of interest plays too large a part in the subsequent stages of Fisher's cumulative process.

On the whole, Keynes's review definitely leaves the impression that, in 1911, his monetary analysis was centered in a much cruder fashion than Marshall's on the problems of the determination of the price-level only. There is no indication that he was working his way towards a monetary analysis of the economic process as a whole. In particular the two crucial elements indispensable for the explanation of the monetary side of the trade cycle are missing. On the other hand, Marshall's elusive attempt to elaborate a systematic analysis of the divergence between the normal rate of interest and the rate of discount is not even referred to. On the other, and like in Marshall's version of the cumulative process, the possibility of 'forced saving' fostering a 'distortion of the time structure of the production' (to use an 'Austrian' terminology) is not alluded to. Or, put in an alternative way, the income approach to the quantity theory was still alien to Cambridge economists[2] despite its appearance in Wicksell's 1907 *Economic Journal* article.

A second pre-war contribution worth mentioning in view of its later influence on Robertson is part IV of Pigou's *Wealth and Welfare* (1912), particularly chap. iv entitled 'The Variability of General Prices' (pp. 423–38).

Two problems which were subsequently to occupy the centre of the analytical stage are touched upon by Pigou in the course of his lengthy discussion of 'the variability of the real earnings of the working classes by the fact that . . . the purchasing power of money is not constant' (1912, p. 423).

First, Pigou briefly refers for the first time to the idea of 'forced saving' in the following terms: 'the issue of new inconvertible notes in payment of their employees affords a means, by which needy governments can exact forced loan, without interest, from their subjects' (1912, p. 433). Of course, this is the most straightforward and obvious case of 'forced saving'. When purchasing power is 'created' in such a way – there being no additional commodities and no corresponding reductions of money-expenditures by savers – prices must rise, first the prices of good on which the new purchasing power is spent, and later on all or nearly all of them. Furthermore in this type of government paper inflation, the new level of prices will last indefinitely unless it is altered by a reduction of the money-supply.

Pigou does not raise in any way the whole set of ideas connected with a bank credit inflation. No attempt is made to show the reallocation process of 'factors of production' fostered by the 'forced loans' exacted from the public by the business men through the newly created purchasing power the banks grant them via new loans. Since this first step is not taken, the logical continuation of the argument is also missing; particularly the ultimate increase of output (and consequently drop of the general level of prices) this 'forced saving' process should lead to.

Second, ten years before Lavington (1921) and eighteen years before Keynes (1930), Pigou discusses with great clarity what Robertson later dubbed the 'threefold-margin-of-preference theory of interest' (1940, p. 17); namely, the fact that the rate of interest is not only the expression of the 'marginal inconvenience of refraining from consumption' (Marshall's reward for waiting), but also measures the 'satisfaction derived from the marginal unit spent on consumption goods' *and the 'marginal convenience of holding money'*. An inquiry into Pigou's treatment of this problem is necessary and important for two reasons, both relevant to our main argument. On the one hand,

Lavington (1921, p. 30) and not Pigou is usually credited with this piece of analysis (see Robertson, 1937, p. 431; 1940, p. 16; Hicks, 1935, pp. 62–3 n. 1; and Patinkin, 1965, pp. 94, 579–80 and 1976, p. 42). Bearing in mind that Marshall already mentioned this idea, this discussion of the same question by Pigou should, on the other hand, strengthen the contention that the loanable-funds theory of interest was already part and parcel of the Cambridge monetary theory well before Robertson suggested it as an alternative to Keynes's liquidity-preference doctrine.[3]

Appropriately Pigou tackles this problem in a paragraph devoted to the 'variability of the quantity of money demanded'. After having discussed along Marshallian lines the demand for money in the form of income deposits, Pigou extends his analysis beyond this straightforward case and has consequently to take account of the influence on this demand of the rate of interest *and* of the general state of expectations.

First, Pigou defines the problem for an exchange economy: 'when the volume of national dividend is given, [the demand schedule for money] rises and falls as the ratio between the satisfactions, which people look for from the *n*th unit of money and the *n*th unit of commodities respectively, rises and falls' (1912, p. 424). Clearly, in that case, there is only a 'twofold-margin of satisfaction': the level of 'satisfaction' (to use Pigou's terminology) yielded by the marginal resources spent on consumption goods must be equal, in equilibrium, to the level of 'satisfaction' yielded by the marginal unit of resources held in the form of money. Or, to express the same point somewhat differently, the choice between present and future consumption (the familiar Marshallian 'thrift' factor) is restricted to a choice, at the margin, between consumption goods and money; what, in turn, implies that the saving-decisions margin and the liquidity-decisions margin are synonymous.

Then Pigou extends this twofold-margin case to the more general threefold-margin case of a production economy. This not only implies the introduction into the picture of an investment decisions margin (namely the rate of interest linked to the 'expectations as to the effectiveness of investment', i.e. 'productivity'), but also necessitates a disaggregation of the magnitude 'commodities' into 'investible' and 'non-investible commodities'.

Then the stage is set for Pigou to restate the theoretical basis of Marshall's earlier version of the loanable-funds theory of interest:

Of those [causes] that bring about variations in the comparative satisfaction, which people derive from the nth unit of money and the nth unit of commodities, the more important are, on the one hand *changes in expectation as to the effectiveness of investment*, and, on the other hand, changes in estimates of the advantage of holding money as security against possible difficulties in meeting obligations shortly to fall due. (1912, p. 424; italic added)

While the first cause is nothing but an early version of Keynes's transactions and precautionary motives, namely, a slightly amended version of the Marshallian k, the second cause is akin to Keynes's speculative motive and involves not only the rate of interest, but also the expectations of how this interest rate is going to evolve.

These 'expectations concerning the fruitfulness of investment', or, in other words, these 'variations in the sentiment of the business world' (1912, p. 425) send us back to Marshall's analysis of the influence of 'bulls' and 'bears' on the demand for securities, and hence on the rate of interest. It appears clearly from Pigou's analysis that if 'expectations concerning the fruitfulness of investment' are high – that is, that the rate of interest is expected to rise, or alternatively the prices of securities to fall (bearish market) – then the demand for money will rise because people are more disposed than before to hold their wealth in the form of money balances, and vice versa. If the demand for money is not increased to meet that extra demand, the rate of interest which, by the virtue of the 'threefold-margin' argument is also the measure of the increased 'satisfaction' yielded by the nth unit of money, will eventually rise.

The fact that the individuals' demand for money is determined by balancing, at the margin, the advantages of holding money with the benefits that could be derived from buying other assets, including securities, undoubtedly reveals that Pigou was aware of the influence of the demand for money on the rate of interest. However, the crucial theoretical consequence of this piece of analysis is definitely *not* explored by Pigou.

Like Marshall, and for the same reasons, he completely fails to recognise in *Wealth and Welfare*, the 'real' impact of variations of the rate of interest resulting from changes in the 'liquidity preference' (and/or from changes in the money-supply): nowhere does Pigou hint at a possible impact of changes in the market rate of interest on the volume of investment, and, subsequently, on the volume of savings.

This total lack of an attempt to integrate 'real' and monetary theory, or, put in another way, to provide a dynamic adjustment process, was still part and parcel of Pigou's analytical framework in his celebrated 1917 paper. Compared with the analysis of *Wealth and Welfare* Pigou even went one step backwards in his 'Exchange Value of Legal-tender Money' article: references to 'Expectations concerning the fruitfulness of investment' are very much reduced (1917 p. 182). The only remaining element of his 1912 analysis Pigou still discusses in 1917 is contained in a rather flat restatement of the 'threefold-margin' argument: 'These three uses, the production of convenience and security, the production of commodities, and direct consumption, are rival to one another' (1917, p. 181).

However, even if in 1917 no allusion is made to the 'bulls' and 'bears' argument, the very fact that the 'threefold-margin' doctrine is discussed with reference to the demand for money is enough to substantiate the claim that Pigou, after Marshall, *also* held a monetary theory of interest. However, in Pigou's general set-up, the separation between the analysis of static equilibrium and the analysis of trade cycle is still too rigidly observed for that integration of 'real' and 'monetary' theories of interest to take place.

In the last analysis this complete dominance of the theory of interest by a twofold-margin between 'productivity' and 'thrift' is simply the mirror image of the absence of any analysis of the influence of money on 'real' magnitudes; namely, the concept of 'forced' or 'abortive' saving. It is in 1923 only that Pigou, shortly after Robertson, was to use this potentially powerful instrument to lay the basis of the saving-investment technique of analysis.

4.2 HAWTREY'S CONTRIBUTION: FROM *GOOD AND BAD TRADE* (1913) to 1925

The year 1913 and the publication of *Good and Bad Trade* marks an important turning-point in the pre-*General Theory* Cambridge monetary theory. Breaking entirely new grounds, and apparently completely independently of the then much more advanced Continental tradition, Hawtrey laid down the basic stepping-stones of the so-called 'income approach' to the problem of the value of money.

Building upon Marshall's cash-balance equation Hawtrey extended the traditional Cambridge analysis by (unknowingly) reverting to Tooke's '13th Thesis',[4] which suggests that the explanation of money prices should start not from the quantity of money but from nominal income. It is well known that both approaches are complementary, or, as Schumpeter puts it that 'the former [income approach] is nothing but another way of writing the latter [cash balance]' (1954, p. 1109).[5] However, Hawtrey's emphasis on the 'aggregate of all money incomes' (1913, p. 6) [the exact equivalent of Wicksell's 'aggregate of money incomes' (1936, p. 44) borrowed in turn from Tooke (1844, p. 123)], on how it varies, is expanded or held, is a crucial turning-point on the road towards an analysis in terms of income, saving and investment. As Schumpeter argues, this shift of emphasis does not in itself solve any important issue, though it provides a starting-point for a stability analysis badly lacking in Marshall's quantity equation:

> The effect of an increase of money upon prices is indeterminate so long as we do not know [as in Marshall's approach] who gets the additional money, what he does with it, and what is the state of the economic organism on which the new money impinges. The income [approach] formula does not in itself take account of all these questions *but it directs our attention toward them and thus helps monetary analysis to step out of its separate compartment.* (1954, p. 1110, italic added; for a similar argument see Leijonhufvud, 1981, p. 152)

However weak Hawtrey's early attempt was, his *Good and Bad Trade* was certainly 'revolutionary' in the proper sense of the term if one compares it with what has just been said of Keynes's (1911) and Pigou's (1912) analyses. Despite the fact that Hawtrey's purely monetary theory of the trade cycle remained at a rather superficial level with an analysis in terms of variations of 'dealers' stocks' to the exclusion of all substantial influence of money and/or credit on fixed capital, its potentialities were great. Coupled with Robertson's 'real' analysis of an 'overinvestment' type, Hawtrey's income approach was to play an important part in the 1920s debate.

As a matter of fact this 'income approach', as independently developed by Hawtrey, laid down the basis for an analysis of the *dynamic process* of monetary saving and investment (the saving-investment technique of analysis) and for a comprehensive and integrated monetary theory of the rate of interest. On top of that already impressive record, Hawtrey's contribution brought home to Cambridge many systematic (though still unconnected) pieces of analysis which were later to take the pride of place in Keynes's, Robertson's and Pigou's subsequent works: a much improved version of the real-balance effect, a systematic analysis of the variability of output and employment, the wage–price lag and the part played by wage rigidities in the cycle, the notion of a credit 'deadlock' as an early version of Keynes's so-called liquidity trap and the interest inelasticity of the investment-demand curve.

Apart from a few articles written during the First World War and collected in *Monetary Reconstruction*, the main complementary source to *Good and Bad Trade* is chap. 3 of *Currency and Credit*,[6] particularly the *Note* to that chapter, which gives the definite algebraic version of the 'consumers' income and outlay and the unspent margin' doctrine (1919, p. 53). Bearing in mind that we are not interested in Hawtrey's trade-cycle theory *per se*, but only in the part played in it by the theory of interest, this section logically falls into three parts. First, it is briefly shown that Hawtrey took over from Marshall the latter's 'normal' interest rate theory. Second, after a brief discussion of the income-approach framework, a detailed analysis of Hawtrey's dynamic adjustment process, i.e. his version of the cumulative process, provides the basic material to appreciate his contribution to the foundations of the Cambridge saving-investment technique of analysis. Third, and last, a systematic exposition of Hawtrey's theory of interest shows more clearly and more decisively than for Marshall's that Hawtrey adopted a loanable-funds version of the determination of the interest rate.

I

Even if Hawtrey's numerous books pay only lip-service to 'pure' marginalist value-theory, it is none the less clear that their general framework of analysis is Marshallian in each and every respect. The Marshallian 'normal' rate of interest is characteristically defined by Hawtrey as the 'cost of production of the capital' (1913, p. 31) and its level is determined relatively to the possibility of substitution of labour by capital goods; namely:

> the rate which represent[s] the actual labour-saving value of capital at the level of capitalisation reached by industry. This ratio of labour saved per annum to labour expended on first cost is a physical property of the capital actually in use, and under perfectly stable monetary conditions is equal to the market rate of interest. It may be conveniently termed the 'natural rate'. (1913, p. 66; see also 1937a, p. 50)

Then, in a very compressed fashion, Hawtrey shows that he is familiar with the main issues raised by Marshall in the latter's discussions of the determination of the 'normal' rate of interest: the quasi-rent versus rate of interest distinction arising in connection with the difference between a stock of 'old capital' (i.e. Marshall's fixed capital) and a flow of 'new capital' (Marshall's 'free capital') (1913, pp. 31 and 47); the long-run tendency towards a uniform rate of interest on capital goods according to 'the ordinary operation of supply and demand in an open market' (1913, pp. 29 and 35); the basic idea of the 'natural' rate of interest as a centre of gravity around which the 'actual' market rate is fluctuating, altered as it is by 'the tendency of prices' (1913, p. 66), the bankers' credit policy (1913, p. 77) or the variations 'in the reserves of working balances of ready money which all recipients of incomes are impelled by prudence to maintain' (1913, p. 14); and the fact that this 'natural' rate of interest fluctuates itself in the long run under the influences of technical progress and capital accumulation.

In the end this 'natural' rate of interest, even if not explicitly determined by the intersection of the schedules of saving and investment, displays the same crucial inverse relation with respect to the volume of investment (see, however, his 1933, p. 130, for an explicit statement of the downward-sloping investment-demand function).

On a more general methodological level Hawtrey is perfectly aware of the fact that his short-run trade-cycle approach is only a 'superstructure' grafted on to the Marshallian long-run analysis of 'normal' prices. Despite the fact that 'Trade is never normal' and that 'the influences which produce fluctuations are not sudden but gradual' and that 'we can [not] postulate an initial condition of stability' (1913, p. 175) Hawtrey clearly considers the economic system as inherently stable around the traditional long-run full-employment equilibrium. Accordingly *Good and Bad Trade* is, in Hawtrey's own words, a theoretically simplified attempt 'to examine certain elements in the modern organization of the world [i.e. money and credit] which appear to be intimately connected with the fluctuations' (1913, p. 3); and to follow 'the effects of the disturbances . . . upon perfectly stable economic condition . . . up to the attainment of a new state equilibrium under the altered conditions' (1913, p. 175). During all his very long life Hawtrey was to remain faithful to this approach which is epitomised in a passage which conveniently shows the extent of his theoretical departure from a strict Marshallian orthodoxy:

the fact that money is merely machinery does not prevent it from having profound and far-reaching effects on the production and consumption of wealth. Though the quantity of money in circulation is not relevant to a consideration of total wealth, *changes* in the quantity of money in circulation react upon the industrial and commercial state of the country, and have effects of the greatest importance (1913, p. 36).

II

In a nutshell Hawtrey's central argument is to show how 'the consumers' income rises and falls with the amount of new credit created; [how] the consumers' outlay [rises and falls] with the consumers' income; [and, ultimately, how] the credit extinguished [rises and falls] with the consumers' outlay' (1919, p. 44).

Put in more familiar terms Hawtrey simply suggests a piece of dynamic analysis showing how an equilibrium is eventually re-established through a mechanism describing how an initial variation in money income, due to changes in the rate of credit creation, is allocated between changes of the consumers' outlays (including consumption *and* investment, i.e. what Hawtrey calls 'effective demand') and changes in the unspent margin (i.e. consumers' purchasing-power balances including cash and credit). This mechanism not only involves a study of how, ultimately, the price-level rises in the same proportion as the quantity of money, but also shows that variations of output and employment are an essential feature of such a short-run 'cumulative process'.

In the last analysis Hawtrey demonstrates that, if ultimately prices change in proportion to the quantity of money, during the adjustment period the price-level is determined by the level of consumers' outlay.

Starting with Marshall's cash-balance version of the quantity theory Hawtrey points out that it is a comparative static instrument only, completely lacking any proper dynamic analysis describing how, once the system has been hit by a change in the money-supply, it finds its way back to equilibrium. Furthermore, Hawtrey rightly sees Marshall's definition of 'money-supply' as too restrictive, particularly in its playing down the crucial part played by bank credit:

It is only at times of equilibrium, when the quantity of credit and money in circulation is neither increasing nor decreasing, that the relation of prices and money values to that quantity of credit and money is determined by the individual's considered choice of the balance of purchasing power appropriate to his income. At all other times one of the most important of the economic conditions which the quantity theory takes to be 'given' will be an acceleration or retardation in the creation of credit. In practice it seldom, perhaps never, happens that a state of equilibrium is actually reached.' (1919, p. 46; see also 1913, p. 23; 1923, p. 58, and 1932, p. 168, where Hawtrey describes monetary equilibrium as 'inherently unstable' and 'balancing upon a razor's edge')

Having thus pinpointed where he thinks the main weakness of the cash-balance equation is, Hawtrey can introduce his basic piece of analysis to study the 'relations between the rate of creation of credit, the consumers' income and outlay and the unspent margin' (1919, p. 53). As a matter of fact, in *Good and Bad Trade* (chaps 2–9) Hawtrey devises a step-by-step argument showing how the 'equilibrium' double equality between the 'total cost of production', the 'aggregate of all money incomes' and the 'total effective demand for all finished commodities' (1913, p. 6) is related to the supply of money. The connection is no longer exclusively between the supply of money and the price-level, but between the supply of money and money-income: 'Since the aggregate of money incomes is proportional to the stock of money, it must be possible to establish some determining relation between them' (1913, p. 9).

After an analysis of the demand for money very much in line with Marshall's (1913, pp. 10–11), Hawtrey concludes that 'the link connecting the [total circulation and the total income of a country] is to be found in the reserves of working balances of ready money [i.e. the 'unspent margin'] which all recipients of income are impelled by prudence to maintain' (1913, p. 14). In other words the Marshallian k is replaced by a concept which is no longer defined with respect to the level of income only, but is equated with 'the margin, up to date, of . . . income over expenditure' (1913, p. 11; see also 1926a, p. 422); or, alternatively, where the money-supply is equated to the unspent margin defined as the sum of 'cash and bank credit balances' (1928, p. 109). In short the *unspent margin* is a *stock* of money balances, the size of which can be altered by the unspent share of any credit creation/destruction (a *flow*) measured by the discrepancy between current income and current expenditure.

Bearing in mind that 'investment is merely expenditure', and that 'the position of a man [with respect to 'working balances'] *qua* consumer and investor . . . is not in essence different [from] his position *qua* producer' (1913, p. 12), it is easy to check that if credit is being created and extinguished at exactly equal rates, the unspent margin will be constant and equal to the Marshallian *k*; and the economic system will be in a state of long-run equilibrium.

On the other hand, any change in the relation between the aggregate money-income and the aggregate consumers' outlay (reflecting a rising/falling effective demand) induces a change in the relative size of the consumers' unspent margin. As Hawtrey puts it:

> If . . . the creation of credit is accelerated or retarded, the consumers' income is increased or diminished. The consumers' outlay will also be increased or diminished, *but not necessarily by an equal amount*. The difference between the consumers' income and consumers' outlay will represent a change in the unspent margin. (1919, p. 41)

Since the level of effective demand *is* the consumers' outlay, it follows that, during the adjusting period, it is not the unspent margin but consumers' outlay which is the proximate cause in the determination of prices (see, e.g., 1926b, p. 130).

Three basic questions immediately arise in connection with the general framework of analysis. First, how are variations in the rate of credit creation brought about?; second, and in Hawtrey's own words, '*how* is the [extra] money used?' (1913, p. 9) (stability analysis including Hawtrey's own version of the cumulative process, and, hence, his theory of interest); and, third, what are 'the consequential changes in production and consumption' (1919, p. 54) brought about by changes in the money supply? ('Real' disproportionalities of the 'forced'/abortive savings type.)

The first question can be readily answered. As a matter of fact it is undoubtedly the weakest link in Hawtrey's framework. Since, as he admits himself, his explanation of the trade cycle is a purely monetary one (1926b, p. 132, and 1937a, p. 124) the initial disturbance driving the system out of equilibrium is to be found in the credit system only. In opposition to Wicksell's 'trailing bank-rate doctrine' according to which 'the loan rate does not adapt itself quickly enough to . . . changes . . . in the real rate of interest' (1935, p. 205, italic omitted), Hawtrey's version of the 'cumulative process, gives to variations of the market rate of interest, and ultimately to the bankers' behaviour, the crucial part to play:

> The real starting-point of the whole [stream of argument] is to be found in the thesis . . . that a depression of trade is in essence a general slackening of the money demand for commodities, and an expansion of trade is a general augmentation of the money demand for commodities. (1913, p. 272)

Hence, ultimately,

> A Depression [Expansion] of Trade occurs when the amount of credit money in existence is more [less] than the bankers think prudent, having regard to their holdings of cash, and they raise [lower] the rate of interest in order to reduce the excess [to encourage borrowing]. (1913, pp. 267–8)

Even if Hawtrey's subsequent analysis was well ahead of the then available version of the part played by the banking system in the trade cycle its strictly short-run monetary starting-point can hardly be seen as a satisfactory explanation of all and every economic fluctuations. This lack of connection with any more fundamental argument in 'real' terms (overinvestment *à la* Robertson or *à la* Hayek, irregularity of technical progress *à la* Schumpeter, or even more 'psychological' theories *à la* Pigou) was to prejudice most of the economic profession against Hawtrey's general approach and blind some of its leading members to the originality of his performance.[7] Before turning to this cumulative process itself it seems worth digressing-slightly from the main argument to show that Hawtrey occupies a niche of his own in the main stream of Cambridge monetary theory. Like Pigou (1917), Robertson (1922) and Keynes (1923) Hawtrey describes with a reasonable degree of accuracy the forces propelling the economy towards its new equilibrium position. He is undoubtedly familiar with the idea that the demand functions of the 'real' sector *are* affected by changes in the real value of cash balances. The analysis in terms of consumers' outlay and unspent margin is nothing but a rather primitive way to explain, how, starting from an equilibrium position where the quantity of money is just at that level which satisfies agents' transactions and precautionary needs, an exogenous increase in the *nominal* quantity of money (bank credit) pushes the *real* quantity above its equilibrium value and thereby creates inflationary pressures in the various commodity markets until the increased price-level has reduced this *real* quantity and removed the disequilibrating inflationary pressures themselves (1935, p. 512).

However, and unlike all other Cambridge economists,[8] Hawtrey seems to have understood the working of the forces stabilising the economy at the new equilibrium position once it is reached. Hence, Hawtrey should be regarded as having recognised the real-balance effect in the fullest sense of the term. As this fact is usually not acknowledged, not even by Patinkin – who, however, does *not* consider Hawtrey as a member of the Cambridge School (1965, p. 167 n. 18) – it seems interesting to ponder it. Our extensive discussion of Marshall's confusion between a demand curve for money and a market-equilibrium curve has revealed that to this confusion corresponds a partial understanding of the real-balance effect, namely, that no proper test of the *stability* of the price-level in terms of real cash-balances is offered. Things can be made perfectly clear by using Patinkin's so-called 'tripartite thesis'. According to this formulation, a complete and systematic statement of the neo-classical monetary theory has to display three distinctive features:

> an increase in the quantity of money disturbs the optimum relation between the level of money balances and the individual expenditures; *this disturbance generates an increase in the planned volume of these expenditures (the real-balance effect)*; and this increase creates pressures on the price-level which push it upwards until it has risen in the same proportion as the quantity of money. (1965, pp. 163–4)

Patinkin then argues that 'only Wicksell (1936, pp. 39–41) and Fisher (1911, pp. 153–4) brought out th[is] crucial intermediary stage' (1965, p. 164) in which the *flow* of extra money expenditures is increased because people feel their *stock* of money is too high. However, without asking too much from the texts it seems possible to add the name of Hawtrey to Patinkin's 'roll of honour':

Textual evidence supporting this claim can be found in *Good and Bad Trade*, even excluding all the other works by Hawtrey. This fact probably explains why Hawtrey's independent discovery has not yet received the same recognition as Wicksell's and Fisher's. *Good and*

Bad Trade is conspicuously absent from Patinkin's bibliography and, when quoted by other writers,[9] it is not in connection with the real-balance effect. In chap V, entitled 'A Monetary Disturbance in an Isolated Community with no Banking System', Hawtrey gives, in a vivid and highly simplified form, the backbone of his demonstration. His discussion of the deflationary case undoubtedly displays the three characteristics of Patinkin's tripartite thesis:

Stage One

Suppose the disturbance to take the form of a sudden diminution [through taxation] of the stock of money . . . After the withdrawal, therefore, . . . members of the community . . . will find that they are in danger of a shortage [of working balances of money].

Stage Two

In the absence (as assumed) of a banking system, it will be necessary for them to restrict expenditure for a time in order to replenish balances.

Stage Three

But though any one may replenish his balance by economising, it is clear that no transfers of money from one individual to another can replenish *all* the balances, the total of which has been definitely reduced by a certain amount. *A new equilibrium can only be found by a change in incomes* [induced by a drop in the price-level] *which will make a reduced scale of balances sufficient.* (1913, pp. 38–9, last italic added)

Clearly 'if the monetary equilibrium . . . is disturbed, the movement will end . . . in a state of equilibrium on *a new scale of incomes* and prices' (1913, p. 44, italic added) compatible with the reduced stock of money.[10]

Let us now revert to our main argument.

The details of Hawtrey's cumulative process can best be understood by following through his standard case, which shows the skeleton of his argument.

Hawtrey starts off by introducing a banking system which 'can create money out of nothing' (1913, p. 57). In this system, there is no longer a direct connection between 'the total of the deposits and the amount of coins which has been paid to the banks'. A 'long and carefully sifted experience' has however taught the bankers what must be the size of their reserves 'to meet the fresh demands for cash to which the creation of new money [i.e. bank credits] may lead' (1913, pp. 56-7; see also p. 81). Finally, like 'a seller encourages or discourages buyers by lowering or raising his prices, . . . the banker encourages or discourages borrowers by lowering or raising the rate of interest' (1913, p. 58) in order to keep his stock of legal-tender currency in due proportion with his outstanding liabilities.

In addition to the 'natural rate of interest' Hawtrey introduces at the start of his demonstration *two* other rates of interest. Thus, instead of analysing *à la* Wicksell, or even *à la* Marshall, the connection between interest and prices, Hawtrey suggests a highly original and sophisticated piece of analysis blending the *normal rate of interest* and the *rate of discount* borrowed from Marshall with *Fisher's 'real' rate of interest*, i.e. the nominal rate corrected for the price increase (1907, pp. 358-60).

This so-called *profit rate* reflects the fact that – even without any intervention of the banking system – 'where monetary conditions are not stable, the market rate diverges from the natural rate according to the tendency of prices' (1913, p. 66).

In brief, Hawtrey's trilogy amounts simply to a 'natural' rate of interest which represents the 'actual labour-saving value of capital' (r_n); a 'rate of profit', i.e. the 'natural' rate corrected for price-changes (r_p); a 'market rate of interest' which represents the only actual market phenomenon; and this rate (r_m) is ultimately determined by the banking system 'according as the bankers wish to discourage or encourage borrowing' (1913, p. 66).[11]

Hawtrey starts off from a position of equilibrium in which the 'natural rate' is identical to the profit rate, these two being in turn equal to the market rate of interest:

$$r_n = r_p = r_m \tag{1}$$

He then assumes that this equilibrium is disturbed either by changes in the quantity of currency or, more likely, by changes 'in the quantity of purchasing power which is based on the quantity of credit money' (1913, p. 74) due to the bankers' failure to differentiate 'a casual increase in their reserves' (1913, p. 74) from a lasting one. For the sake of his argument Hawtrey chooses a straightforward contraction of the stock of money through government taxation.

Initially this causes a contraction of the 'working balance' of money (or 'unspent margin') of each and every individual subject to that new tax. The relation between the level of his income and his stock of money (cash balances) being upset, every individual takes steps to replenish his working balance (real-balance effect). As the existence of a banking system is assumed, individuals need not reduce their expenditures to make the reduced balances sufficient: they simply turn to their bankers and draw out enough cash to restore their working balances. This sudden withdrawal obviously depletes the bankers' reserves and diminishes the community's purchasing power by the amount of currency withdrawn. Before the bankers react to that diminution of their reserves, the very contraction of the volume of currency induces a 'relatively small depression' (1913, p. 59). Dealers' stocks start increasing following the diminished volume of effective demand (consumers' outlay) and the market rate of interest may even be slightly reduced, the dealers borrowing less as they try to reduce their stocks which are suddenly out of proportion with a flagging demand. Hence,

$$r_n > r_p = r_m \tag{2}$$

Then, finding themselves with reserves below the level demanded by their liabilities (another illustration of the real-balance effect), banks desire to reduce their loans. In order to discourage borrowers, they increase the bank rate: 'On the contraction of the currency occurring the bankers raised the market rate above the natural rate' (1913, p. 68). That is,

$$r_n > r_p < r_m \quad (\text{with } r_m \lessgtr r_n) \tag{3}$$

Once that initial intervention by the bankers has been made, Hawtrey is quite clear not only about its cumulative consequences, but also about the inherent instability of an economic system with a banking network:

the equilibrium which the bankers have to maintain in fixing the rate of interest is essentially 'unstable', in the sense that if the rate of interest deviates from its proper value [i.e. the rate of profit] by any amount, however small, *the deviation will tend to grow greater and greater until steps are taken to correct it.* (1913, p. 76; italic added; see also p. 263)

This rise in the bank-rate affects two classes of borrowers: the producers and the dealers. The producers' cost of production is, of course, increased and they quote higher prices to the dealers in order to cover this extra cost. But, adds Hawtrey – and this is crucial for his subsequent position in the debate between Keynes, Robertson and himself up until 1939 – 'changes in the rate of interest such as we are considering are too small to affect retail prices immediately' (1913, p. 62). In other words, increased costs of production reduce stocks rather than prices.[12] Despite side-discussions on the impact of changes in the bank-rate on saving and investment, Hawtrey's entire analysis of the consequences of such variations is concentrated on changes in dealers' stocks.

It is only through such dealers' attempts to reduce their stocks that the production sector is hit. As a matter of fact, 'the money which the dealers would otherwise have been using to pay the manufacturers for goods, they are using to extinguish their indebtedness to their bankers' (1913, p. 62).

Faced with a slackening of demand the producers lower their prices as far as costs of production permit, hoping to avoid restriction of output and employment. This cut in prices is seen by the producers as a way to beat the dealers' attempts to reduce their stocks, by allowing them to stimulate the consumers' demand with lower retail prices.

However, and this marks the start of the most interesting part of Hawtrey's cumulative process, in the meanwhile (i.e. before the producers' initial and *limited* reduction has had time to stimulate demand) a reduction of stocks by dealers and a reduction of output by the producers will *already* have taken place. This crucial step of Hawtrey's argument needs careful examination.

What dealers and producers try to achieve is 'a diminution of [their] indebtedness to the bank, and this diminution of bankers' assets [is synonymous with] a diminution in their liabilities, i.e. in the supply of credit money' (1913, p. 63). Hence, 'the balances of money in the hand of the public [i.e. the unspent margin] are therefore decreasing, and the superstructure of incomes erected thereon is simultaneously shrinking' (1913, p. 63). In other words, the money-supply is partly demand determined. We are back to Hawtrey's basic income approach: a contraction of the dealers' indebtedness implies a drop in the volume of aggregate *money* income, unspent margin, and ultimately consumers' outlay. However, as the 'curtailment of one's man expenditure means a curtailment of another man's receipts' (1913, p. 64), the cumulative contraction of nominal income *and* prices fostered by the contraction of the dealers' and producers' indebtedness has not only to start immediately, but prices and incomes (mainly wages) also have to fall in the same proportion to avoid reductions in output and employment. Realistically, Hawtrey takes account of both elements.

On the other hand, he is well aware that firms cannot continue producing at an unchanged level until prices and wages start falling, for this would require them to accumulate inventories at levels increasing with the decreasing dealers' demand (1913, p. 267). On the other hand, 'if the producers do not receive sufficient orders to employ their capital and labour at full time, *they must either reduce their output, or reduce their prices, or both*' (1913, p. 40, italic added). In short, changes in output and employment, or, in other words, *quantity adjustments* arise from the fact that prices of consumption goods are not immediately adjusted to changes in demand, and from the lack of flexibility of money wages.

This analysis is certainly Hawtrey's finest achievement given the state of economic and monetary theory in pre-1914 England.[13] He not only provides a very interesting and novel discussion on the brunt respectively born by price and quantity adjustments, but he also clearly gives priority to quantity adjustments over price adjustments. Prices react only to *actual* contractions of output, incomes and employment following a reduction of dealers' demand.

In other and rather anachronistic words, producers are first hit by quantity rationing and are no longer responsive to price-signals only. In total opposition to Wicksell's and Marshall's version of the cumulative process, time-lags, wage- and price-rigidities are explicitly introduced in the picture. It allows Hawtrey to discuss the influence of the related quantity adjustments (output and employment) on the length of the adjustment process. Hence, 'throughout the period of high interest there [will be] *a progressive restriction of output and fall of prices*' (1913, pp. 64–5, italic added).

To understand how and why Hawtrey's cumulative process is lengthened and how and why the economic system nevertheless reaches a 'perfectly stable full-employment position', it is now necessary to examine in more detail the respective influence and working of the price and quantity-adjustment mechanisms.

In so far as the adjustment is only made by laying off workers, the total output will be diminished without change in the price-level:

> This process could, theoretically, be pushed so far that the proportional decrease in the number employed and in the national output would be equal to the proportional decrease in the money circulation . . . the old scale of incomes and prices could be maintained; but the incomes would be shared among a portion only of the community, upon whom would be thrown in some form or other the burden of supporting the unemployed. (1913, p. 41)

On the other hand

> if the adjustment could be made entirely by a suitable diminution of wages and salaries, accompanied by a corresponding diminution of prices, the [economic system] could be placed . . . in a new position of equilibrium, in which the output would continue unchanged, and distribution would only be modified by the apportionment of a somewhat larger share of the national product to the possessors of interest, rent, and other kinds of fixed incomes. (1913, p. 41)

The reality, of course, lies somewhere between these two extreme cases. The initial contraction of output and employment does eventually foster a reduction of the price-level, which, however, is curbed by the rigidity of money-wages. In Hawtrey's model it is clear that 'Wages . . . are the key to the situation' (1913, p. 65; see also p. 63).

Despite a more explicit consideration of quantity adjustments alongside the traditional price-level argument, the logic of Hawtrey's cumulative process is the same as Wicksell's. Hawtrey simply shows that, in the 'real world' the cumulative process is not as simple and straightforward as in theory, and that, in particular, it can be a long-drawn-out one.

The disruptive consequences on prices and output resulting from *a given* discrepancy between the market-rate and the profit-rate are – to use Wicksell's (1935, p. 208) or Marshall's (1926, p. 274) terminology – 'cumulative'. That is, if that discrepancy is maintained it will bring about a *continuous*, and not only a given, decrease in prices and/or in output.

Two questions now arise: are there forces which bring Hawtrey's cumulative process to an end? If so, how?

The fundamental restrictive element preventing the process going

on for ever is the mirror image of the initial element which started it
all; namely, the intervention of the banks to adapt the volume of
their reserves (reduced by the initial tax increase) to their liabilities
(1913, p. 64).[14] As soon as the ratio between banker's loans is back to
its original level, bankers will take steps to decrease the market rate
of interest. Hence

$$r_n > r_p = r_m \tag{4}$$

As soon as the system is in such a situation there will be no further
reduction in the money-supply, the bankers having restored their
reserves to a satisfactory level. However, and it is a corollary of the
novelty of Hawtrey's mechanism, the system is not yet back in
full-employment equilibrium. The price-level has not yet fallen
enough to correspond to the reduced money-supply.

The inequality in equation (4) is simply the expression of Hawtrey's assumption that wages and prices are sticky and do not decline
in the same proportion. In that unemployment disequilibrium 'the
symptom of incomplete adjustment is the diminution of employment'
(1913, p. 41). The more prices and wages are rigid the longer the
adjustment process; or, in other words, the more rigid are prices and
wages, the larger the gap between the natural rate of interest and the
now equal profit and market-rates.

Hawtrey describes this *period of unemployment disequilibrium* in
the following terms:

> The bankers have restored their reserves and are satisfied . . . .
> The aggregate of purchasing power is on the reduced scale corre-
> sponding to the reduced stock of money; the productive resources
> of the community will not be fully employed until the level of
> prices is reduced in the same proportion; prices cannot be reduced
> until the cost of production is sufficiently reduced; and the cost of
> production can only be reduced as wages are reduced. Wages,
> therefore, are the key to the situation. (1913, p. 65)

In short, as long as the price-level (and ultimately the wage-rate) is
not reduced in proportion to the reduced stock of money the economic system must remain in a state of unemployment disequilibrium.
The progressive reduction of prices and wages leads the system
back to the full employment of all factors of production *because* the
resulting decrease in the market-rate gradually affects planned invest-

ment as to make it eventually equal to full-employment saving. In Hawtrey's own words:

> As wages fall, prices fall, *output increases* [namely investment increases because r_m diminishes] and employment improves, until at last all money values have completed a fall proportional to the original diminution of the stock of money and equilibrium is restored. (1913, p. 94, italic added)

Hence

$$r_n = r_p = r_m \tag{5}$$

A last element must be added to Hawtrey's cumulative process: the situation Hawtrey later dubbed 'credit deadlock'. This early version of the 'stagnation thesis' anticipates in a way some arguments later raised in connection with the inelasticity of the rate of interest linked with Keynes's so-called 'liquidity-trap'.

After his discussion leading to equation (4) Hawtrey sums up his argument in the following way:

> for the banker's purpose, a 'high' rate of interest is one which is above the profit rate, and a 'low' rate of interest is one which is below the profit rate, and it is only when the rate of interest is equal to the profit rate that there is no tendency towards either an increase or decrease in temporary borrowing. In any of the three cases the rate of interest may be either above or below the natural rate. (1913, p. 67)

This can be readily expressed in the symbolic way used in equations (1) to (5):

$$\text{'high' rate:} \qquad r_n \lessgtr r_p < r_m \tag{6}$$
$$\text{'low' rate:} \qquad r_n \lessgtr r_p > r_m \tag{7}$$
$$\text{'equilibrium' rate:} \qquad r_n \lessgtr r_p = r_m \tag{8}$$

However, one condition has to be added to warrant the validity of this set of equations. The rate of depreciation of prices (i.e. the rate of deflation) cannot be greater than the natural rate of interest. Or, put in a different way, the difference between the natural rate of interest and the rate of profit has to be smaller than the natural rate of interest itself.

$$r_n - r_p \lessgtr r_n \tag{9}$$

Alternatively it is equivalent to saying that the 'rate of profit' has to be greater than zero:

$$r_p > 0 \tag{10}$$

Should this condition not be fulfilled bankers would then be power-less to stimulate new demand for credit even with a market rate of interest equal to zero. In such a situation, the ordinary means of banking policy would prove wholly ineffective and the rate of interest – as the adjusting mechanism *par excellence* between saving and investment – would have completely broken down. Variations of the market rate of interest would simply fail to stimulate the demand for loanable funds and 'the depression [would be] exaggerated to the point of stagnation' (1913, p. 186). However, this 'stagnation case' is but a 'special case' which entirely depends on a high '*expected* rate of depreciation of the prices of commodities' (1913, p. 187).[15] In later works (see, e.g., 1937a, pp. 77–82) Hawtrey qualifies substantially this 'extreme case' of his cumulative process which, otherwise, gives the pride of place to the market rate of interest and to the traditional weapons of credit policy.[16]

III

Hawtrey's idiosyncratic piece of analysis connecting changes in the rate of interest with variations of dealers' stocks, instead of pro-ducers' investment, should not obscure the fact that eventually (and despite his strong denials) the rate of interest *is* the price which ultimately brings into equality the demand and supply for saving.

However, the system of interest rates is proximately determined by the supply-and-demand for loanable funds, and no longer directly by the supply and demand for saving only: 'The essential function of the capital [i.e. investment] market is to equalize the demand and supply of investible funds' (1926a, p. 54). Hawtrey reverses the order of emphasis put by his predecessors on each of these determinants. In so far as the normal rate of interest is concerned, the working of the twin factors of productivity and thrift is simply taken for granted. Hence, the whole of Hawtrey's undertaking is clearly to show that the influence of monetary factors in the investment market, banking policy, wages and prices rigidities, expectations about future prices, variations of output and employment can only temporarily endanger the basic claimed tendency to the full employment of the factors of production.[17] The low flexibility of money wages assumed by Hawtrey is the best illustration of that approach. If the economic system remains bogged down in an unemployment disequilibrium, it is because money wages have not fallen in proportion to the initial contraction of bank credit.

However, Hawtrey fails to see that an expansionary monetary policy could by-pass this difficulty. In the chapter 'Can Trade Fluctuations be Prevented?', not a word is said about the impact of an 'open market' policy on the rate of interest. Moreover, all direct government interventions are banned on the grounds of 'Treasury View'.[18]

Hawtrey's theory of interest is nothing but a particular version of the loanable-funds theory of interests. As he puts it himself, three 'distinct elements have to be taken into consideration in calculating the rate of interest: the "natural" rate, the monetary conditions, [and] the bankers' wish to discourage and encourage borrowing' (1913, pp. 65–6). We may therefore confidently visualise Hawtrey's rate of interest as being determined by the intersection of the supply-and-demand curves for 'loanable' or 'investible funds'; or, by what Hawtrey calls 'the opening offered by the producer and the money offered by the investor' (1913, p. 208).[19]

Using Hawtrey's terminology the market rate of interest can also be seen as the price that equates the supply-and-demand for the 'unspent margin':

> The requirements of the community for reserves or purchasing power may be regarded as constituting the demand for credit and money. The supply of credit emanates from the banks. The supply of money is determined by the legal and administrative arrangements for regulating the coinage and the issue of legal tender proper. (1919, p. 38; see also 1938, p. 175).

Thus, Hawtrey's rate of interest can clearly be seen as determined by the intersection of a demand and a supply schedule for loanable funds.[20] However, one important question remained to be solved: the influence of 'monetary disturbances' on the volume of saving and investment in 'real' terms, and ultimately on the rate of capital accumulation. Hawtrey does not deny altogether that a credit expansion/contraction has an influence on the volume of investment;

but he holds it to be unimportant when compared with the direct influence on the 'dealers' stocks'.

In the *Treatise on Money*, quoting from *Good and Bad Trade*. Keynes pinpoints with remarkable accuracy where Hawtrey has gone wrong, or more precisely where he has wrongly put the emphasis:

> When we come to the earlier writings of Mr. Hawtrey, we seem to get much nearer to the idea of bank rate as affecting the rate of investment but the whole emphasis is placed on one particular kind of investment, namely, investment by dealers and middlemen in liquid goods – to which a degree of sensitiveness to changes in bank rate is attributed which certainly does not exist in fact. (JMK, v. p. 173; see also vii, p. 76)

As a matter of fact dealers' stocks act as *buffers* between variations of the level of aggregate effective demand and changes in the price-level. Despite the fact that dealers' stocks are much more sensitive to changes in the market rate than manufacturers' investments, in the end, the level of the latter cannot but be entirely dependent of the former. If, in the long run, the inverse relation between the volume of investment and the rate of interest actually does hold good, Hawtrey's adjustment process obscures that connection behind this unwarranted 'stock' assumption.[21]

In the 'deflationary case' this hypothesis simply introduces a time-lag between a rise in the market rate of interest and a drop in the price level and/or a contraction of the volume of investment and output.[22] Despite the fact that Hawtrey never substantiated his thesis, he was so mesmerized with it that it barred him from later taking a more constructive part in the heated discussion over the saving-investment technique of analysis. He not only stuck to his purely monetary theory of the cycle but went also as far as to deny the possibility of 'forced saving' on the very ground of stock availability. In the end Hawtrey's analysis does not depart in that respect from the most traditional quantity theory; despite all his claims, outside the adjustment periods, the homogeneity postulate holds good and money is neutral:

> If the monetary equilibrium . . . is disturbed, the movement will end . . . after a greater or less interval of time, in a state of equilibrium on a new scale of incomes and prices, but with the whole system of production and distribution very nearly unchanged. (1913, p. 44)

HAWTREY'S ARGUMENT SO FAR

Hawtrey remained faithful all his life to that general approach outlined as early as 1913. He never altered substantially his conceptual
framework, even after the long and protracted discussions he had
with Robertson and Keynes.[23] This consistency has provided him
with a particular niche in the Cambridge tradition, quite separate
from both the Pigou–Lavington–Robertson and the Keynes approaches. However, and despite Pigou's and Robertson's dismissive
reviews, Hawtrey brought home to Cambridge two main stepping-
stones on which the saving-investment technique of analysis was to be
built from 1924 onwards:

1. the income approach to the quantity theory of money involving
   a reasoning in terms of nominal income, saving and investment;
2. the first detailed analysis of the financial working of the 'cumulative process' to be put in writing in England.

The main weakness of Hawtrey's contribution is, of course, his
strictly monetary explanation of the causes of the cycles, and the
parallel lack of analysis of the influence of money on saving, investment and capital accumulation in *real* terms. In that respect, and with
characteristic wit, Robertson sums up very aptly Hawtrey's contribution:

> The greater part of his elaborate scaffolding [i.e. his cumulative
> process] seems to be of the nature of a mere 'tour-de-force'; the
> main line of his argument amounts to little more than the conten-
> tion that if there is a monetary disturbance, there will be a monet-
> ary disturbance. (1913, p. 63)

To that Hawtrey might have certainly be justified to answer that the
erection of a scaffolding – however elaborate it may be – is a
necessary preliminary to the construction of the building itself; and,
in 1913, such a 'monetary scaffolding' was badly missing.

Despite all these reservations and weakness, and when all is said
and done, the rate of interest is undoubtedly for Hawtrey the price
which, in the long run, equates 'the net amount of investment [with]
the openings offered to it in the form of capital raised' (1937, p. 62).[24]

The ultimate proof of that is given by Hawtrey himself. In a letter
written to Keynes barely a month after the publication of the *General
Theory*, Hawtrey outlines clearly himself the extent of his departure
from the traditional Marshallian interest theory:

I believe my treatment of the theory of interest . . . is quite in accordance with classical doctrine. . . . In regard to unemployment. . . . I accept the doctrine that unemployment is in general due to wages being . . . too high. . . . I depart from the classical tradition in laying special stress upon monetary conditions. (JMK, xiv, p. 19)

4.3 ROBERTSON'S EARLY CONTRIBUTION: FROM *A STUDY OF INDUSTRIAL FLUCTUATION* (1915) TO *MONEY* (1922)

The theory of fluctuation put forward by Robertson is usually classified as a non-monetary overinvestment one (see, for example, Haberler, 1952, pp. 85–7). Crises are seen to be caused by structural maladjustments resulting from overinvestment; the factors generating these fluctuations are non-monetary in nature and can be associated with inherent characteristics of the capitalist mode of production. The core of the monetary complement to that 'real' analysis suggested in *Industrial Fluctuation* (1915) was added from 1925 onwards, starting with *Banking Policy and the Price Level* (1926). However, some interesting suggestions pointing in this direction can be found in part ii, chap. iii of *Industrial Fluctuation* and in the first edition of Robertson's well-known textbook on *Money* (1922).

Accordingly, this section falls into four parts. In Section I a brief outline of Robertson's 'real' theory of cycles provides the necessary background to understand its monetary complement, which was, paradoxically to occupy Robertson during the rest of his life. This section also provides a brief account of Robertson's early discussion of the theory of the 'normal' rate of interest. In Section II an analysis of Robertson's early 'real'-saving theory tries to assess the impact of such a concept on subsequent developments of his theory of interest. Section III examines the sketchy monetary theory contained in *Study*; and Section IV discusses Robertson's first attempt to tackle the concept of 'forced saving' (*Money*, 1922).

I

Paradoxically Robertson's theory of the trade cycle is substantially free from Marshall's own 'monetary' version. Following Pigou's encouragement provided during the early stage of his research on his *Industrial Fluctuation* Robertson always tried 'consistently and thoroughly to dig down behind money appearances to real facts'.[25] His mode of analysis is firmly entrenched in real factors since the monetary variables cannot instigate the trade cycle on their own: *real* forces only can set the cycle on its way.

The best summary of Robertson's 'real' analysis is the one he offers himself in the *New Introduction* to the 1948 reprint of his *Industrial Fluctuation*:

> As regards my own treatment, it will be seen that I was at pains to argue that the collapse of investment is not *always* precipitated by a 'shortage of saving', but is essentially due rather to a temporary saturation with instrumental goods, the decline in whose utility furnishes in turn a rational inducement to the producers of consumption goods to restrict their production, and that to an extent inconsistent with the desires and interests of their workpeople. I was thus led to combine my 'under-saving' propositions with 'over-saving' or 'under-consumptionist' propositions of a quasi-Hobsonian type. (1915, pp. xiii–xiv)

Although, in *Industrial Fluctuation*, Robertson defines savings as the stock of consumer-goods available to finance investment – a fact of the utmost importance in the subsequent conceptualisation of his theory of interest – he does not fully support the view that the shortage of real saving is responsible for all crises.

If the availability of consumer's goods is inadequate to meet consumers' demand until the increased output of consumption goods is brought to the market, investments have to be abandoned before they have had time to bear any of their expected returns. The capital-goods sector is thus plunged into depression and left with a large amount of half-finished and useless investment-goods. Even if Robertson readily admits this argument, he does not consider it either as a necessary or unique explanation of the cause of the cycles.

For him the downturn of the cycle mainly results from overinvestment inducing a decline in the marginal utility of acquiring capital-goods (the marginal utility of consumption goods being relatively stable); or, put in other words, a decline in the desire to purchase the flow of capital-goods coming on the market (1915, pp. 180–1 and 240).[26] This downturn of the marginal utility of capital goods would arise even if plenty of real saving was still available. Crises which are caused by a shortage of savings merely advance the timing of the downturn. Hence, with or without shortage of saving, the crisis is inevitable because expansion always leads the economic system to a point where 'the increasing cost of instruments, or the decline in the desirability caused by their increasing numbers, would . . . prescribe a revaluation of the net advantage of acquiring instruments' (1926, pp. 90–1).

Thus the cycle is primarily one in the demand for investment goods. The temptation for overinvestment results mainly from the repercussions on the volume of investment of its 'period of gestation': namely, the length of time necessary for investments to be realised and for the additional supply of consumers' goods to be available.

Eventually depressions are aggravated by what Robertson calls 'the imperfect divisibility and intractability' of investment and the 'longevity' of the instruments of production. In less an abstruse terminology it is nothing else but the producers' inability to increase their productive capacity exactly in the proportion needed to meet demand; to alter without cost the physical compostion of their capital stock (i.e. capital is not 'malleable') and to ignore the influence of the length of the life of capital goods on the periodicity and the duration of the cycle. These characteristics of the capital goods industry clearly mean that fluctuations in output and employment are not only part and parcel of Robertson trade-cycle theory, but are also to some extent necessary and desirable in a dynamic economic system which knows technical progress and inventions.[27]

In all this, if monetary factors (together with other psychological or even agricultural factors) may only be responsible for undesirable changes in output, they cannot be seen as instigating the trade cycle on their own. These forces are additional to those creating overinvestment and need the prior impact of these 'real' forces to set the cycle on its way. Monetary expansion or contraction cannot eliminate the cycle, and any attempt to remedy for undesirable fluctuations by such means may well be more damaging than the disease. This conception of the role of money is the very antithesis of Hawtrey's purely monetary theory of the cycle. This was obviously to have a very potent influence on Robertson's 'vision' when from 1925 onwards he comes to deal more specifically with monetary factors in the cycle.

This vision of 'a quasi-rhythmical movement in the level of prices, in the level of money profits, and the level of employment' (1926, p. 6) as 'inherent in the modern system of large-scale capitalistic industry' (1915, p. 13) makes Robertson believe that he had severed crucial links with the Marshallian tradition. In particular his claim to have subjected 'Say's Law of Markets . . . to some rough handling' (1915, p. xiii) certainly can not be considered as a rejection of the whole self-adjusting supply-and-demand apparatus inherited from Marshall. As a matter of fact it is widely different to suggest a sophisticated analysis of the inevitability and 'quasi-rhythmical move-ment' of the cycles in terms of short-run fluctuations around a centre of gravity and to reject the marginalist approach altogether. Robert-son's 'rough handling' of Say's law is nothing more than a critique of its short-run validity during each and every phase of the cycle. Indeed, it seems possible to go even further and to argue that the very nature of the theory is no more than a clever application of Marshall's 'normal' versus market price distinction to the problem of the trade-cycle theory. In particular it is not because Robertson 'dared to criticise the still living master . . . [on the grounds] that his . . . famous account of the genesis and operation of "cheap money" had tended to exaggerate its influence in promoting "investment"' (1915, pp. xii–xiii)[28] that he denied that investment is no longer a monotonic function of the rate of interest. Similarly Robertson casts no doubts on the validity of this inverse relation when he argues that 'the payment of high real rate of interest is not a decisive deterrent to the business man if he is still convinced of the high future satisfaction productivity of investment' (1914, p. 218).

On the contrary the entire logical structure of a theory devised to demonstrate the recurrent succession of booms and recessions in terms of rise and fall of the utility of investment goods is precisely based on the long-run tendency of the rate of interest to adjust the volume of saving to cyclical variations of the demand for capital as a flow.

Similarly the so-called 'secondary cause' of cycles – i.e. the 'short-age of saving' – makes use of the same adjusting mechanism, the impulse coming this time not from a sudden downward shift of the investment-demand function, but from a sudden upward shift of the saving-supply function.

Very little indeed is said about the rate of interest in *Industrial Fluctuation*. At first it seems rather suprising in a book the *Preface* of which contains the first clear call for an analysis in terms of saving and investment to be heard in Cambridge (1915, p. xx).

Except for a few rather unoriginal remarks on the natural versus market rate of interest argument (1915, pp. 213–38) Robertson offers no explicit analysis of the determinant of the 'normal' rate of interest. The explanation of that apparent gap is very simple and is given by Robertson himself in his *Preliminary Chapter*:

> In some of the more abstract portions of this essay I shall make use, *without further explanation or apology*, of the processes and terminology in common use among the school of economic thought associated in this country chiefly with the name of Dr. Marshall. (1915, p. 11; italic added)

Hence, Robertson simply takes for granted Marshall's general economic theory, and his theory of the 'normal' rate of interest in particular. He even goes as far as to assert that 'one cause of the obscurity which still surrounds this problem [i.e. trade cycle] is that, in the attack upon it, full and systematic use has never hitherto been made of the weapons supplied by this particular intellectual armoury' (1915, p. 11).[29]

When all is said and done Robertson's overinvestment crisis is characterised by a downturn of the interest rate induced by businessmen's drastic revisions on the 'productivity side' of the 'capital market'; a drop, or an expected drop, of the rate of interest fosters a fall in the volume of investment according to the principle incorporated by Marhall in his investment-demand function. Eventually variations (or expected variations) around the natural rate of interest are nothing but the signal which sums up and transmits to the body of investors the scattered information on the state of the capital market and, hence, on the phase of the cycle the economy is in.

Paradoxically this novel theory of the cycle was to play second fiddle to monetary theory and to the related question of the 'kind of savings' in Robertson's analysis of the cycle from 1925 onwards. However, despite this fundamental reorientation of his research programme, Robertson never lost sight of his grand design outlined in *Industrial Fluctuation*; he always looked at his contribution to monetary theory as a refinement of 'some part of the analytical framework of my *Study of Industrial Fluctuation*' (1926, p. vii).

II

Even if in 1915 Robertson had little sympathy with these overinvestment theories which lay the blame upon the failure of the banking system to provide the loanable funds necessary to meet investment demand, this 'shortage of real-saving' theory anticipates in many

vays criticisms which Robertson was to level against Keynes some
wenty years later. The argument is simple. If the *real* stock of saving
ιvailable *ex ante* is inadequate for the community to live on while a
ςreater proportion of resources is devoted to capital-good produc-
ion, investment has to be postponed or abandoned altogether,
ɔlunging the production sector into depression.[30]

Two important remarks can be made here on the inner logic of this
eal-saving theory in view of future developments of Robertson's
ɪnterest theory.[31]

First, this stock of consumption goods, or *real* saving, needed to
ɪnance investment, has to be accumulated *prior* to the investment
ɔrocess. In 1915 the size of this lump could not be altered by banking
ɔolicy, or at least, Robertson showed no interest in that line of
ɪnquiry. It is only with *Money* (1922) that this crucial idea received its
ɪrst treatment, which was to lead to the decisive break-through of
Banking Policy and the Price Level (1926).

Second, and despite his strictly real-saving theory, Robertson was
ιble to mount the first formal attack ever on the 'Treasury View'
1915, p. 253). Hawtrey's defence and illustration of this principle
vhich, according to Robertson 'scarcely deserves formal refutation'
1915, p. 253 n. 1), is submitted to some rough criticisms. As shown
ςarlier Hawtrey held the same lump-of-savings theory[32] but was
ɪnable to escape from this old forebear of the modern 'crowding out'
ιypothesis. Well ahead of most economists, Robertson was able to
ɟemonstrate – in a strictly orthodox framework – that 'the whole
ɔoint is that in times of depression [if an 'artificial elevation of the
ɟemand for constructional goods' does not take place] savings are *not*
ɔtherwise so applied' (1915, p. 253 n.1). Hence, far from withdraw-
ɪng from the market savings which would otherwise have gone into
ɔrivate investments, public works are theoretically justified by
Robertson: the government merely puts back into circulation a part
ɔf that lump of savings which would have otherwise remained idle.

III

ɪn *Industrial Fluctuation* Robertson adopts a very sketchy monetary
theory. In a somewhat hasty fashion he dismisses any attempt at
providing a pure monetary theory of the trade cycle for fear of
ɾelapsing into what he calls somewhere else 'the time-honoured
[conclusion] that crisis and depression are due entirely to scarcity of
ɔurrency' (1914c, p. 878).

Robertson's discussion of the 'cumulative process' following an increase in the money-supply (currency or credit) is very brief indeed. As a matter of fact Robertson is more at pains to repeat time and again that 'neither general reasoning . . . nor the evidence of facts supports [the] view . . . that an influx of [money] tends to synchronize with [the boom] and with no other phase of the industrial cycle' (1915, p. 228). The general tone of his argument is one of irritation against monetary cranks who argue at length in favour of a theory that every sensible person knows to be only superficial. The quantity equation and the validity of the homogeneity postulate *à la* Hume are dealt with in a mere twelve lines. Marshall's two-rate-of-interest mechanism is seen as 'now sufficiently well established' (1915, p. 213) to deserve no more than a brief discussion: the lowering of the discount rate places a larger volume of credit currency in the hands of businessmen. Four main results ensue: the service of bankers are cheaper; a falling market rate is combined with a rising price-level (Gibson's paradox); money-wages are lagging behind prices and borrowing savings is made cheaper. None of these results is indeed original in itself. These various sources of gain for businessmen are short-lived and Robertson only offers a vague mixture of psychological and anticipatory elements to explain the reversal of tendency and the rise in discount rates (1915, pp. 217–18). All this is rather vague and has nothing in common with Hawtrey's careful step-by-step analysis.

The fact that, for Robertson, money is not an essential cause of the cycles explains his apparently contradictory approach to Marshall's monetary theory. On the one hand, Robertson submits Marshall's 'cheap money' argument to some rough handling: 'it is most necessary to adopt a sceptical attitude towards Dr. Marshall's generalisation' (1915, p. 235); namely, towards the ability of a bank-rate policy to stimulate investment. On the other, when, by chance, an increase of the money-supply coincides with the upward phase of the cycle,[33] Robertson adopts the same dismissive attitude as that of Marshall, Pigou and Hawtrey as far as 'forced saving' and an increase in the rate of accumulation are concerned.

Clearly, for Robertson, 'any temptation to over-investment that may exist will be aggravated by an increase in currency' (1915, p. 215). However, even if money only accelerates a real process in the origin of which it plays no part, Robertson briefly comments on the influence of money *during* this process. First, and this is the closest he comes to the idea of 'forced saving', Robertson readily recognises that 'the transference of resources to business men [through an increase in the credit supply] is a transference to those who are more prone to use resources in investment' (1915, p. 215). Second, the next step is not taken. Even if a hint at the idea of 'forced saving' may be detected in the previous quotation, Robertson's next move clears any doubt in that respect. As a matter of fact, using Marshall's own words, Robertson asserts two pages later that such an 'increase of resources in reckless or incompetent hands . . . aggravated perhaps by some conspicuous failure' is the only result to be expected from this transfer of real resources. Like Marshall and Keynes, in 1915 Robertson is only aware of the distribution effects fostered by an increase in the money-supply and ignores completely its influence on the volume and the structure of the production.

IV

A discussion of chaps IV and VIII of the first edition of *Money* (1922) is the last element needed to complete the picture of Robertson's pre-*Banking Policy* contribution to the saving-investment technique of analysis. A development of his sketchy 1915 analysis of the role of money in the course of industrial fluctuations was the next natural step Robertson had to take before ultimately coming to grips in 1926 with an attempt to integrate 'real' and monetary factors into a complete theory of the cycle. Robertson describes in the following way this two-tier development between 1915 and 1926:

> it was not till a later period . . . that the endeavour to make plain to myself and others what bankers are really up to (*Money*, 1922, ch. IV), led me on to try to re-integrate the theory of money into that of the trade cycle. . . . (1915, 'New Introduction', p. xv)

The fact that the 'forced-saving' thesis was introduced in the first edition of *Money* is the only reason why this little textbook has a place of its own in the saving-investment story. Even if this analysis is restricted to one page (pp. 90–1), even if no explicit connection is drawn between 'forced saving' and the gap between the 'normal' and the market rate of interest, even if the two-rate-of-interest argument is skeletal, and even if the idea of real capital creation is not present either, a crucial step is taken for the first time at Cambridge. The volume of saving available for investment is no longer equal to an accumulated stock of consumption goods available at the start of the investment process. Or, put in other words, the rate of interest no longer equates investment with saving *stricto sensu*. On the contrary, as loans in excess of the 'real stuff to lend' (1922, p. 90) are made available by banks, the volume of savings available for investment is now equal to saving *stricto sensu* plus the amount of saving 'forced' upon the general public through the rise in prices fostered by the increase in demand resulting from the extra purchasing power provided by additional bank loans. Accordingly the demand-and-supply schedules for loanable funds determine the rate of interest and 'forced saving' is the expression of the divergence between the 'normal' rate of interest determined by productivity and thrift and the market rate of interest determined on the market for loans. Hence 'forced saving' is also the link between Robertson's price and monetary theories.

This first version of the 'forced-saving' doctrine puts more clearly in evidence than later or fuller statements the crucial connection it has with the investment period of gestation at the root of Robertson's overinvestment theory in *Industrial Fluctuation*. As a matter of fact it is more important to realise that the 'forced-saving' doctrine is nothing else but an extension to a monetary economy of Robertson's basic and simple idea that 'investment takes time'. If the levels of production of investment and consumption goods were to respond immediately to a net addition to loans, the very idea of 'forced saving' would be meaningless. Hence time-lags are essential if 'forced saving' is to occur; and, it is in this sense that this phenomenon is the fundamental link between the long-run overinvestment doctrine of *Industrial Fluctuation* and the systematic period analysis of *Banking Policy* and after. As a matter of fact this 'step-by-step analysis' (1926, pp. ix and xi) inaugurated by Robertson in 1922 is nothing else but one of the first pieces of dynamic analysis.[34]

The 1922 version of the forced-saving process can be summarised in a way which conveniently highlights Robertson's step-by-step method.[35]

Starting from an equilibrium position, for whatever reason (e.g. increased 'normal' rate of interest), the demand for loanable funds rises. The volume of voluntary saving (i.e. the *real* saving of *Industrial Fluctuation*) offered via the market for loanable funds is inadequate to support the planned volume of investment at the current rate of interest; however, if banks accept to finance this additional volume of planned investment, it means 'that [they] "lend" money without ensuring that at the date the loan is made there is any real stuff to lend' (1922, p. 90); or, put in other words, the market rate of interest is not raised to the new higher level reached by the 'normal' rate. Since these additional loans are used to finance the production of capital goods this production will not be ready before the end of the average period of production. Hence during this period of time the production of consumer goods is *fixed* and has to be shared between a larger number of productive consumers (the wage bill in the capital goods industries increases.) An additional flow of money (equal to the volume of extra loans) creates an additional demand on the goods market. Since the supply on the consumer-goods market is given, the price-level goes up; and consumers are 'forced' to share the available output with the businessmen financing new ventures with the additional loans made available to them by bankers; in other words, the average real consumption has dropped and 'forced saving' is taking place:

> [if] there is [no] corresponding preliminary accumulation of goods [to match additional loans], any saving that is done is done during the currency of the loan . . . by the members of the general public, who find the value of their money diminished, and are forced to abstain from consumption which they would otherwise have enjoyed. The community is in effect compelled, by the extra purchasing power put into the hands of the borrower, to share with him its current income of real things, and such hoards of real things as it may possess. (1922, p. 90)

A number of important conclusions follow from the preceding. First, 'forced saving' implies a transfer of *real* resources from one group of individuals to another; it cannot result from a transfer of purchasing power held in the form of hoarding or/and securities by one group to another.

Second, the crucial piece of stability analysis, i.e. the real-balance effect is missing; nowhere does Robertson explain that the *only* reason why 'forced saving' takes place lies in the consumers' attempt to keep constant the value of their real balances.[36]

Third, Robertson's sketchy discussion of the consequence of 'forced saving' on the 'real' side of the economy is not clear at all. In a sense he readily recognises that 'the additional loan will presumably justify itself by and by, by adding to the flow of real goods' (1922, p. 90). However, he does not carry his argument to its logical end; namely, he does not link that increase in the rate of accumulation with a subsequent drop in the 'normal' rate of interest (1922, pp. 173–4).

Fourth, the length of the 'forced-saving' process is clearly related, for Robertson, with the length of the period of production of the capital goods for which additional loans have been granted. The longer the period of production, the higher the necessary volume of additional loans, the longer the 'forced-saving' process, and, ultimately, the higher the risk of a 'shortage of saving' during the period of gestation (1922, p. 90).

Fifth, and last, Robertson is the first Cambridge economist to state clearly that the rate of interest on such additional loans is no longer the reward for waiting: 'the interest does not necessarily go to those who, under the pressure of rising prices, do the real "abstinence" ' (1922, p. 91). As innocent as it may seem it is quite a big step away from the Marshallian orthodoxy to realise that the effect of such additional loans 'may be that the community has to stint itself temporarily to meet not only the claim on goods exercised by the borrower, but also that exercised by the receivers of money interest' (1922, p. 91).

ROBERTSON'S ARGUMENT SO FAR

Between 1913 and 1924 Robertson can eventually be credited with three major pieces of analysis, all of which were to play an important part in the coming saving-investment debates of the late 1920s and 1930s:

— a *trade-cycle theory in real terms* in which the 'period of gestation', the 'indivisibility' and the 'intractability' of investment explain why 'it is in capitalism as an economic . . . system that the seeds of crises are inherent' (1914b, p. 89);

— a *real-saving theory*, making the volume of investment a function of a pre-existing amount of saving in physical terms;

— an analysis of the *'forced-saving'* process showing how banks can alter the volume of real saving available for investment.

5 Early Contributions II: Keynes, Lavington and Pigou (1913–24)

5.1 KEYNES: FROM OVERINVESTMENT (1913) TO UNDERINVESTMENT (1924)

Keynes's writings on business fluctuations and monetary theory during the period under review are far less original than Robertson's and well within the Marshallian orthodoxy. From his two *strictly* theoretical contributions (his 1913 paper given to the Political Economy Club, JMK, xiii, pp. 1–14 and section I of the third chapter of *A Tract on Monetary Reform*, 1923, JMK, iv, pp. 61–70), the first one only brings new elements of interest to our argument. In the *Tract* the refinements brought to the Cambridge equation do not alter in any substantial way the conclusions reached earlier by Marshall and Pigou.

Accordingly this section falls into two parts. In Section I, an analysis of 'How far are Bankers responsible for the Alternations of Crisis and Depressions?' shows Keynes much in agreement with Robertson's 'secondary thesis'; namely, the 'shortage-of-saving' doctrine. Section II is devoted to a brief discussion of the theoretical chapter of the *Tract* and to an even briefer analysis of the rationale of the economic policy argument contained in that book.

I

Keynes's paper starts with a critique of Fisher's version of the credit cycle very much in line with that of Robertson's,[1] and, consequently, completely different from the constructive criticisms levelled at Fisher's cumulative process in the 1911 review of *Purchasing Power of Money*.

In fact Keynes takes a surprising step if one bears in mind both his 1911 review of Fisher and all what was to follow in the 1920s and 1930s:

> This kind of theory holds, . . . to a great extent, the academic field. I do not say that it has not sometimes been applicable to

affairs. . . . But for my own part I have always felt it clever, rather than satisfactory. It strikes one as diagnosing symptoms rather than causes. (JMK, xiii, pp. 2–3)

The bulk of the paper is then devoted to showing how bankers have the power to encourage the tendency to overinvestment inherent in the economic system. However, it does *not* suggest an analysis of the forced-saving process. As a matter of fact a careful perusal of that paper reveals that Keynes only holds *a quasi-forced*-saving doctrine: banks can force people to invest more than they have deliberately planned to; namely, they can lend their deposits to investors; but what they cannot do is to force people to save more (in real terms) than the sum of their deliberate saving plus their bank deposits. Keynes is still very far indeed from the credit-creation process and the general rise in prices forcing people to consume less; namely, to save more. All that is pretty basic and it is difficult to understand why Keynes saw it as ' a superb theory about fluctuations' (JMK, xiii, p. 1, letter to Robertson).

However, on one particular point, Keynes goes one step further. This is not enough to transform his theory into an analysis of the forced-saving process, but it certainly sets the stage with all the necessary elements for the subsequent post-war developments.

Bankers are repeatedly accused of encroaching 'on the community's reserve [of] free resources' (JMK, xiii, p. 6) beyond what the savers have deliberately decided to invest. However, Keynes explains in at least three different passages that 'it is exceedingly difficult for a banker to know for certain when a period of over-investment is in progress' (JMK, xiii, p. 8), or that bankers are 'unwittingly led into transforming into fixed capital too high a proportion of their assets' (p. 10) or, simply that they do not 'know in what way those who have borrowed from them are using their funds' (JMK, xiii, p. 7). In short, bankers are completely in the dark. However, and this is the other idiosyncracy of the model, 'a point must soon come when further increases [of investment financed by bank credit) are impossible' (JMK, xiii, p. 6). This remark removes any remaining doubts about Keynes's lack of forced-saving analysis in his 1913 paper. As a matter of fact if bankers do not know exactly where they stand when they grant credits backed by real resources actually saved, how could they know when they have depleted the whole available lump of real saving? It is, however, exactly what Keynes argues; and he stops his argument precisely at the point where he could have broken new ground.[2] In all, the only novelty Keynes suggests is that banks can *accelerate* a process they are powerless to alter and the timing of which they even do not know.

Two further remarks may be added. First following Robertson's lead, Keynes shows a very marked suspicion towards a systematic interest-rate policy as a mean to alter the volume of investment; in other words, he raises doubt about the short-term elasticity of the investment-demand curve:

> the demand [for investments] is exceedingly inelastic and it is most difficult to choke them off by a slight increase of charge. . . . I am doubtful how much power [bankers] really have to put a serious brake on the tendency to over-investment. (JMK, xiii, p. 13)

Second, it is rather ironic to note that in his first theoretical contribution using the concepts of saving and investment, Keynes is light-years away from his latter-day 'stagnation' thesis. As a matter of fact the whole of his argument reflects his fears of overinvestment; and in the reference made to the real world to back his theory Keynes goes as far as to argue that in the pre-1913 period 'the investment of the world's free resources in fixed capital works has been very appreciably in excess of the amount saved and deliberately set aside for such purpose' (JMK, xiii, p. 11). However, the experience of the war years was soon to alter radically Keynes's version of the working of the economic system, in particular his conception of the respective behaviour and role played by savers and investors. On this drastic revision which led him to embrace for the rest of his life an 'underinvestment' or quasi-stagnationist approach, from 1924 onwards Keynes was to build the whole of his theoretical contribution to the saving-investment technique of analysis which, ultimately culminated in the principle of effective demand.

II

A discussion of some aspects of the theoretical apparatus of chapter 3 of *A Tract of Monetary Reform* is necessary as a prelude to a discussion of the theoretical framework underpinning the policy proposals made in *The Economic Consequences of the Peace* (1919), the *Tract* (1923) and various articles in *The Nation and Athenaeum* (1923–4). The fact that, for the first time in print, Keynes shows a clear awareness of the 'threefold-margin' argument is of great interest:

> [The community's] habits are fixed by its estimation of the extra
> convenience of having more cash in hand as compared with the
> advantages to be got from spending cash or investing it. The point
> of equilibrium is reached where the estimated advantages of keep-
> ing more cash in hand compared with those of spending or invest-
> ing it about balance. (JMK, iv, p. 64)

Clearly in equilibrium and at the margin the rate of interest is not
only the measure of the rate of return on investment (i.e. the
marginal productivity of capital), but also the measure of the 'level of
satisfaction' yielded by the marginal resources spent on consumption
goods (time preference) and by the marginal unit held in the form of
money (liquidity preference). However, like Marshall, Pigou and
Hawtrey, Keynes still fails to recognise the full implication of this
piece of analysis; namely, the influence of the rate of interest on the
demand of money, or, alternatively, the existence of an asset-
demand for savings deposits, despite his assigning an important role
to monetary changes on the rate of interest. Let us consider how, two
pages before the passage quoted above, Keynes discusses the impact
of a monetary increase:

> When people find themselves with more cash than they
> require . . . , they get rid of the surplus by buying goods or
> investments, or by leaving it for a bank to employ, or, possibly, *by
> increasing their hoarded reserves*. (ibid. p. 62; italic added)

The italicised words clearly show the individual as using his extra cash
to increase his 'idle balances'. However, Keynes makes no mention
whatsoever of the fact that to induce the individual to hold this extra
supply of cash, *the rate of interest has to drop*. In other words, he fails
to understand the main implication of the 'threefold-margin' argument which he clearly restates in a systematic form two pages later:
the link is established between the increase in the stock of money and
the increase in demand for the flow of commodities (wealth-effect)
without any reference being made to the portfolio-adjustment substitution effects. Or, put still in different terms, Keynes (like Marshall
and Pigou) fails to extend the analysis of the demand for money
beyond money in the form of income deposits neglecting thus the
influence of this demand on the rate of interest.

The failure to extend the 'threefold-margin' argument to its logical end can be usefully illustrated in terms of a modern optimum port-folio approach from which some implications would be missing.

The sharp stock-flow distinction underlying the optimum portfolio approach implies two sets of decisions on the part of economic agents (consumers, producers, bankers, etc.):

How to hold their stocks of wealth at a given point in time? (Of particular interest is of course the proportion of this total wealth to be kept in money.)

At which rate should they add to these stocks of wealth over time? (Namely, the decision as to the volume of the flows of saving and investment.)

Keeping in mind this crucial distinction the main emphasis of the portfolio approach is on the optimal relationship between the stock of money and the stocks of other assets as influenced primarily by the alternative rates of return yielded by these assets. Hence, the individual's holdings of money should be optimum not only with respect to income (the Marshallian k), but also with respect to wealth.

Two main building-blocks of this approach, which conceives the individual as optimising the composition of his portfolio of assets subject to an income (flow) and a wealth (stock) constraint are obviously missing in the pre-*Treatise* Cambridge monetary theory.

First, it results clearly from our previous discussion that Marshall, Pigou and Keynes were none too clear whether the individual is optimising his cash holding with reference to his stocks of other assets or with reference to his income, or with reference to some combina-tion of both wealth and income. Despite the fact that all of them alluded with various insistence to wealth[3] in their analysis of the determinants of the demand for money, they did so in a way showing a complete ignorance of the fundamentally different influence income and wealth have on such demand.[4] Marshall, Robertson and Keynes, the most explicit of the Cambridge economists about wealth, simply include it in their analysis as a simple extra-determinant playing the same role as income.

Second, this uncertainty about the specific role of wealth could not but blind them to the crucial consequence of that stock-flow distinc-tion. Monetary changes induce not only a wealth (real-balance) effect, but also a substitution effect between assets.

The failure to understand these two crucial pieces of analysis reduces the many references by Cambridge economists to the 'threefold-margin' argument to mere wishful thinking. However, the fact that this question was to be satisfactorily answered by Keynes in 1930 only, does not mean either that Cambridge economists previously ignored the interaction between money changes and the rate of interest or that such a failure to grasp the full implications of this argument barred them from working with a monetary theory of interest of the loanable-funds type. As a matter of fact it will be shown that, between 1924 and 1930, Robertson and Keynes managed to lay the foundations of the saving-investment technique, including the all-important 'forced-saving' doctrine, despite their very incomplete understanding of the two most important components of this type of monetary stability analysis; namely, the real-balance effect and the 'threefold-margin' argument.

Apart from this theoretical section of the *Tract* the economic policy arguments contained in that book, and indeed in the numerous papers written at that time for *The Nation and The Athenaeum*, are based on the familiar idea that a stabilisation of the price-level is what is urgently needed – even at the cost of deliberate state interventions – to remove the short-lived forces which prevent 'voluntary savings of the community [to be drawn] into "investments" ' (JMK, iv, p. 16). As a matter of fact, this mechanism is based on nothing other than the idea that, in a system in which the price-level is stable, investment would adjust to full-employment saving (ibid. p. xiv).

However, the post-war succession of inflationary and deflationary years had modified 'social psychology towards the practice of saving and investment' (ibid. p. 16); namely, and very broadly speaking, on the one hand, the 'typical English investor' is no longer prepared to turn his savings into long-term gilt-edged bonds and to run the risk of being redeemed in a depreciated currency; on the other, the depression, which 'in due course has to come', fosters 'a fall in the value of money [which] discourages investment' (ibid. p. 25). Accordingly an active monetary and financial policy (bank-rate and open-market operations) should aim at stabilising the price-level to restore to its pre-war efficiency the mechanism which brings into line decisions to save and decisions to invest. Since the social and economic organisation which made it possible before 1914 had disappeared (JMK, ii, pp. 11–13), Keynes saw no other solution but 'to bring in the State' (1924b, p. 312). Once the price-level is stabilised, 'unemployment, the precarious life of the worker, the disappointment of expectation, the sudden loss of savings, the excessive windfalls to individuals, the speculator, the profiteer [which] all proceed, in large measure, from the instability of the standard of value' (JMK, iv, p. xiv) will disappear.

The theoretical framework underlying such policy recommendations is wholly Marshallian. Saving and investment may be relatively interest inelastic, unemployment may be seen not as temporary but as *lasting* problem of society, price and wage rigidities may delay the adjustment process, etc., but Keynes shows no sign whatsoever of casting doubts on the long-run adjusting capacities of the economic system once these aberrations have been removed by means of a proper monetary policy:

> The object of monetary policy is to keep the price-level stable, – which is our main point . . . – and no one has a firmer belief than I in the relation between unemployment and monetary policy. (1923, p. 530 and 1924a, p. 235)

Keynes adds to this strictly monetary argument a plan in favour of public works. Such investments, by reducing the share of the available 'lump of saving' which, 'from lack of an outlet at home [is] . . . drifting abroad' (1924a, p. 236) would compensate for the private investments which would not be undertaken even at low rates of interest. Hence, once these short-lived forces have been removed by proper policy measures, nothing else will stand between the tendency to full employment of the factors of production and its *actual* fulfilment. In that respect, Keynes is perfectly clear in one of his articles in *The Nation and the Athenaeum*:

> I look, then, *for the ultimate cure of unemployment, and for the stimulus which shall initiate a cumulative prosperity, to monetary reform* – which will remove fear [of falling prices and/or expectations of falling prices] – and to the diversion of the national savings from relatively barren foreign investment into State encouraged constructive entreprise at home – which will inspire confidence. (1924a, p. 236; italic added)

This epitomises the complete reversal by Keynes over trade cycles which took place during the war and was first expressed in print in *The Economic Consequences of the Peace* (1919). All his pre-war fears of 'over-investment' have vanished and are replaced by the 'under-investment' – an argument which is the main theme of Keynes's policy discussion of the early 1920s and was to become the main theme of his theoretical investigations up until and including the *General Theory*. It is only in mid-1924, when he sat down to write what was to become, after six years of drafting and re-drafting, the *Treatise on Money* that Keynes for the first time gave a systematic elaboration of the theoretical framework to the policy recommendations contained in the *Tract*. In November 1924, in a draft 'Summary of the Author's Theory', Keynes explicitly establishes such a link. Before arguing 'that the general price level can be stabilised by giving the Bank of England a control over the volume of bank money created . . . and by using this control to cause the volume of bank money to vary in the same proportion as that in which the volume of real balances varies', Keynes warns his reader that '[t]his conclusion is the same . . . as the leading tenet of my *Tract on Monetary Reform*' (JMK, xiii, p. 21).

For the first time in a series of notable occasions, Keynes's policy proposals were ahead of their strictly theoretical rationalisations.[5]

5.2 LAVINGTON'S *ENGLISH CAPITAL MARKET* (1921): THE 'THREEFOLD-MARGIN' ARGUMENT AND THE IDEA OF A GAP BETWEEN SAVING AND INVESTMENT

Despite Robertson's (1937, p. 431; 1940, pp. 16–17) and Hicks's (1935, pp. 62–3 n. 1; 1937, p. 132 n. 1) attempts to rescue Lavington's *English Capital Market* from oblivion, this book always suffered from a general and rather surprising neglect. Neither Keynes, nor Hawtrey, nor indeed Marshall make a single reference to Lavington's writings, though they are very much relevant to Cambridge monetary theory. On two issues of interest to our argument, Lavington improved the Cambridge analytical framework.

First, Lavington's discussion of the 'general principles on which [people] allocate their resources among competing uses' (1921, p. 31) is by far the clearest statement so far of the 'threefold-margin' argument:

Resources devoted to consumption supply an income of immediate satisfaction; those held as a stock of currency yield a return of convenience *and security*; those devoted to investment in the narrower sense of the term yield a return in the form of interest. In so far therefore as his judgement gives effect to self-interest, the quantity of resources which he holds in the form of money will be such that the unit of resources which is just and only just worth holding in this form yields him a return of convenience *and security* equal to the yield of satisfaction derived from the marginal unit spent on consumables, and equal[6] also to the net rate of interest. (1921, p. 30; italic added; see also p. 66 for a similar treatment and p. 181 for an adaptation of this argument to the banking system along Hawtreyan lines)

Given our previous discussion of this argument, three brief remarks are sufficient here to bring out the crux of Lavington's improvement to it.

To begin with, and most importantly, the individual's demand for money is no longer exclusively determined by the level of income. To the traditional transactions-motive (Marshall's k) is added a 'security motive' according to which part of the total demand for cash is held against 'the uncertain events of the future' (1921, p. 30), or, alternatively, 'on the degree of uncertainty in his business situation' (1921, p. 31). As Lavington puts it:

It seems reasonable . . . to regard this latter part of the aggregate money stock as a *reserve* whose size is regulated largely by the general level of confidence – a reservoir from which money flows into active circulation when times are good, and into which money flows from active circulation when times are bad. (1921, p. 33; italic added)

Another proof of the importance of this new separate motive to hold money is the care with which Lavington draws a distinction between the accumulation of 'idle balances' (to use Hawtrey's terms) and a demand for money for a 'security–uncertainty' motive:

the characteristic of a hoard is its usefulness, and the characteristic of a *reserve* lies in the fact that it does money work, though of a rather different kind from that of money in active circulation. (1921, p. 33; italic added)

Hence, for the first time in Cambridge, the total volume of cash balances is determined *'in some measure independently of the volume of payments'* (1921, p. 33; italic added).

Next, despite his adding 'the general level of confidence' (1921, p. 33) as the second determinant of the demand of money, Lavington makes no explicit mention of the individual's wealth as yet another determinant of this demand for cash. Hence, he fails to break really new ground. The 'wealth-motive' being still missing, there is no way in which Lavington can formally relate variations of the demand for money either to the price of securities that can be held as alternative assets or indeed to the rate of interest.

Lastly, Lavington nevertheless realises that his analysis of the demand for money, though different from the traditional quantity theory of the Marshallian type proceeds from the same logic: 'These considerations [on the *contingency* determinant of the demand for cash] lead to a definition of the demand for money rather different (though not inconsistent) with that laid down by the Quantity theory.' (1921, p.32) Clearly despite his new departure from the Cambridge equation, Lavington was still light-years away from a full understanding of the implications of the 'threefold-margin' argument Keynes was to reach in the *Treatise*.

Let us turn now to the general framework underpinning Lavington's use of the concepts of saving and investment – the second important element in his contribution. The very first sentence of the *Preface* to *Trade Cycle* places Lavington firmly in the Marshallian tradition[7] of cycle theory as a study 'of the main causes which underlie the rythmical variations in the activity of business' (1922, p. 7). The very logic of Lavington's theory is to study the causes of the short-lived influences which make the economic system temporarily depart from its long-run equilibrium position. In the case of monetary changes Lavington is at pains to underline that 'their effect is not to co-ordinate, but rather to disturb the existing co-ordination of supply and demand' (1922, p. 26). Accordingly it is no surprise to find some strong restatements of the long-run adjusting abilities of the 'normal' rate of interest:

> although there is a recondite sense in which there can be an 'excess of savings', there cannot be such an excess in the sense that new supplies of capital are not marketable; history and common sense alike show that indefinite quantities of new capital can be absorbed and can be made to yield a return, *though possibly of smaller amount than before*. (1922, p. 71; italic added)

Thus, for Lavington, when the volume of saving is growing less rapidly than the possibility of investment, or vice versa, the rate of interest will promptly bring them back into equilibrium: 'For this and other reasons, no explanation of the termination of boom is looked for on that line of inquiry' (1922, p. 71).

However, despite this strong assertion that nothing can theoretically be gained from a closer look at the short-lived cyclical gap between saving and investment, Lavington displays in a few essentially descriptive passages an acute understanding of the relations between the direction and the magnitude of that gap and variations in the level of output and employment:

> [If people] save continuously but . . . invest only after a period of accumulation when a favourable opportunity occurs . . . they withdraw currency from active circulation . . .; in effect money is being hoarded. . . . The immediate effect is that, in consequence of fewer purchases, of a smaller effective demand for goods, production slows down. As second effect is a general fall in prices, which tends to proceed until the diminished quantity of money in active circulation again controls and sets in action the whole supply of social resources. It seems clear that this latter compensatory effect [namely, none other but the real-balance effect] must proceed more slowly than the former and that in the interval during which it is proceeding social resources are imperfectly employed. In other words, in spite of the banking system, variations in the interval between saving and investing, are, or may be, causes of fluctuation in the employment of capital and labour. (1921, p. 70)

Thus, for the first time in print, the idea of a temporary gap between saving and investment (however loosely these concepts are actually defined) is connected with a lack of effective demand. In fact Lavington's argument is nothing else but an improved statement of Marshall's elementary idea of a temporary lack of co-ordination between saving and investment decisions.[8] Such a 'different-decision hypothesis' is certainly not allowed to alter the basic Marshallian long-run equilibrium towards which the system is tending. In the closing paragraphs of his analysis of the 'real' and 'monetary' causes of the gap between saving and investment Lavington is keen on stressing that 'in the long run, the stream of waiting, or saving, is *identical* with the monetary stream of investment; and changes in the volume of the one tend to produce corresponding changes in the volume of the other' (1921, p. 71). Furthermore it is clear that, for Lavington, the *ex ante* existing lump-of-saving dictates the size of the prospective volume of investment.[9]

Eventually Lavington's conviction that nothing theoretically useful can be gained from a study of temporary gaps between saving and investment is coupled with a somewhat confused and sketchy discussion of the 'forced-saving' doctrine.

On the one hand, in his *English Capital Market*, Lavington understands that any divergence between saving and investment, regardless of its origin, contributes to business cycles 'by increasing the rapidity with which resources are diverted to or from the production of capital goods' (1921, p. 72). This includes the case where banks, expanding their loans, 'transfer to borrowers a control over resources greater than that lodged with them by the public' and hence allow these borrowers 'to make a forced levy on the community' (1921, pp. 181–2).[10]

On the other hand, there is equally no doubt that Lavington does not understand the implication of such a piece of analysis; namely, he does not realise that such a 'forced levy' may actually increase the volume of real investment and hence the rate of accumulation:

> an expansion in bank loans cannot increase the quantity of real resources available for production; it can only increase the quantity of *control over resources* [Marshall's command over capital]; it can only supply business men with increased quantity of money, wherewith they compete for the available supplies of materials and so force up their prices. (1922, p. 109; see also 1921, p. 173, for a similar argument)

In the final analysis, and despite the refinments brought to the theory of the demand for money and despite the fact that most of the elements of the 'forced-saving' doctrine are present in his work, Lavington is unable to cut through the Gordian knot of the Marshallian version of the relations between money, prices and interest.

5.3 PIGOU'S INDEPENDENT CONTRIBUTION (1920–4)

Two little-known, though important, contributions by Pigou must be dealt with to complete the picture of the state of the saving-investment technique of analysis before the 'decade of high theory'.

On the one hand (Section I), and for the first time in Cambridge, Pigou brings home the all-important distinction between 'increased bank balances' and 'accumulation of things'; or in less abstruse terms, between monetary and real savings.

On the other hand, the rarely quoted essay[11] on *Correctives of Trade Cycle* (1924) displays in a very compressed form a 'forced saving' argument improving on several points Robertson's 1922 version. It is argued that Pigou should be considered as an independent discoverer of the main building-blocks assembled by Robertson, with Keynes's help, between 1924 and 1926.

I

In the 1948 *New Introduction* to his *Study of Industrial Fluctuation* Robertson lists Pigou and Cassel as 'the midwives' (1915, p. xv) who helped him to understand that, during a depression, an accumulation of bank balances 'is not an accumulation of things, and does not imply any accumulation of things, or, in other words, any real savings, on the part of those who make it' (Pigou, 1920, p. 812). Since this assertion by Pigou was instrumental in Robertson's discovery of the concept of 'abortive saving' (the opposite of 'forced saving') in *Banking Policy and the Price Level* it is necessary to examine the relevant original discussion in Pigou's *Economics of Welfare* (1920, pt vi, chap. iii, pp. 809–15). Furthermore, in doing so, we appear to fulfil at last a wish expressed in 1948 by Robertson himself: 'The whole passage in which this sentence [quoted above] occurs . . . is well worth looking at by those interested in the history of doctrine' (1915, p. xvi'n. 1).

Pigou's argument is made in the course of a very critical appraisal of Tougan-Baranowsky's thesis, according to which booms result from the sudden release on the investment market of lumps of gradually accumulated savings. According to Tougan-Baranowsky (1913, p. 273) and Lescure (1913, p. 505), such a disrupting process is rendered inevitable by the sheer size of industrial investments, which cannot be performed unless there is a corresponding amount of 'unused savings' previously accumulated in the banking system.

For Pigou this central idea that savings are made, stored up in the form of non-industrial capital and eventually converted into industrial capital may give a true picture of the reality either in a Robinsonian or in a slightly less primitive society (1920, pp. 810–11)in which Robinson hires 'ignoble savages'. But, as soon as a banking system is introduced into the picture, it is no longer tenable to argue that savings are accumulated in periods of depression and used up in periods of boom. Such a theory simply confuses accumulation of purchasing power with accumulation of real things. In Pigou's own words:

> By accumulating unused purchasing power people have not
> automatically accumulated also unused savings of real things.
> What they have done by not spending their money has been to
> *reduce prices in general* below what they would otherwise have
> been, thus making the money of other people worth more goods
> than it would otherwise have been, and thus *enabling these
> other people to buy more goods*. What they have accumulated by
> this proceeding is, not things, but the power, when they' choose
> later on to spend the money, to raise prices, reduce the purchasing
> power of other people's money, and absorb for themselves the
> goods which have in this way been rendered inaccessible to others.
> The accumulation is, thus, an accumulation of claims upon other
> people. It is not an accumulation of . . . real savings, on the part of
> those who make it. (1920, p. 812, italic added)

Clearly, though not yet explicitly, 'savings cannot be saved'; or,
savings lodged in the banking system are 'abortive savings' – to
anticipate Robertson's terminology, 'hoarding' or 'abortive lacking'
does not necessarily involve saving. As a matter of fact the deflationary process set in motion by the increased volume of bank deposits
simply transfers an amount of purchasing power equal to these extra
deposits from the section of the community which accumulates claims
upon other people to the section of the community which takes the
opportunity of the lower price-level to increase its consumption of
real goods. Barring the difficulties extensively discussed later by
Robertson under the general heading 'Saving and Hoarding', such an
accumulation of purchasing power, as opposed to 'real saving' may
well leave unchanged the aggregate volume of consumption. That is,
to put the same argument in a somewhat more familiar fashion, the
money-supply being given, an increase in the Marshallian k does *not*
necessarily implies that real savings have taken place.

II

The main argument of Pigou's *Correctives of the Trade Cycle* is to
provide a set of remedies to smooth out cyclical movements in prices,
output and employment.[12] The discussion of the 'forced-saving'
argument takes place partly in the section devoted to a sketchy
outline of the *causes* of the cycle and partly in the section devoted to
a theoretical argument in favour of price stabilisation. It is worth
remembering that, like Robertson, but for very different reasons,

Pigou always views as *secondary* monetary causes of trade fluctuations. Psychological and confidence motives form the core of his trade-cycle theory. Monetary factors inducing a 'succession of wave-like movements [of the price-level] which constitutes the trade cycle' (1923, p. 93) act only as proxies for 'excessive optimism and excessive pessimism [which] have an inherent tendency to engender one another, and, therefore, a natural rhythm' (1924, p. 97). Bearing this in mind it is easy to understand that a suitable policy would remove fluctuations in business confidence and, ultimately, economic fluctuations altogether.

Accordingly, Pigou's discussion of the 'forced-saving' process starts with a wave of optimism, whatever its origin may be, which induces businessmen to spend a larger proportion of their balances and/or to borrow from their bank on a larger scale. Thus, a larger volume of purchasing power (money and bank credit) being offered against a given volume of goods and services, the general level of prices rises. Next, for the first time in Cambridge, Pigou argues explicitly that such a process is best understood through a period analysis: 'In the course of this [upward movement in general prices] the prices of different things are not all affected equally at the same instant, but *in successive* stages. (1924, p. 99; italic added)

Not surprisingly the analytical framework underlying Pigou's 'forced-saving' process is the same as that Robertson uses in *Money*. However, Pigou adds to this basic theoretical structure a certain number of original points.

First, the levy extracted from the owners of fixed incomes by the businessmen putting on the market an extra volume of monetary purchasing power puts the latter at the command of more real resources (1924, pp. 100, 107) which enable them to expand the volume of their investments and to offer a larger demand for labour. For the first time in Cambridge, Pigou establishes thus a link between an inflationary 'forced-saving' process and more productive investments and more jobs:[13] 'This [process] means that a forced levy is raised from the receivers of fixed incomes *and goes to swell the supply of capital*' (1924, p. 111; italic added).

Second, the connection between the 'normal' equilibrium rate of interest, the rate of discount and the higher rate of accumulation fostered by the 'forced-saving' process is made much clearer than in any previous Cambridge contribution to the subject. The forced levy can only take place if there is a discrepancy between 'the rate of interest on real capital' (1924, p. 110) and the rate of discount.

Furthermore, if the original upward movement is expected to be a continuing one this will in turn induce businessmen to extent their demand for new loans thus perpetuating, though at a higher level of prices, the gap between the 'two rates':

> Business men may rightly expect that lenders of money will realise the situation less clearly than they do themselves, and will not increase the price of money to the full extent needed to offset its fall in value. (1924, p. 100)

Hence, anticipations of higher prices fuel a new demand for loans which, in turn, 'reopen' the gap between the 'rate of interest on real capital,' and the discount rate. This cumulative process, akin to the Wicksellian (and German) doctrine of the 'trailing bank rate' will go on as long as the 'wave of optimism' lasts. Clearly Pigou does not view the 'forced-saving' process as a once-and-for-all shift of real resources between fixed incomists and the investment-good sector, but as a cumulative process fuelling itself as long as the gap between the 'two rates' is not closed.

Third, apart from this lagging bank-rate, two other 'rigidities' lengthen this cumulative process, and hence the total volume of forced saving: the fact that money-wages are lagging behind real-wages, and the idea (akin to Robertson's) that the additional workers employed thanks to the 'forced levy' get their money *before* prices have risen and *before* any new investment good, and *a fortiori* any new consumption good, has had time to reach the market. Both elements fuel the businessmen's optimism by widening the profit margins.

Fourth, apart from his idiosyncratic reversal of the 'wave of optimism', Pigou suggests no built-in self-adjusting mechanism whatsoever in terms say of the real-balance effect. However, he displays an unusual confidence in the discount policy to prevent upward movements of the price-level and the simultaneous discrepancy between the 'real' rate of interest and the rate of discount:

> If the banking and monetary arrangements are so altered that prices are kept stable when the demand for new capital rises, there will be no forced levy. Consequently, the supply of capital will be smaller, and the [normal] rate of interest required to balance demand and supply will be higher that it is when there is a forced levy. Thus, to manipulate the discount rate with a view to price

stabilisation is not to remove it away from the rate to which the demand and supply of real capital point; it is to conform it to this rate, but, by eliminating forced levies, to make this rate itself somewhat different from what it would otherwise have been. (1924, p. 111)

Here, and explicitly for the first time in Cambridge, Pigou makes use of a loanable-funds theory of interest framework to show how a proper discount policy can stabilise prices by raising up the market-rate to its 'natural' level, which, in turn, implies that the supply schedule of 'new capital' (or saving) and the demand schedule for 'new capital' (or investment) are respectively *identical* to the curve and the demand curve for loanable funds. Such a systematic discount policy can certainly not be seen as 'artificial' or against the 'irrevocable economic law' (1924, p. 111). Quite the reverse. Such a policy allows the dominant forces of productivity and thrift to be adjusted by variations of the 'normal' rate of interest without being hampered by short-lived monetary forces, 'because, after all, to doctor the supply of capital by the addition or substraction of forced levies is not a natural proceeding!' (1923, p. 111).

Fifth, Pigou's confidence that – once the monetary disturbances have been disposed of, the 'normal' rate of interest will adjust planned investment to full-employment saving – is slightly altered by the relative inelasticity of the investment-demand curve, even if there is no sign whatsoever of Pigou giving up that fundamental relation. However, Pigou clearly detects an asymmetry between the 'forced-saving' and the 'abortive-saving' case. While a higher market-rate of interest will always dispose of the excess demand for real capital, and hence of the 'forced levy', a drop in that rate below the 'normal' rate may not be powerful enough to stimulate investment and prevent savings 'running to waste' in the banking system:

when confidence has broken down, business men's demands for new loans may be not only small, but also highly inelastic, and it may require a very large reduction in the rate to produce any marked effect. (1924, p. 113)

Pigou goes even further and suggests that a negative rate of interest may be required to equate investment to full-employment savings. However, as long as it costs nothing 'for a banker . . . to hold his money in his own vaults' (1924, p. 113), the market rate of interest is

unlikely to become negative. Accordingly the volume of investment
may fail to use the available amount of savings, the uninvested part of
which is 'lost' in swollen bank deposits.[14]

Thus, between 1920 and 1924, Pigou can be credited with providing three new elements preparing the ground for Robertson's crucial
break-through in *Banking Policy and the Price Level*: the question of
the 'kinds of savings' and the necessity to distinguish between 'real'
saving and the accumulation of bank balances (or, alternatively,
between saving and hoarding); a clear demonstration that 'forced'
saving' does mean more productive investments and more jobs; a
skilful discussion of the interactions between 'forced saving', the
'normal' rate of interest and the discount rate by means of a
loanable-funds type of interest theory.

5.4 PRINCIPAL CONCLUSIONS

The principal conclusions of this chapter may be summed up in five
main points:

First, Cambridge economists' preoccupations with short-run adjustments pre-date 1914 and show that, though along Marshallian
lines, some basic elements of the long and protracted debates of the
1920s and 1930s were already being discussed. Despite a lack of
awareness of the necessity of altering the long-run Marshallian equilibrium framework to cope in a more satisfactory way with short-run
adjustment processes, the main ideas (already hinted at by Marshall)
underlying the cumulative process, the optimum portfolio approach
and a monetary theory of interest are already discussed by Keynes,
Pigou and Robertson.

Second, Hawtrey's 'income approach' is the first important move
away from the strict Marshallian cash-balance orthodoxy towards an
analysis of monetary changes in terms of income, saving and investment. Moreover, this novel pre-war piece of analysis includes a very
sophisticated cumulative process akin to Wicksell's and Fisher's in
which the real-balance effect, a 'three-rate-of-interest' adjustment
mechanism, quantity adjustments, wage and price rigidities and
temporary unemployment disequilibria play a central part.

Third, Robertson's 'overinvestment' cycle theory provides a long-
run antidote to Hawtrey's purely monetary theory. Notwithstanding
short-run secondary monetary causes, Robertson devises a 'grand
dynamic' of the instability of the capitalist system based mainly on

he 'ebb and flow' of the marginal utility of capital goods, and
accessorily on a 'shortage-of-saving' theory. Both arguments lead to
he idea of a cyclical collapse of investment, which, in turn, contains
in embryo all the necessary elements to foster the revival which
cannot but follows.

However, and fourth, these three early formulations of widely
different aspects of economic fluctuations all share a basic common
monetary theory of interest of the loanable-funds type. Whatever
may be the cause of the cycle (monetary, banking or 'real') the
discrepancy between market and 'normal' rate of interest is only
temporary *and* self-adjusting. Instead of being the factor which
equates saving and investment *stricto sensu* at the so-called 'natural'
full-employment level determined by productivity and thrift, the
market-rate of interest not only equates the supply-and-demand for
loanable funds, but also operates (however primitive and unsatisfactory this piece of analysis still was) on the investment decision
(marginal efficiency of investment), on the consumption decision
(time preference) and on the size of money-holdings (liquidity preference). However, in the long run, through variations in the price-
level, the market-rate *always* tends towards the long-run 'normal'
full-employment rate of interest determined by the dominant forces
of the economic system. Despite Lavington's extension of the
analysis of the demand for money beyond money in the form of
income deposits, the stock – flow distinction necessary to a proper
understanding of the speculative demand for money, and hence of its
influence on the rate of interest, is still absent in 1925 from the
Cambridge version of the loanable-funds theory of interest.

Lastly, all the basic elements of the 'forced – abortive' savings
doctrine are present, though still unco-ordinated, in pre-1925 writings. However, despite a clear-cut distinction between 'saving and
hoarding' (Pigou), an understanding of how banks can alter the
supply of real saving available for investment (Pigou, Robertson), a
grasp of how the 'real' rate of capital accumulation is altered by
'forced saving' and an explicit recognition of the 'different decision'
hypothesis, all the implications from these still largely unconnected
building-blocks are far from being drawn, and even less understood.
In particular, and this is probably the result of the absence of a
clear-cut distinction between equilibrium and stability analysis (or
alternatively between long-run and short-run analysis), a *real-saving*
doctrine still dominates the picture. It implies, *inter alia*, that the
investment process can only take place if there exists *ex ante* a

physical 'lump-of-savings' large enough to match the volume of planned investment, allowing however for an amount of saving to be 'forced' upon the general public *during* the investment process. In other words, it is equivalent to saying that the total amount of savings (to which the level of investment is ultimately made equal through variations of the rate of interest) is made up of a *stock* of *ex ante* savings which may be altered by a *flow* of 'forced' (or 'abortive') savings.

6 *Banking Policy and the Price Level* and the 'Kinds of Savings'

Since the history of the working relationships between Keynes and Robertson, and their mutual theoretical indebteness, has been told several times in recent years,[1] only a few remarks are relevant here; particularly in connection with Keynes's successive adoption, improvement and final rejection of Robertson's 'forced-saving' doctrine.

The first of these three stages broadly corresponds to a period starting immediately after the publication of the *Tract* (autumn of 1924) and finishing by May 1925 when Keynes and Robertson started in earnest to discuss the first drafts of chapters 5 and 6 of *Banking Policy*. During this nine-month period Keynes seems to have worked out independently a 'forced-saving' argument more or less akin to Robertson's 1922 version. A good example of that evolution is given by the comparison of two early drafts of what was to become the *Treatise*. On 1 November 1924, in his 'Summary of the Author's Theory', Keynes is clearly *not* aware of the fact that the banking system can alter the supply of real-saving made available for investment (JMK, xiii, pp. 20–1).

However, barely a month later, an early draft of chapter 3 (dated 30 November 1924) contains the first written mention by Keynes of a 'forced-saving' process: 'It is true . . . that rising prices may increase the flow of current savings by inflicting a levy on consumers and wage earners for the advantage of producers' (JMK, xiii, p. 22). Unfortunately it is impossible to find more than this isolated, and in itself not very significant passage, before Keynes actually starts discussing Robertson's manuscript – the early drafts and correspondence have not survived.

The second stage of the Keynes–Robertson relationship is the most fruitful period of collaboration between them. Starting with an intensive exchange of notes and letters, supplemented by countless discussions between May and November 1925,[2] the beginning of this period saw the two men working in complete harmony, busy refining the basic framework laid down by Robertson in his first drafts. At a very general level Robertson's celebrated account of Keynes's role in the development of the ideas contained in *Banking Policy* gives an unusually vivid picture of the extent of their collaboration:

> I have had so many discussions with Mr. J. M. Keynes on the subject of chapters V and VI, and have rewritten them so drastically at his suggestion, that I think neither of us knows how much of the ideas therein contained is [*sic*] his and how much is [*sic*] mine. I should like to, but cannot, find a form of words which would adequately express my debt without seeming to commit him to opinions he does not hold. I have made a few specific acknowledgments in footnotes: happily there is the less need for meticulous disentanglement as his own version of the Theory of Credit is to be published very soon. (1926, p. 5; see also 1928b, p. ix, and for some of Keynes comments on this collaboration JMK, xiii, pp. 39–40, 273, and xxix, p. 2)

Keynes's final rejection of the framework he had helped Robertson to create marks the start of the last, and longest period, of their relationship. Keynes's formal dismissal of the 'forced-saving' framework coincides with his ultimate extensive rewriting of the central theoretical Books III and IV of the first volume of the *Treatise* during the winter 1929–30.

However, if the draft of a chapter 23 (dated August 1929), which subsequently disappeared in later revisions, clearly displays the *Banking Policy* theoretical framework, including the 'forced-saving' process (JMK, xiii, pp. 87, 104–8), the subsequent drafts together with Robertson's cool reception of them during the autumn of 1929 and the following winter make plain that Keynes was groping towards the substantially different approach of the fundamental equations. For example, in a letter dated 4 March 1930 Robertson is already aware of Keynes's progressive departure from the analysis of *Banking Policy*: 'I'm disappointed to find myself still full of resistances on certain points – not, I think, on the main structure' (JMK, xiii, p. 122).

Suffice it to notice at that stage that, in opposition to the traditional wisdom (e.g. Hicks, 1964, pp. 310–11), Keynes already substantially disagreed with Robertson *before* the publication of the *Treatise*.[3] The best testimony of Keynes's early departure from the 'forced-saving' doctrine is given by Robertson himself. In the new 1949 preface to *Banking Policy* he did not resist expressing *a posteriori* the bitterness ie felt when he realised that Keynes was moving away from the forced-saving' doctrine:

> While Keynes must at the time [of the publication of *Banking*] have understood and acquiesced in my step-by-step method, it is evident that it never, so to speak, got under his skin; *for in his two successive treatments of the saving-investment theme in his two big books he discarded it completely*. This was naturally a great personal disappointment to me. (1926, p. xi; italic added)

From the early months of 1930 when he and Keynes parted way, Robertson fought a constant rear-guard action against him; and his attacks on both *Treatise* and the *General Theory* can only be properly understood when read in the light of the step-by-step 'forced-saving' model of *Banking Policy*.

5.1 ROBERTSON'S MODEL

The fundamental aim of this unusual little book is to make explicit the still vague definitions of saving and investment. In fact, and bearing in mind what has already been said in the previous chapters, during the 1920s, the theoretical discussion is centred not so much on investment, or investment decisions *per se* (the volatility of which is admitted by practically everybody), but on a redefinition of the concept of saving in a monetary economy; and consequently on the influence of money on saving and on the role of this new concept in the cycle.

Robertson's systematic analysis of 'The kinds of savings' (1926, chap. 5) is basically linked with a sequential analysis of the lagged adjustments of output to monetary expenditure flows. The time-lag of some money incomes behind price-changes are responsible for savings being not only spontaneous, or voluntary, but also *forced*. Without delving into some over-subtle distinctions touched upon at length by Robertson, the essential features of *Banking Policy* (chap. 5) can be outlined in five points.

First, the relation between income and 'spontaneous lacking' (which 'corresponds pretty well to what is ordinarily thought of as Saving'; 1926, p. 47) is based upon a period analysis (Robertson's famous 'day'): 'A man is lacking if during a given period he consumes less than the value of his current economic output' (1926, p. 41; see also 1933a, p.

66). Thus the amount of 'spontaneous lacking' on 'day$_t$' is determined by the amount of disposable income received on 'day$_{t-1}$,' in relation with the amount of consumption on 'day$_t$; namely, $S_t = Y_{t-} - C_t$. Clearly, though the voluntary saving process takes place during 'day$_t$', the amount of goods (or disposable income) to be allocated during that day between consumption and saving does physically exist *before* the process starts, even if part of it is still 'in progress' at the end of 'day$_t$'. 'Spontaneous lacking' is thus the monetary expression of the *ex ante* 'lump-of-saving' defined by Robertson in his 'real'-saving doctrine.

Second, and this is the crucial point in the whole analytical exercise, spontaneous lacking and *total* saving (or lacking) need not be equal. If for one reason or another (e.g. an increase of the supply of money and/or credit) some individuals can expand their consumption at the expense of others, the ensuing higher price-level forces the rest of the community to consume less, and thus to add its lacking beyond that which is voluntary. Total lacking is thus in excess of voluntary saving by an amount equal to *automatic lacking*. In fact, automatic lacking is the equivalent of the 'forced saving' introduced by Robertson in 1922 in *Money*. The only difference between these two concepts lies in the fact that, in *Banking Policy*, Robertson makes explicit that – like a straightforward credit creation process – a change in the propensity to hoard (namely, the determinant of the Marshallian k) can also generate 'forced saving'.

Third, and under the direct influence of Keynes[4] (see 1926, pp. x, 49 n. 1 and JMK, xiii, pp. 36–7, 293),[5] Robertson introduces the completely new idea of 'induced lacking' as a complement to 'automatic lacking', both forming together 'imposed lacking'. In fact induced lacking is a remote ancestor of the modern real-balance effect *à la* Patinkin.[6] As a result of an increase in the flow of money on to the goods markets, prices will rise and 'forced saving' (or, more properly 'automatic lacking') will occur. *Additional* saving will, however, be induced on top of automatic lacking by a decline in the real value of the individual's money-holdings and, as consequence, people may refrain from consuming (namely, increase their lacking) in order to restore their cash balances to their previous *real* value:

> Induced Lacking occurs when, the same process that imposes Automatic Lacking on certain people having also reduced the real value of their money stocks, these people hold money off the market, and refrain from consuming the full value of their current

output, in order to bring the real value of their money stocks up again to what they regard as an appropriate level. (1926, p. 49)

It is remarkable that this piece of analysis (which was eventually to play such a crucial role in the 'neo-classical synthesis' interpretation of the *General Theory*) was actually suggested to Robertson *by Keynes himself*! In fact it is even more remarkable when one realises that 'induced lacking' is the only *substantial* improvement of the 1926 'forced-saving' analysis on the previous 1922 version. Though Keynes's argument was couched in terms of variations of the Cambride k it sounds quite familiar to modern economists bred on Patinkin's *Money, Interest and Prices*. It is well worth quoting Keynes at length in this respect:

> '*No* position of equilibrium can be reached [after an initial increase of the money-supply] until someone is induced to replenish his hoard, i.e. to do *some new* hoarding out of current income. It is only when this occurs that new short lacking is provided.
>
> This inducement to effect new hoarding comes about, in general, in one of the three ways:
>
> (i) The *real* [bank] deposits of the public may fall to a highly inconvenient low proportion of their real income, so that they prefer to do new hoarding so as to raise them, rather than to maintain their current expenditure at its previous level.
> (ii) Inflation may effect a redistribution of current real income into the hands of people whose incentive and ability to hoard is greater than those from whom it is taken.
> (iii) A higher bank rate may increase the incentive to hoard'. (JMK, xiii, p. 36, letter from Keynes to Robertson, 31 May 1925)

However, in the same letter to Robertson, Keynes is equally convinced that the case for 'induced lacking' should *not* be overstated:

> though powerful motives may come into cooperation to promote it, it remains just as voluntary as any other form of saving; . . . my *caveat* . . . is that new hoarding is not the *only* form of saving . . . [and] that there are other and better ways of [increasing the supply of new short lacking]. (JMK, xiii, p. 38).[7]

Incidentally, and given the countless criticisms levelled at Keynes, first by Pigou (1943, pp. 349–50, and 1947, pp. 249–51) and Haberler (1952, pp. 241–2, 491–503) and then by everybody writing in the field of monetary theory, and accusing him of assuming 'that the real-balance effect does not directly influence the commodity market' (Patinkin, 1965, p. 634), it is rather piquant to see Keynes discussing such a piece of analysis as early as 1925. Furthermore, it is even more surprising to realise that he even explicitly draws the connection between the money market and the commodity markets: '[Induced lacking] is a result of individual decisions balancing the advantages of maintaining hoards at a given level as against those of maintaining consumption at a given level' (JMK, xiii, p. 38). What could be a better anticipation of Patinkin's central contention that through the real-balance effect, monetary changes have a direct influence on the level of consumption as a direct implication of utility maximisation (see, for example, his 1948, p. 268)?

Fourth, in view of later discussions Robertson was to have with Keynes about the *Treatise* fundamental equations, and in order to emphasise the connection between 'forced-saving' and sequence analysis it is essential to get an idea of the meaning of *capital* in *Banking Policy*. To three types of capital, fixed, circulating and imaginary, correspond three types of lacking, long, short and unproductive. This threefold distinction is obviously linked with different lengths of time and, thus, plays an important part in Robertson's dynamic sequential analysis.

The *fixed capital*, provided by '*long* lacking', is the existing stock of investment goods which can be used in the future to produce goods and services. In fact it is nothing else but Marshall's 'specialised capital' (or capital as a *stock*) yielding a quasi-rent.

The notion of *circulating* (or working) *capital* is at the heart of Robertson's 'forced-saving' doctrine; it is also central to his step-by-step analysis. As expected this concept is nothing else but a sophisticated version of Marshall's 'free' or 'floating' capital (i.e. capital as a flow) (1926, p. 42).

Moving away from the then strict traditional 'real-saving' doctrine, for Robertson, the amount of saving necessary for investment is no longer equated to a stock of consumption goods accumulated before the start of the investment process (1915, p. xv; letter to Keynes, JMK, xiii, p. 122). On the contrary, only a small proportion of circulating capital consists of finished consumer-goods; the bulk of it is made up of goods and services 'in progress, in all stages of their

passage from the soil to the ultimate user' (1926, p. 42). Robertson
attributes this 'conversion' to Cassel (1923, p. 38) and to Henderson
(1922, pp. 124–5). Since there is no need for the whole circulating
capital to be accumulated at the start of the investment process in the
form of stocks of consumption goods, all that is required before the
production starts is to know that the community has the *power* to
produce these goods (or circulating capital) as the needs arise.

However, it is important to stress here that, analytically, it does *not*
alter the traditional Marshallian relation between saving, investment
and the rate of interest.

If the equation $S_{t-1} = Y_{t-1} - C_{t-1}$ (in which S_{t-1} is the stock of
consumption goods available *ex ante* for investment during the period
t) reflects the essential argument of the 'real-saving' doctrine, Robertson's equation $S_t = Y_{t-1} - C_t$ reflects the fact that the rate of interest
brings current investment in line with current saving *out of the income
available at the end of the previous period*. Put in a nutshell, the
concept of spontaneous lacking as a *stock* of accumulated consumption goods is replaced by a notion of a *flow* of working capital the size
of which is determined *ex ante*.

Imaginary Capital (i.e. the stock of paper securities not backed by
physical assets) does not play a large part in Robertson's theory.
Unproductive savings are in fact a mere transfer of purchasing power
from the public to the government (as opposed to productive saving
made up of spontaneous, automatic and induced lackings).

Fifth, it is now possible to understand fully the crux of Robertson's
analytical model. The whole exercise in *Banking Policy* amounts to
an appraisal of the influence of variations in (and the interaction
between) the amount of bank credit and the amount of hoarding on
the volume of circulating capital made available during a given
production period. Put in other words, and we are back to the
traditional Marshallian short-run method, the amount of *spontaneous
short lacking* planned *ex ante* with reference to the disposable income
(namely, the income earned during the previous period) and the then
current rate of interest can be altered during the current period
through changes in the amount of cash balances and/or bank credit.
As Robertson puts it: 'Lacking . . . of the short variety . . . is provided either by the entrepreneurs in charge of the production and
marketing of the goods, or by the general public under the compul-
sion of the monetary system' (1926, p. 85). However, and despite an
extremely refined analysis of the influence of the interactions between cash balances and bank credit on the volume of savings,

Robertson's elaborate framework is nothing more than another theoretical variation on the basic 'quantity-theory' theme.

6.2 THE 'FORCED-SAVING' PROCESS

Starting from an equilibrium position between the supply and demand for short lacking, for whatever reason, the demand for circulating capital rises. In consequence, and in Robertson's own words, since 'there seems no doubt that . . . the supply of Short Lacking is not sufficiently elastic to cope with such pronounced and discontinuous increases in demand and that the responsibility for meeting them rests almost entirely upon the banking system' (1926, p. 72), the demand for loanable funds (and/or the reduction of money-holdings) exceeds supply and the volume of voluntary saving is inadequate to support planned investment at the existing rate of interest.

Banks respond to the demand and increase their supply of credit (and/or a section of the community dishoards). The stream of money directed on to the markets for circulating capital increases, leaving the 'market'-rate of interest unchanged and 'trailing behind' the 'normal' rate. Since this additional stream of purchasing power is directed towards the purchase of a fixed available supply of circulating capital (made up of a small part of finished consumption goods and a large part of goods 'in progress'), and since *ex definitio* the production of circulating capital is perfectly inelastic – namely, cannot be increased before the end of the period of production – the increased wage-bill in the capital-goods industry induces competition by consumers for the fixed available output of circulating capital; the price-level rises.

Some agents are thus forced to lack, i.e. to have their consumption 'reduced both below what they intended and below the value of their current output' (1926, p. 48). This 'forced lacking' is divided between 'automatic lacking' (i.e. forced saving *stricto sensu*) and 'induced lacking' ('semi-voluntary-forced-saving') by agents reducing voluntarily their consumption to keep the *value* of their real balances (a stock) intact. These two elements (making up together 'imposed saving') are both real transfers from one section of the community to another.

As long as the 'normal' rate of interest is higher than the market rate, or alternatively as long as prices are rising (or still in another way, as long as people's *stocks* of cash have not been restored to their previous *real* value through a contraction of the consumption *flow*) this forced-saving process goes on even if during the subsequent time-periods, it is complicated by the arrival on the market of an increased volume of circulating capital.

The above schematic outline of Robertson's 1926 'forced-saving process' raises a number of important questions to which we may now turn.

(1) *The concept of hoarding.* Together with induced lacking and the new definition of circulating capital, Robertson's analysis of the concept of *hoarding* is the third major new element of *Banking Policy*. Not only can a change in hoarding habits generates forced saving, but Robertson's skilful analysis of the implications of the interaction between hoarding and credit creation and the distinction between general and 'sectorial' changes in hoarding habits bring in new variations on the 'quantity-theory' theme.

Given the random and unco-ordinated influences of variations of bank credit and levels of hoarding on the volume of savings, and, hence, on the purchasing power of money, how can monetary equilibrium be preserved in order to bring 'to fruition the thrifty intentions' of the community? (Robertson, 1959, p. 33). Or, eventually, put in another way, given the respective influences of bank credit and hoarding on the supply and demand for loanable funds, how can the market-rate of interest be held at its 'normal' or 'natural' level?

Two examples drawn from the various cases discussed by Robertson illustrate this connection between bank credit and hoarding.

The first case is a variation on the 'saving-running-to-waste-in-the-banking-system' argument; namely, the mirror image of the 'forced-saving process'. If *all* members of the public increased proportionately their hoardings, the real income of each (and consequently the purchasing power of money) may suffer *no* diminution. The planned saving involved in each and every individual's spontaneous new hoarding may be exactly cancelled by an increased volume of consumption fostered by the drop in the price-level following the general increased demand for cash (1926, p. 49). Clearly, in this case, as in the 'sectorial' spontaneous hoarding one, though for entirely different reasons, hoarding does not imply saving.

The second case illustrates in another way the (partial or total) mutual cancelling effect variations in the volume of credit creation and variations in hoarding habits can have on planned decisions to save. If some or all members of the community plan to raise the volume of their cash balances, the usual 'saving-lost-in-the-banking-system' consequence would arise, following a fall in the price-level and a subsequent rise in the volume of consumption from some members of the community; or, respectively, a subsequent unex-pected maintained consumption on the part of the community as a whole. In both cases, such a 'loss of saving' can be prevented by the banks making a suitable increase of their loans. Thus, instead of getting lost in the banking system, this additional volume of hoarding would be turned into 'actual' saving; the additional bank loans preventing the price-level from falling and hence the aggregate volume of consumption to rise (1926, pp. 53–4).

(2) *The equilibrium conditions.* By gathering together the various threads of Robertson's argument discussed so far it is now possible to give a formulation of Robertson's *monetary equilibrium theorem.* As expected, the criteria and the requisites for the existence of such a monetary equilibrium reflect nothing else but a straightforward, though much glorified, quantity theory.

Let us first assume the following conditions:

a. the velocity of circulation of money is given: in every and each period of production, the stock of money changes hands once in final exchange for one of the constituents of the community's real income or output (1926, pp. 57–8; 1933a, p. 65; 1959, pp. 47–8);
b. the only kind of money in circulation consists of balances with the banking system (1959, p. 47);
c. the proportion of the real income over which people wish to keep command in the form of money is constant (i.e. k is given);
d. the whole working capital has been built up in the *past* with the aid of the banks; namely, no working capital has been built by entrepreneurs out of their own (or out of the public's) saving;
e. the banks have not used any of their powers of money-creation for any other purpose than building up working capital.

Given then the following set of definitions:

Y = the real annual income;
k = the proportion of Y kept in the form of money;
kY = the aggregate of bank deposits;
D = the fraction of the year covered by the process of production

(in the simplest case, it is equal to 0.5);

C = the circulating (or working) capital during D;

n = the ratio of D to Y;

DY = the real income during the period of production;

we get the following relations ('those four crucial fractions', Samuelson, 1963, p. 527):

I) $C = nDY$ (i.e. the real value of bank assets);

II) $kY = nDY$

III) $k = nD$

Under the assumptions made above, equation III expresses the equilibrium condition between two different periods of time: the period of circulation of money against output and the period of production process. According to Robertson such equilibrium conditions are unlikely to be fulfilled except 'as a fortunate accident' (1959, p.48) because saving and investment decisions 'are determined by entirely separate and independent forces' (1928b, p. 106) which make highly unlikely in the short run the equality between saving and investment (see also 1959, p. 48).

Now, if we relax conditions c and e, and hence, admit that, on the one hand, part of the working capital has been accumulated through voluntary savings and, on the other, that some bank balances are used for other purposes than the building of working capital, we have to introduce two additional concepts:

a = the proportion of kY (bank assets) which is represented by working capital;

b = the proportion of C (circulating capital) which has been built with the aid of the banks.[8]

Then, Robertson's equilibrium conditions become:

(IV) $ak = bnD$ (or, alternatively, $k = b/a \, nD$).

In Robertson's own words this equation marks 'the climax of this part of the discussion' (1928a, p. 48).

If the equilibrium conditions postulated by equation IV are fulfilled the economic system will be in a situation of monetary equilibrium. This has a number of implications. In particular it implies the stability of the price-level together with the equality between voluntary saving and investment. The latter in turn implies both an equilibrium on the market for loanable funds (or, under the restrictive assumption (b) above the equality between the demand and supply for bank balances) and the equality between the 'normal' and the market-rate of interest. From this arises the neutrality of money in the sense that 'money does not introduce disturbing or dislocating factors, but permits and assists the real underlying forces making for general equilibrium, as expressed in the theories of value and distribution, to work themselves out' (1959, p. 32). In this equilibrium profits will be at a 'normal' level (namely, a level free of windfall losses/profits due to a reduced/increased money-stream) and there will be an equality between the time preference, the marginal productivity of capital and liquidity preference (the 'threefold-margin argument').

This crucial monetary equilibrium condition between 'saving in monetary form' (namely, Marshall's k) and the demand for circulating capital (D), clarifies a good deal Robertson's basic methodological dictum, which, at first, might have looked rather strange:

> I think myself that to find a concept of 'savings' in which their divergence from investment can be treated as a criterion of disequilibrium we must have recourse to a device by which the savings of one period are regarded as the excess, over the consumption of that period, of the income received not in that but in the preceding period. This is the method which I adopted . . . in my *Banking Policy and the Price Level* and elaborated later in my 'Saving and Hoarding'. (1959, p. 35)

In simple words, Robertson's whole exercise relies entirely on the fact that since production takes time, i.e. since the supply curve for working capital is inelastic, the volume of voluntary saving available *ex ante* for investment during a given period can only be altered through changes in the volume of consumption, i.e. through changes in the price-level fostered by variations in the volume of bank credit.

(3) *The connection between idle resources and the price-level.* Robertson's treatment of the connection between his 'forced-saving' process, the existence of idle resources and the price-level is a mixture of two earlier traditions.

Actually Robertson readily admits the existence of idle resources (capital and labour) during the recession phase of the cycle, and so is led to reject the most commonly held version of the 'forced-saving' doctrine of Thornton, Malthus, Lauderdale, Ricardo, and Walras among others.[9] This version implied *full employment* of resources. However, an increase of investible funds would no doubt increase employment (through overtime via increase of factor prices) and output at the expense of fixed income members of the community through a rise in the price-level. With his period analysis Robertson is also at odds with the other major version of the 'forced-saving' doctrine of Thompson, Burgess, Poulett Scrope and Joplin. This approach is assuming that there are idle resources and that an increase of loanable funds would raise both consumption and investment *at nobody's expense,* i.e. the price-level would remain constant.

Clearly Robertson's views are half-way between these two earlier traditions. He explicitly admits the existence of idle resources *but* makes clear that every expansion of output can only *follow* a rise in the price-level. The concatenation is as follows: if output is to be expanded, this result can only be done through a *prior* increase in the available volume of circulating capital; if spontaneous lacking does not provide for this extra circulating capital (i.e. if a 'thrift campaign' does not take place) it is left to the banking system to meet the demand for it through credit creation; this will enlarge the purchasing power competing for a *given* available amount of circulating capital in the current price period, bringing thus an increase in the price-level, and, eventually, automatic and induced lacking. Thus, since production takes time, an increase in the volume of circulating capital, and hence of lacking, must always *precede* any expansion of output; however, for its part, the volume of employment can in fact increase immediately, *during* the 'forced-saving' process (see Presley, 1979a, p. 197, for a similar argument). Thus, we are back willy-nilly to the concept of 'saving prior investment' as an entity or 'substance' that has to be converted, or incorporated, into investment. Dishoarding and credit expansion simply provide *alternatives* to increased saving as sources of working capital. Hence, the ensuing compulsory reduction of consumption (i.e. 'forced saving') is the only logical way to conform to the fundamental marginalist view that the only way to prepare for increase of investment is to save more at an appropriately *prior* date.

(4) *'Forced saving' and changes in the structure of production.* At first sight one may be genuinely surprised by the lack of interest displayed by Robertson towards changes in the structure of production, a question forming the core of Hayek's trade-cycle theory. Indeed, when this question is put in the proper and wider perspective of Robertson's general theory of industrial fluctuations, everything

falls neatly into place. Obviously Robertson is perfectly aware of the changes in the structure of production that take place following changes in the relative prices of capital and consumer goods. After all, 'forced saving' is nothing else but an addition to voluntary savings, the primary task of which is to allow for a lengthening of the production process (1926, pp. 72 and 74).

However, while, in Hayek's framework, 'forced saving' is the villain of the piece to be blamed for crises and subsequent changes in the structure of production (1933, p. 226, 1935, p. 135) Robertson only sees it as a relatively minor component of his trade-cycle theory outlined in *Industrial Fluctuation*. At the cost of some simplification it seems possible to argue that, for Hayek,[10] the cause of an expansion is the provision of additional bank credit, while for Robertson, the factors at the root of this 'credit inflation' are the *real* cause of this expansion.

In Robertson's theory of industrial fluctuations, of which *Banking Policy* examines only the strictly monetary aspects, 'forced saving' and the ensuing changes in the structure of production are brought into the picture at two different stages only, each of them being of secondary importance if compared with the overwhelming influence of *real* forces. On the one hand, during the recovery phase, forced saving is the means of financing a sudden burst of investment unmatched *ex definitio* by voluntary saving, but it is *not* the cause of the upturn itself.

On the other hand, in Robertson's secondary cause of crises, namely the shortage of saving case, the extraction of 'forced saving' from the public may temporarily postpone the downturn resulting from a failure of spontaneous saving to match investment demand. However, it cannot be overstressed that this shortage-of-saving thesis, postponed or not by 'forced saving', may only accelerate on occasion the inevitable downturn resulting from a devaluation of the marginal utility of acquiring capital goods. In other words, the cause of the downturn is the fall in the *demand* for saving, and hence for 'forced saving', and *not* the failure of supply to match demand (1926, pp. 90–1).[11]

(5) *The part played by the rate of interest.* The last problem to be examined in connection with Robertson's 'forced-saving' process is why the rate of interest still plays a very minor role in *Banking Policy* compared to the position of extreme importance it was to acquire in the 1930s.

On the one hand, Robertson simply takes for granted Marshall's theory of interest. Given the existence and stability theorems outlined by Marshall, Robertson's task amounts to a 'mere' step-by-step disequilibrium analysis taking into account the influence of various short-run factors *on the length* of the adjustment process between saving and investment.

On the other hand, it is only with Keynes's development in the *Treatise* of some major features of what was to become the liquidity preference theory of interest, Hayek's concentration on the gap between natural and market rates as the *cause* of the forced-saving process (1931a, 1933, 1935) and the various discussions which sur-rounded these two sets of contribution that *new elements* were added to Marshall's standard-interest theory.[12] Thus it is no wonder that Robertson did not feel necessary to return to the 'fundamentals' of interest theory before 1934.

For the sake of completeness one brief remark may, however, be added in connection with Robertson's use of Marshall's interest theory. Like Pigou and Hawtrey, Robertson discusses with great clarity the inelasticity of the investment-demand curve which, together with the liquidity trap and the wage-rigidity cases, are often considered by the 'neo-classical synthesis' as the hallmarks of Keynes's contribution to economic theory (see, e.g., Blaug, 1968, pp. 643–6): 'while there is always *some* rate of money interest which will check on an eager borrower, there may be *no* rate of money interest in excess of zero which will stimulate an unwilling one' (1926, p. 81).

7 Saving, Investment and the Theoretical Framework of the *Treatise* (1930)

This chapter has two primary aims: to appreciate Keynes's departure from the Robertsonian 'forced-saving' doctrine and to understand the originality of the theoretical framework of the *Treatise*.

The whole idea of 'forced saving' has a very *minor* part indeed to play in the *Treatise* (see JMK, v, pp. 269–70). This is interesting because as late as August 1929 Keynes was contemplating including a chapter which not only displayed support for it but refined Robertson's argument on many a minor point (JMK, xiii, pp. 83–113). In view of the 'big theoretical switch' that took place between the *Treatise* and the *General Theory*, it seems necessary to have a closer look at Keynes's first steps away from a theory which, in his own words:

> believed that inequalities between saving and investment . . . only arose as a result of what one might call an act of inflation or deflation on the part of the banking system. (Letter to Robertson, 6 October 1931, JMK xiii, p. 273)

The thirty pages which make up the draft of chapter 23 – a very minor part of which actually appeared in the *Treatise*[1] – is a lengthy and detailed restatement of 'The Part Played by the Banking System' in the adjustment of 'the supply of working capital' to the demand for it (JMK, xiii, pp. 83 and 92). They show that Keynes was then working along purely Robertsonian lines (see, e.g., ibid. pp. 93 and 104).

The first signs of Keynes's discontent with Robertson's argument appeared in the autumn of 1929. By Keynes's own admission his extensive rewriting of the fundamental chapters of Books III and IV of the *Treatise* 'were primarily devised to meet what seemed to me misunderstandings on the part of Pigou and Robertson' (JMK, xiii, p. 138). Unfortunately, at this crucial point of the evolution of

Keynes's thought, the evidence of the nature of those misunderstandings is very scarce, practically all records of this attempt having
not survived (see JMK, xiii, p. 135 n. 1). It is only in July 1930 that
Keynes gives a clue to what is for him his central point of disagreement with Robertson and Pigou:

> My attempt to explain to Pigou and Robertson *the difference
> between excess hoarding and excess saving*, about which they have
> been making obstinate misunderstandings, has led me to what
> seems to be a very great improvement of exposition and some
> slight change of substance. (JMK, xiii, p. 135; italic added)

Before trying to disentangle what is for Keynes the meaning of
Pigou's and Robertson's confusion, it is worth noting that even if
Keynes has clearly the impression of departing from Robertson's
'forced-saving' doctrine he makes equally clear that his new theory
'looks a great deal more different from the old version than it really
is' (JMK, xiii, p. 135; see also p. 138). In other words, the 'slight
change of substance' brought in by the fundamental equations does
not render his theoretical framework at all incompatible with the
standard Cambridge quantity-equation approach.

In so far as Pigou's and Robertson's misunderstanding is concerned, it seems to be connected with the basic stock–flow (or
wealth–income) confusion linked in turn with the analysis of the
demand for money beyond money for income deposits. In other
words, during the winter 1929–30 Keynes was already well aware that
there is *no* direct connection between what he called later 'a growth
of inactive deposits and an excess of saving' (JMK, xiii, p. 226).
Clearly this amounts to denying Robertson's and Pigou's thesis that
whenever there is an increase in saving more money would be passed
to the stock exchange and used to finance a corresponding increase in
investment (following a drop in the interest rate), this transfer
inducing in turn a rise in the prices of investment goods and a drop in
the prices of consumption goods. Thus Keynes had grasped at the
time what was to become the central novelty of the *Treatise*: the
price-level of investment goods and the price-level of consumption
goods are largely determined independently of each other. This
analysis implies a theory of the demand for money beyond money in
the form of income deposits; a connection with the influence on this
demand of the rate of interest (liquidity preference) and the general

state of expectations; and, eventually, a complete new formulation of the optimum portfolio analysis and a simultaneous revision of the 'threefold-margin' analysis.

As far as the saving-investment technique of analysis is concerned, it should be clear that even if Keynes made a substantial departure from the 'forced-saving' approach he remained faithful to the logic of the traditional Marshallian analysis: a gap between saving and investment reflects a disequilibrium situation and is the potential instrument *par excellence* of economic prognosis. As Schumpeter put it a few years later, commenting on the gap between the 'natural' and the market-rates of interest (the corollary of a gap between saving and investment), it is 'a kind of *coefficient of tension in the system* which . . . expresses the degree of disequilibrium present in the latter' (1939, p. 126). In a nutshell, if Keynes disagreed with Robertson (and Hayek) on how this gap comes into existence he certainly did not disagree on the meaning of this gap itself.

7.1 THE FUNDAMENTAL EQUATIONS

More explicitly than in Robertson's *Banking Policy* the main critical thrust of the *Treatise* is directed (in a somewhat Hawtreyan fashion) at the long-run equilibrium character of the quantity-theory equation. In Keynes's own words the duality of this approach is very clearly stated. On the one hand, '*in equilibrium* . . . there is a unique relationship between the quantity of money and the price-levels of consumption-goods and output as a whole, of such a character that if the quantity of money were double the price-level would double also' (JMK, v, p. 132). However, the traditional quantity equations (both the Fisherine and the Cambridge versions) 'do not . . . have the advantage of separating out those factors through which, in a modern system, the causal process actually operates *during the process of change*' (JMK, v, p. 120; italic added). Obviously we have here a direct echo of Keynes's 1911 review of Fisher's *Purchasing Power of Money*: without a proper stability analysis the quantity theory has little to say about the 'real' world.

Thus, Keynes's prime aim is 'to treat the problem dynamically, analysing the different elements involved, in such a manner as to exhibit the causal process by which the price-level is determined, and the method of transition from one position of equilibrium to another' (JMK, v, p. 120); or, in other words, to determine nothing less than 'the dynamical laws' of the disequilibrium process (JMK, v, p. xvii).

Eventually the link with Marshall's long-run value theory is established through the idea of windfall profit/loss (i.e. profits above those representing a 'normal' uniform return on capital). These profits/losses measure the difference between the 'demand-price' (i.e. market-price) of a unit of output and its 'supply price' (i.e. cost of production). As in Marshall's set-up, such unexpected profits/losses cause firms to expand/contract their respective outputs, and, hence, their demand for factors of production. Profits being thus the driving force of the economy (JMK, v, pp. 126, 141, 163, and xx, p. 107) the study of cyclical movements in employment and output between two equilibrium situations is nothing else (as, for example, in Walras, 1954, p. 225) but a study of the causes of the differential movements of prices and costs (JMK, xx, p. 82).

Casting their nets beyond the narrow part played by the banking system the fundamental equations extend to a wider range of causes the sources of inequality between saving and investment; they also disaggregate the variations of the price-level between 'purely monetary' (second part of the right-hand side of both equations) and 'real' cost-of-production causes (first part of the right-hand side of both equations).

Despite the somewhat awkward task of 'translating' Keynes's definitions in more familiar a terminology the basic idea underlined by the fundamental equations is simple: the main reason for the existence of windfall profits/losses – or identically for a gap between investment and saving to exist – is the 'result of the public changing their rate of saving or the entrepreneurs changing their rate of investment' (JMK, xiii, p. 251); or, put in other words, the main cause for this gap to arise comes from the fact that the division of total income between the part earned in the consumption-goods sector and the one earned in the investment-goods sector respectively *differs* from the division of that income between consumption and saving.

Given the following set of definitions (JMK, v, pp. 121–2):

E = current money-income = factor earnings = costs of production (all including 'normal' profits);

O = the same, at base-period prices;

I' = that part of E earned in the investment-goods sector = current money-costs of producing investment-goods;

C = the same at base-period prices;

I = the same at current market-prices, i.e. the current market value of investment-goods produced;

$E - I'$ = the part of E earned in the consumption-goods sector
= current money costs of producing consumption-goods;

R = the same, at base-period prices;

P = current price-level of consumption-goods;

P' = current price-level of investment-goods;

π = current price-level for output as a whole (i.e. the weighted average of P and P').

If the equilibrium assumed in both sectors in the base-period (i.e. per unit cost = per unit price) should remain undisturbed, any change in the price of consumption-goods could only arise from a change in the per-unit costs of production of these goods; what Keynes calls 'the rate of efficiency earnings':

$$\frac{E}{O} = \frac{W}{e} = W_1$$

where W = index of money wage-rate (price of a unit of factors-of-production-in-general);

e = 'coefficient of efficiency' (i.e. index of output per worker);

W_1 = 'rate of efficiency earnings'.

From all these definitions – and reversing Keynes's order of derivation – we eventually reach two alternative formulations of the fundamentals equations:

$$\text{(i)} \quad P = \frac{E}{O} + \frac{Q_1}{R} = \frac{W}{e} + \frac{Q_1}{R} = W_1 + \frac{Q_1}{R}$$

$$\text{(ii)} \quad \pi = \frac{E}{O} + \frac{Q}{O} = \frac{W}{e} + \frac{Q}{O} = W_1 + \frac{Q}{O}$$

and, given Keynes's definition of saving as 'the sum of the differences between the money incomes of individual and their money-expenditure on current consumption' (JMK, v, p. 113), i.e. in algebraic terms

$$S = E - PR;$$

we can derive two equations – corresponding to (i) and (ii) above – to define Q_1 and Q:

$$Q_1 = PR - (E - I') = I' - S$$

$$Q = (PR + I) - E = I - S.$$

Thus the fundamental equations can be rewritten in their usual form:

$$P = \frac{E}{O} + \frac{I' - S}{R} \qquad \text{and} \qquad \pi = \frac{E}{O} + \frac{I - S}{R}$$

Keynes infers from his first equation that 'the price-level [of consumption-goods], as determined by the first term, is upset by the fact that the division of output between investment and goods for consumption is not necessarily the same as the division between savings and expenditure on consumption. For workers are paid just as much when they are producing for investment as when they are producing for consumption; but having earned their wages it is they who please themselves whether they spend or refrain from spending them on consumption. Meanwhile the entrepreneurs have been decided quite independently in what proportions they shall produce the two categories of output.' (JMK, v, p. 123)

If we assume the price-level of investment-goods P' as given, the second fundamental equation can be easily derived as above; or conversely, by subtracting the first from the second equation, we can easily get P'. Questions arise as soon as we want to know what are the determining factors of the price-level of investment-goods. As a matter of fact, Keynes assumes that the price-level of consumption-goods are determined *independently* of each other. Indeed, this is *the* fundamentally new argument suggested in the *Treatise*.

The novelty of this idea is only matched by the novelty of its analytical underpinning. By arguing that the price-level of investment goods (P') 'is that price-level at which the desire of the public to hold savings deposit is equal to the amount of savings-deposit which the banking system is willing and able to create' (JMK, v, p. 129), Keynes eventually brings to fruition the 'threefold-margin' argument. As a matter of fact, the *Treatise* offers the first analysis of the demand for money beyond money in the form of income deposits and fills the gaps left by Pigou and Lavington in the general theory of the choice of an optimum portfolio of assets. It provides both a sharp distinction between stocks and flows (and the two corresponding ideas of an asset-demand for saving *deposits* as an alternative for an individual to hold his wealth and the explicit addition of *wealth* as a determinant with respect to which, together with income, the individual's holdings of money are determined) and also the first complete statement of the implications of the 'threefold-margin' argument; namely, the influence of the rate of interest on the demand for money (or, to express the same point slightly differently, to the *wealth*-effect of money-changes is added the portfolio-adjustment *substitution*-effect). It is essential to have a clear idea of this analysis, since it anticipates some major features of what was to become the liquidity-preference theory in the *General Theory*.

As Shackle puts it, save the emphasis put on uncertainty in the *General Theory*, the 'liquidity-preference theory of interest [is] stated in the *Treatise on Money*' (1967, p. 314; see also pp. 173–4; Kahn, 1974, pp. 6–7, and 1984, pp. 33–4, and Patinkin, 1976, p. 40). The central and controversial part played by liquidity preference as an *alternative* theory of interest in the *General Theory* compels us to examine the role Keynes gave to a similar piece of analysis in the entirely different theoretical framework of the *Treatise*.

It will be appreciated that if Keynes had mastered before the *General Theory* a theory substantially similar to the one Robertson and Hicks suggested in 1937 as a more 'general case' including the liquidity-preference interest theory there would be a prima facie evidence that this loanable-funds theory of interest is incompatible with the principle of effective demand, in so far as Keynes repeatedly asserted that the source of the difference between the *General Theory* and orthodox thinking (including the *Treatise*) is to be sought in the theory of interest (JMK, xiv, pp. 202, 212; see below, Chapter 9).

Basically Keynes's idea in his discussion of the price-level of investment-goods (P') is to extend the theory of demand for money beyond the traditional income approach (the Cambridge k). When comparing in Book III, chapter 14, his fundamental equations with 'the older methods' of the alternative quantity equations, Keynes concentrates his critique of the Cambridge equation precisely on the fact that it does *not* explain the demand of money for savings-deposits (see JMK, v, p. 200).

Putting together Marshall's (1887), Pigou's (1917) and his own version of the Cambridge equation (1923), Keynes makes clear where Cambridge economists, including of course himself, had gone wrong before the *Treatise*:

the introduction of . . . the current income of the community, suggests that variation in this is one of the two or three most important direct influences on the demand for cash resources. In the case of the income deposits this seems to me to be true. But the significance of [current income] is much diminished when we are dealing, not with income-deposits in isolation, but with the total deposits. Indeed the chief inconvenience of the 'Cambridge' Quantity Equation really lies in its applying to the total deposits considerations which are primarily relevant only to the income deposits, and in its tackling the problem as though the same sort of considerations which govern the income deposits also govern the total deposits [namely, income plus saving-deposits]. . . .

The prominence given to k, namely the proportion of the bank deposits to the community's *income*, is misleading when it is extended beyond the income deposits. The emphasis which this method lays on the point that the amount of real balances held is determined by the comparative advantages of holding resources in cash and in alternative forms, so that a change in k will be attributable to a change in these comparative advantages [i.e. the 'threefold-margin' argument], is useful and instructive. *But 're-sources' in this connection ought not to be interpreted* as it is interpreted by Prof. Pigou [and by Marshall, Robertson and myself could have added Keynes], *as being identical with current income.* (JMK, v, pp. 207–8; last italic added)

Clearly it remains now to be shown that, in his discussion of the determinants of P', the idea of '*resources*' is interpreted by Keynes as *wealth*, and that the volume of this demand of money for savings-deposits (or speculative demand) is connected with the rate of interest (or conversely with the price of securities) and with the general state of expectations.

Given the crucial importance of that analysis, another lengthy quotation from the *Treatise* decisive Book III, chapter 10, does not seem out of place here:

When a man is deciding what proportion of his money income to save, he is choosing between present consumption and the ownership of wealth. . . . [I]n so far as he decides in favour of saving, there still remains a further decision for him to make . . . between 'bank deposits' and 'securities'. . . .

The decision as to the volume of saving . . . relates wholly to current activities. But the decisions as to holding bank deposits or securities relates, not only to the current increment to the wealth of individuals, but also to the whole block of their existing capital. Indeed, since the current increment is but a trifling proportion of the block of existing wealth, it is but a minor element in the matter.

Now when an individual is more disposed than before to hold his wealth in the form of savings deposits and less disposed to hold it in other forms, this does not mean that he is determined to hold it in the form of savings *at all costs*. It means that he favours savings deposits . . . more than before at the existing price level of other securities. But his distaste for other securities is not absolute and depends on his expectations of the future return to be obtained from savings deposits and from other securities respectively, which is obviously affected by the price of the latter – and also by the rate of interest allowed on the former. If, therefore, the price level of other securities falls sufficiently, he can be tempted back into them. If, however the banking system operates in the opposite direction to that of the public and meets the preference of the latter for savings deposits by buying the securities which the public is *less* anxious to hold and creating against them the additional savings deposits which the public is *more* anxious to hold, then there is no need for the price level of investments to fall at all. Thus the change in the relative attractions of savings deposits and securities respectively has to be met either by a fall in the price of securities or by an increase in the supply of savings deposits, or partly by one and partly by the other.

. . . [W]e may sum up the matter thus. The price level of investments as a whole, and hence of new investments [i.e. P'] is that price level at which the desire of the public to hold savings deposits is equal to the amount of savings deposits which the banking system is willing and able to create.' (JMK, v, pp. 127–9)

All this carefully worded analysis suggests that Keynes's 'resources' can beyond doubt be interpreted as meaning 'wealth'. This theoretical development can be summarised as follows: the decision as to the flow of saving (i.e. the rate at which to add to the stock of wealth) is a function of income; or, $S = S\,(Y)$;[2] the decision as to the forms in which to hold a stock of wealth is function of the size of that stock, the rate of interest on savings-deposits, the rate of interest on securities, the level of income (for a 'trifling' proportion) and eventually the expectations as to the future of the two rates of interest just mentioned; hence, the demand for money is made up of income and savings deposits, the latter being a function of total wealth and of the rate of interest:

$$M^D = M_1(Y) + M(r)^3$$

therefore, according to the 'threefold-margin' argument, any change in the rate of interest following a monetary change not only affects the amount of the community's borrowing (changes of the *flow* of expenditures via a *wealth* effect) *but also* affects the quantity of money it chooses to hold in order to re-establish the equilibrium – the 'balance at the margin' – between these holdings of money and the stocks of other assets (changes of the stock of money via a substitution-effect in a portfolio of a given size).

To summarise the *Treatise* basic framework in Keynes's own words:

> It follows that the price-level of output as a whole and the amount of total profit depend on . . . the two factors
> 1) the excess of saving over cost of investment, and
> 2) such excess of bearishness on the part of the public as is unsatisfied by the creation of deposits by the banking system. (JMK, v, p. 129)

To close the circle of his 'disequilibrium analysis' Keynes restates the equilibrium conditions under which his fundamental equations are equivalent to the Cambridge (or Fisherine) equation:

> in equilibrium – i.e. *when the factors of production are fully employed*, when the public is neither bullish nor bearish and is maintaining in the form of savings deposits neither more nor less than the 'normal' proportion of its total wealth, and when the volume of savings is equal both to the cost and to the value of new investments – there is a unique relationship between the quantity of money and the price levels of consumption-goods and of output as a whole. (JMK, v, p. 132)

It is equivalent to saying:

equilibrium conditions: $I = I' = S$

first fundamental equation: $P = \dfrac{E}{O} (= W_1)$

second fundamental equation: $\pi = \dfrac{E}{O}$ $(= W_1)$

This leads us (JMK, v, p.135) to Fisher's familiar equation if E (money-income) is equated to MV:

$$\pi = P = \frac{M_1 V_1}{O}$$

To recapitulate, it can be seen that two results very much at odds with the then received doctrine stem from these two fundamental equations. Both of these are in fact *corollaries* of the extension of the analysis of the demand for money beyond money in the form of income deposits. On the one hand, the idea that the price-level of investment-goods may decline owing to an excess of saving over I', there being *no* parallel increase in the disposition to hoard unspent money (Robertson's 'buckets-in-a-well' fallacy). On the other hand, the idea that the price level as a whole can depart from equilibrium *without* any change having occured in the quantity and/or velocity of circulation of money (JMK, xiii, p. 251; Hayek's 'neutral money' issue). These two results illustrate the fact that the *Treatise* breaks with more than two centuries of tradition. Keynes no longer asserts in the short run a direct relationship between the quantity of money (or for that matter its velocity of circulation) and the price-level.

Accordingly monetary changes no longer foster *ipso facto* a forced/abortive saving process; and, from the crucial and exclusive part this process played in Robertson's and Hayek's frameworks, Keynes reduced its range of validity to a very particular case in which the bearishness of the public and the volume of savings-deposits are constant (see Keynes's ultimate attack against 'forced saving' along the same line in his preface to the 1931 German edition of the *Treatise*; JMK, v, pp. xxiii–xxiv).

7.2   THE EXTENT OF THE DEPARTURE FROM THE 'FORCED-SAVING' DOCTRINE: 'BUCKETS-IN-A-WELL' AND 'NEUTRAL MONEY'

The crux of Robertson's review of the *Treatise on Money* is what he calls 'Mr. Keynes's paradox' (1931b, p. 400), or what Keynes later called 'buckets-in-a-well' (JMK, xiii, p. 223):

if *P* declines owing to an excess of *S* over *I'*, then, *even though there is no increase in the disposition to hoard money unspent*, there need be no counterbalancing rise in *P'*, there will be a fall in π, the price of output as a whole. (Robertson, 1931b, p. 400; italic added)

Hayek, for his part (1931b, 1931c, 1932a), espoused a similar view, which, according to Keynes, implies 'that an act of monetary expansion . . . is not merely a possible cause of investment exceeding saving but (1) that it is a necessary cause of this and (2) that the amount of the monetary expansion *exactly measures* the excess of investment over saving and hence is exactly equal to the amounts of profits (in my terminology)' (JMK, xiii, p. 246).

In his replies to both Robertson and Hayek, Keynes displays a very clear understanding of the crux of their disagreement with his own thesis. By disconnecting the direct and proportional relationship between variations of the money-supply, variations of the price-level and the opening of a gap between the 'normal' and the market-rate of interest (and ultimately between savings and investment) Keynes struck the most destructive blow at the 'ancient ceremony' (Robertson, 1959, p. 11) of the Cambridge equation ever launched from within its own limits. In other words, Keynes's contribution ruined the apparently straightforward and mechanistic stability analysis postulated by Marshall, Pigou and Robertson.

In particular, it introduces a destructive element of uncertainty into Robertson's analysis of the 'kinds of savings' which, in turn, proved deadly to the entire 'forced-saving' argument.

After months of argument and counter-argument Keynes was in a position to deny Robertson's thesis that there must be a relationship between the prices of consumption and investment goods (assuming an unchanged propensity to hoard) which ensures that 'the one must go down when the other goes up, like buckets in a well'. By an alternative route, Keynes's reply to Hayek reaches the same conclusion, this time not in terms of hoarding, but in terms of quantity of money:

saving and investment (as I define them) can get out of gear without any change on the part of the banking system from 'neutrality' as defined by Dr. Hayek, merely as a result of the public changing their rate of saving or the entrepreneurs changing their rate of investment, *there being no automatic mechanism in the economic system* . . . to keep the two rates equal, provided that the effective quantity of money is unchanged. (JMK, xiii, p. 251, italic added)

The absence of such an 'automatic mechanism' (Hayek) and the 'buckets-in-a-well' fallacy (Robertson) amounts eventually to the same thing. On the one hand, the rate of saving and the rate of investment can get out of gear *without* being accompanied by changes in the money-supply because the same volume of income deposits can circulate a smaller/larger volume of production, leaving the volume of saving-deposits unchanged (JMK, xiii, p. 222–4). On the other hand, a gap between saving and investment is no longer *measured* by variations of inactive deposits – put in more general terms, the idea that there is no 'invariable association in experience between a growth of inactive deposits and an excess of saving' (JMK, xiii, p. 226)[4] results from the fact that, in the *Treatise*, the 'decision to hold inactive deposits is not . . . an absolute one irrespective of the price of other assets' (JMK, xiii, p. 221). The introduction of a 'speculative' demand for money keeps thus at bay the supply-and-demand mechanism (Hayek's 'automatic mechanism') underlying the orthodox quantity equation. More properly speaking, Keynes had laid bare an additional, important and intricate source of disequilibrium neglected (if not ignored) by all previous writers.

Durbin put this very clearly in his much-neglected *Problem of Credit Policy* :

If there exists in the economic order large stocks of property rights, the exchange of part of which gives rise to an important volume of monetary business, the equilibrium of the industrial circulation is *inherently unstable*, and with it that of output and employment. . . . Large stocks of securities, just as much as large stocks of commodities, constitute a continuous and serious threat to monetary equilibrium. (1935, p. 103)

However, once again these large stocks of securities do not put in jeopardy the long-run validity of Marshall's traditional equilibrium analysis more than large stocks of commodities do (like in Hawtrey's model).[5]

7.3   THE ROLE OF PROFITS AS AN EXPRESSION OF THE
      GAP BETWEEN SAVING AND INVESTMENT

At this stage of the argument three comments need to be made which give even stronger support for what has just been said. First, Keynes's final remarks about his fundamental equations are not over-enthusiastic:

> all these equations are purely formal; they are mere identies; truisms which tell us nothing in themselves. In this respect they resemble all other versions of the quantity theory of money. Their only point is to analyse and arrange our material in what will turn out to be a useful way for tracing cause and effect, when we have vitalised them by the introduction of extraneous facts from the actual world. (JMK, v, p. 125)

Thus, windfall profit/loss is introduced as *the* 'extraneous facts from the actual world':

> It is the introduction of this *fact* from the real world which gives significance to the particular fundamental equations which we have selected and saves them from the character of being mere identities. (JMK, v, p. 141)

Hence, while in a long-run equilibrium this windfall profit/loss has a zero value (JMK, v, p. 141), to an excess of saving over investment corresponds a windfall loss and to an excess of investment over saving a windfall profit (JMK, v, p. 74). However, the only really interesting problems connected with the nature of this $(I - S)$ gap – i.e. the reasons why windfall profit/loss engineers variations of output – are barely touched upon by Keynes, except by way of reference to Marshall's traditional approach. Keynes simply assumes as a matter of fact from the real world that, to positive or negative profits corresponds an increase or a decrease of the volume of employment which entrepreneurs offer at the existing rates of remuneration of the factors of production.

Second, thanks to this rather elementary artifact, Keynes can claim that his equations are not truisms or mere identities. Instead they are clearly able to isolate temporary changes linked with the existence of Q_1 and Q_2 – and thus with I', I and S – from a long-run 'normal' equilibrium norm which is itself allowed to vary. Conversely, in equilibrium, both Q_1 and Q_2 are equal to zero. It then follows from this that $P = \pi = E/O$ shows in a pure Marshallian fashion that the 'long-period or equilibrium norm of the purchasing power of money' (JMK, v, p. 137) is given by the cost of production. These fundamental equations are thus able to give 'the clue to the way in which the fluctuations of the price-level actually come to pass, whether they are due to oscillations about a steady equilibrium level or to a transition from one equilibrium to another' (JMK, v, p. 137).

Third, the savings habits of the community being pretty stable (JMK, v, pp. 251, 257), entrepreneur's decisions to invest are largely determined by the terms of credit (or market-rate of interest). The Marshallian two-rate mechanism is then introduced in order to develop a full-blown cumulative process. The rate of interest which makes the value of investment equal to saving (i.e. $I = S$, or alternatively $Q_1 + Q_2 = Q = O$) is the long-run norm, the so-called 'natural rate of interest'. As soon as there is a discrepancy between these two rates, there is a tendency 'to set up a disturbance of the price level by causing the second term of the equation to depart from zero' (JMK, v, p. 39), and, as long as they differ, the price-level will continue to rise/fall 'without limit' (JMK, v, p. 176). Nothing could be more akin to Marshall's cumulative process despite the lack, in the *Treatise*, of a proper analysis of the determination of the natural rate of interest itself; namely, the absence of a capital theory proper.[6]

The famous chapter on 'The "modus operandi" of Bank rate' is a brilliant piece of analysis showing bold confidence for the rate of interest as the adjusting mechanism to fill any gap between I and S, to correct all temporary divergences from the long run-equilibrium norm:

> I believe that the root of the trouble [in the late 1920s] is to be found in the long-term rate of interest held far above its equilibrium level. . . . Our task is to bring down the rate of interest to whatever extent is necessary to bring about an equilibrium balance in demand for loans and supply of current savings. (JMK, xx, pp 353 and 553; see also pp. 71, 78, 95, 272, 469 and 518)

As in Robertson's model this standard piece of analysis implies not only that saving and investment are interest-elastic, but also that gaps between saving (out of full-employment income) and planned investment can be bridged as the rate of interest changes.

Keynes provides the reader with a very clear answer to both of these Marshallian hypotheses. On the one hand,

> a rise . . . in the market rate of interest upsets the balance between the value of investment and saving, unless a corresponding rise in the natural rate occurs at the same time. It may do this either by stimulating saving or by retarding investment. (JMK, v, p. 180; see also xx, p. 80)

On the other, since, 'in equilibrium . . . the factors of production are *fully employed* . . . and . . . the volume of saving is equal both to the cost and to the value of new investments' (JMK, v, p. 132; italic added), any gap between saving and investment (induced by a discrepancy between market- and natural-rate) will yield 'a state of unemployment [which] may be expected to ensue, and to continue, until the rise in bank-rate is reversed or, by a chance, something happens to alter the natural rate of interest so as to bring it back to equality with the new market rate' (JMK, v, p. 184).

Keynes's strong belief in the theoretical capacity of bank-rate to adjust saving to investment in the long run, does not blind him to the practical difficulties of such a policy at the time he was writing the *Treatise*. In the winter of 1929–30 one of his leitmotiv in his evidence before the Macmillan Committee is precisely to show how the gold exchange standard precludes a fall of the interest-rate (JMK, xx, pp. 84, 348, 351, 374–5, 435, 445):

> if you jam the machine half way through [and] put the Bank rate at a level at which savings are in excess of investments, . . . you have a chronic condition . . . of unemployment, a chronic condition of waste; and the excess savings are spilled on the ground. (JMK, xx, p. 75)

However, Keynes is equally clear when he adds that, even if 'it has broken down as a practical instrument for restoring true equilibrium, bank-rate policy [is] still *theoretically* intact' (JMK, xx, p. 71; italic added).

One final remark can now be added:

In order to explain what he sees already in the *Treatise* as severe persistent unemployment[7] Keynes uses the only available device he could use in his analytical set-up, i.e. the length of the 'short-period' deviation around the long-run full-employment norm.[8] He simply extends the so-called 'short' period to an extremely long period of time. But the inner logic of the theory remained unchanged. The three following passages seem to convey such an idea of a 'very long short period':

> Finally, under the pressure of growing unemployment, the rate of earnings – *though, perhaps, only at long last* – will fall. (JMK, v, p. 185; italic added)

And perhaps more explicitly in the applied theory volume:

> A 'short period', it would seem, thinks nothing of living longer than a man. A 'short period' is quite long enough to include (and, perhaps to contrive) the rise and fall of the greatness of a nation. (JMK, vi, p. 141; see also p. 388)

And in his evidence before the Macmillan Committee:

> Economists spend most of their time discussing what happens in a position of equilibrium, and they usually affirm that a position of disequilibrium is merely transitory. . . . We have behaved as though the intermediate 'short periods' of the economist between one position of equilibrium and another really were short, whereas, they can be long enough – and have before now – to encompass the decline and downfall of nations. (JMK, xx, pp. 72 and 379)

In that respect Keynes holds an approach very similar to Robertson's:

> If we trust for a cure [too high interest-rates] to time, and nature and a happy accident, we have no right to expect this cure *soon*. . . . Time and natural forces [will not] lead us with an invisible hand to the economic harmonies; . . . there is no design but our own, and . . . the invisible hand is merely our own bleeding feet moving through pain and loss to an uncertain and unprofitable destination. (JMK, xx, 474 and 519)

Let us now turn precisely to some further discussions about 'natural'- and 'market'-rate which took place in the years preceding the publication of the *General Theory*.

8 Further Reflections on the Rate of Interest (1930–5)

It is necessary now to make explicit the theoretical consequences of the extension of the analysis of the demand for money beyond income deposits on the theory of interest Keynes took over from Marshall. In his well-known parable of the *banana growers* Keynes describes the consequences of a thrift campaign in what was formerly an Eden of stability and full employment. Consumers reduce their expenditures. This has the effect of occasioning losses to the manufacturers of consumption-goods. These producers then try to meet their losses by selling part of the stock of existing securities they keep as a class of assets or means of holding their wealth. By the sale of these securities they can maintain their payments to the factors of production.

Despite the facts that the outflow of money to financial circulation (speculative motives) is occasioned not by a change in financial circulation, but by events taking place entirely within industrial circulation (transaction and precautionary motives), the situation in industrial circulation becomes deflationary. In other words, despite the fact that the money-incomes of the consumption-good factors are maintained at their old level, the situation cannot be but deflationary because the sale of securities on the part of producers of consumption-goods prevents the rise in the price-level of securities which would otherwise have taken place. Had it not been offset by this increase in the supply of securities, the price-level of securities would have risen as a result of the increased rate of saving. Put in a slightly different way, *the rate of interest* remains unchanged despite the increase of saving. As a matter of fact since new savings are merely used by consumers for the purchase of old securities (thrown on to the market by producers of consumption-goods in order to meet their losses), this does *not* lead to a rise in prices of securities – i.e. to that fall of the rate of interest necessary to restore equilibrium (JMK, v, p. 159).

As a result savings will exceed investment, income will fall and there will be no position of equilibrium until either (a) all production

ceases and the entire population starves to death; or, (b) the thrift
campaign is called of . . .; or (c) investment is stimulated by some
means or another so that its cost no longer lags behind the rate of
saving' (JMK, v, p. 160).[1]

Durbin summarises with great clarity this piece of analysis which
for the first time ever, brought to the forefront changes in stocks of
securities as the major cause of fluctuations in income:

> The rate of interest will . . . be held up despite the increase of
> saving and will arrest any stimulus to the volume of investment or
> prevent any adjustment to the new situation from taking place.
> Saving has risen, losses are being made in the production of
> consumption goods, but part or all of the new saving is necessarily
> being used to buy the securities newly brought to the market and
> *the Rate of interest cannot fall to the point at which it induces an
> equal outflow of new money for the purchase of new capital.*
> Despite the maintenance of the Consumers' Incomes, losses are
> steadily being made in the production of consumption goods, there
> are no profits in the manufacture of capital and the Rate of Interest
> is not falling. This disequilibrium will exist however sensitive the
> dependence of the volume of investment upon the Rate of Interest.
> (1935, p. 96; italic added)

Clearly, without any creation or cancellation of bank credit, the
forces of demand-and-supply expressed in the investment-demand
function and the saving-supply function can be kept at bay for
substantial periods of time by means of 'liquidity preference'. The
uncertainty concerning what lenders will in fact get back later from a
given sum lent now may foster alternative 'changes in the relative
attractions of savings deposits and securities respectively' (JMK, v
p. 128). These, in turn, may induce changes in the actual rate of
interest dictated not by the dominant forces of productivity and
thrift, but by the will to re-establish equilibrium (the balance 'at the
margin') between money-holdings and stocks of other assets (which
include, of course, securities).

However, this liquidity-preference approach is seen by Keynes (as
it was to be later by all subsequent economists of the 'neo-classical
synthesis') as altering only *temporarily* these traditional forces of
productivity and thrift.

Ultimately, and despite temporary disturbances introduced no only by mistaken banking policy and changes in the volume of hoarding, but also by a speculative demand for money, it is variations in the rate of interest which adjust decisions to invest with decisions to save:

> [Since] booms and slumps are simply the expression of the results of an oscillation of the terms of credit about their equilibrium position . . . [the rate of interest] is the instrument by which a disturbance is set up or equilibrium restored between the rates of saving and of investment; for to raise it stimulates the one and retards the other, and conversely if it is reduced. (JMK, v, pp. 165–6)

Thus one may safely conclude that in 1930 Keynes had not only solved the liquidity-preference issue left open by Marshall, Pigou, Lavington, Hawtrey and Robertson, but that he had also integrated his entirely new piece of analysis into a theory of the forces which determine the rate of interest anticipating in each and every respect both Robertson's and Hicks's post-*General Theory* version of it; namely, the loanable-funds theory of interest.

Two important papers respectively written by Robertson (1934) and Hicks (1935) must be touched upon now in order to complete the picture of the 'state of the art' before 1936 as far as the saving-investment technique of analysis and the theory of interest are concerned.

On the one hand, Robertson discusses for the first time the fact that the 'normal' rate of interest might *not* be unique. On the other, Hicks's paper suggests the first neo-Walrasian attempt to reconcile in a general equilibrium framework the theory of value and the theory of money by means of the central theoretical contribution of the *Treatise*.

8.1 ROBERTSON'S 'INDUSTRIAL FLUCTUATION AND THE "NATURAL" RATE OF INTEREST' (1934)

Robertson's paper is in fact a comment upon the Wicksellian conception of the natural rate of interest as developed by Hayek and discussed by Keynes in the *Treatise*. Surprisingly enough, this article is the only attempt ever made by Robertson to examine this concept.

To be charitable – and to use the words of Presley, one of Robertson's most sympathetic commentators – 'this major problem . . . was not satisfactorily resolved' (1979a, p. 158).

The whole exercise amounts to showing that, in a moderately 'progressive economy', there is no such thing as *one* static natural rate of interest towards which the market-rate is drawn. Robertson's argument is in fact a rationalisation, by means of his disequilibrium analysis and the 'forced-saving' process discussed in *Banking Policy*, of his overinvestment trade-cycle theory.

Instead of adopting Marshall's version of a *unique* 'normal' rate of interest determined by long-run forces Robertson focuses his attention on the medium-run alterations generated in the underlying forces of productivity and thrift by 'quasi-rhythmical movements' in the marginal productivity of capital goods. Logically this procedure leads him to focus the whole of his analysis on the instability of *the* natural rate over the cycle. In fact this unique Marshallian rate is replaced by a succession of *quasi-natural rates* (1934, p. 86).

Merging his concept of a fluctuating marginal productivity of capital (discussed in *Industrial Fluctuation*) with the impact of monetary factors (discussed in *Banking Policy*), Robertson visualizes the natural rate of interest as moving through booms and slumps from one position of *temporary* equilibrium to another, never returning to its original position and never being *actually* attained despite the fact the market rate is still pulled towards each of these successive quasi-natural rates by the dominant forces of productivity and thrift.

Graphically (Figure 8.1) this amounts to inserting a medium-run locus *QR* depicting successive quasi-natural rates between the two traditional long-run (*LR*) and market-rate (*MR*) curves[2]. This implies that when one of these quasi-natural rates coincides with the market-rate, full employment is not necessarily one of its features. The quasi-natural rate ruling, for example, at the bottom of a slump (*A*), if equal to the market-rate, will be characterised by the price stability *and* unemployment. Thus, full employment and price stability may not be possible within a single definition of equilibrium. Or, still in other words, due to an overinvestment crisis, the economy is stuck for an appreciable length of time at a quasi-natural rate which corresponds to a kind of 'unemployment disequilibrium'. However, and in sharp contrast with dominant neo-classical interpretations of Keynes,[3] this means that saving is *not* equal to investment at point *A* despite the stability of the price-level and of the quasi-natural rate of interest. Conversely, at point *B*, saving would be equal to investment

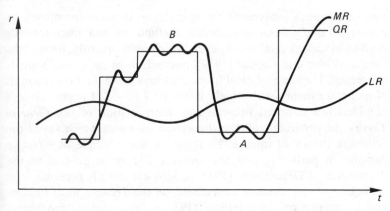

Figure 8.1

thanks to a 'forced-saving' process synonymous with a rising price-level.

Hence, it is only when the system temporarily reaches a point on the long-run curve *LR* that Marshall's double condition of full employment and price stability would be met – viz., when Robertson's quasi-natural rate is not only equal to the market-rate, but also to the traditional long-run 'normal' interest rate.

Finally, movements from one quasi-natural rate to another are explained according to the familiar Robertsonian approach: the downturn of the cycle is caused by the saturation of the economy with capital goods; a phenomenon which can be, in some occasions anticipated and/or accelerated by a shortage of saving crisis. All of this is a variation on Marshall's basic theme. Robertson simply reworks Marshall's interest theory to make it compatible with his vision of the inherent instability of the economic system which 'proceeds discontinuously – in lumps and by jumps' (1931d, p. 122). The introduction of this 'intermediate' notion of quasi-natural rate does not alter in any way the self-adjusting part played by the rate of interest between saving and investment. This simply shows that his adjustment process may be a long-drawn-out one.

8.2   HICKS'S 'SUGGESTION FOR SIMPLIFYING THE THEORY OF MONEY' (1935)

Hicks's famous article is of interest here for two main reasons. First, Hicks's simplified monetary theory is nothing else but a generalisation of Keynes's analysis of the speculative demand for money by means of the general equilibrium method he had then recently revived in various celebrated papers which, subsequently, formed the basis of *Value and Capital* (1939). Second, in so far as our topic is concerned, Hicks's analytical framework lays down the fundamentals of monetary theory with which, in his 1937 *IS – LM* paper, Hicks's heralded the standard neo-classical interpretation of the *General Theory*. In particular, all the theoretical elements which saved the orthodox theory of interest by reducing the principle of effective demand in particular and the *General Theory* in general to the 'Economics of Depression' (1937, p. 138) are already present.

Hicks was very quick in capitalising on the *Treatise* 'most important . . . theoretical contribution' (1935, p. 64); namely, the 'three-fold-margin' argument linked with the speculative demand for money. As a matter of fact his attempted reconciliation between value and monetary theory is no more than a rigorous restatement of Keynes's main argument.

The first section of Hicks's paper offers the first clear account by a non-Cambridge economist of the sixty years of groping by Cambridge economists with their analysis of the demand for money. Considering Wicksell's and von Mises's parallel failures to work out a marginal utility theory of money, Hicks comments:

> A more subtle form of the same difficulty appears in the work of Marshall and his followers. They were aware that money ought to be subjected to marginal utility analysis; but they were dominated by the classical conception of money as a 'veil' . . . that they persisted in regarding the demand for money as a demand for the things which money can buy – 'real balances'. As a result of this, their invocation of marginal utility remained little more than a pious hope. For they were unable to distinguish, on marginal utility lines, between the desire to save and the desire to hoard; and they necessarily overlooked that indeterminateness in the 'real balance' . . . which occurs when the prices of consumption goods are expected to change.

He adds: 'On the other hand, I must admit that some versions of the Marshallian theory come very close to what I am driving at. Cf. Lavington, *English Capital Market*, ch. VI' (1935, pp. 62–3 n.).

Besides this quite accurate assessment of the Cambridge monetary theory before 1930, it does not take Hicks much time to realise that

Keynes had solved in his *Treatise* this sixty-year-old riddle by means of the marginal utility theory as *a general theory of choice*:

> Mr. Keynes's *Treatise*, so far as I have been able to discover, contains at least three theories of money. One of them is the savings and investment theory, which seems to me only a quantity theory much glorified. One of them is a Wicksellian natural rate theory. But the third is altogether much more interesting. It emerges when Mr. Keynes begins to talk about the price-level of investment goods; when he shows that this price-level depends upon the relative preference of the investor – to hold bank deposits or securities. . . . Here at last we have a choice at the margin! And Mr. Keynes goes on to put substance into [the idea of the marginal utility of money] by his doctrine that the relative preference depends upon the 'bearishness' or 'bullishness' of the public, upon their relative desire for liquidity or profit. . . .
>
> It seems to me that this third theory of Mr. Keynes really contains the most important part of his theoretical contribution; that here, at last, we have something which, on the analogy . . . of value theory, does begin to offer a chance of making the whole thing easily intelligible; that is from this point, not from velocity of circulation, natural rate of interest, or Saving and Investment, that we ought to start in constructing the theory of money. (1935, pp. 63–4)

Hence, the whole article is centred on 'the central issue in the pure theory of money' (1935, p. 66); namely, the explanation of the decision to hold assets in the form of idle money rather than of interest - or profit-yielding securities. The passage just quoted shows how eagerly Keynes's central theoretical contribution was welcome (and not only by Hicks; see also Lundberg, 1937, pp. 33, 59–60).

Hicks provides many a hint at the approach which was subsequently to form the cornerstone of the neo-classical synthesis. The portfolio analysis taken over from Keynes is systematised in terms of expected rate of interest, cost of investment and expected length of the period of investment – the value of these three factors being in turn heavily dependent on the elements of risk and uncertainty linked with people's expectations. The nub of Hicks's argument anticipates in fact his *method of expectations* connected with his notion of intertemporal equilibrium.[4] Like Hayek and Robertson, but with the much more powerful general-equilibrium analysis behind him, Hicks suggests for the first time a solution to the trade-cycle problem using *equilibrium analysis* methods. It is quite clear, when he argues that 'the whole problem of applying monetary theory is largely one of deducing changes in anticipations from the changes in objective data which call them forth' (1935, p. 76), that he is not very far from an analysis in terms of *short-period positions in sequence over time* on which is based the idea of temporary equilibrium so crucial in *Value and Capital*. Indeed, the very fact that the equilibrium on the money-market is, for the first time, clearly connected through marginal utility analysis with the $(n - 1)$ other markets, and since expectations of future prices (including the rate of interest) are crucial in the determination – with current prices – of this equilibrium on the money-market, the basic conceptual framework subsequently used by Hicks in his temporary equilibrium model (1946, pt III) is unmistakably here. In a way, the reintegration of money into the general theory of choice – together with all the elements of risk and uncertainty to which it is bound – can be seen as the *first* step taken by Hicks (with Keynes's help) towards his framework of intertemporal equilibrium. Such an approach examines indeed the determination of nt market clearing prices (for n commodities over t time-periods) to establish one of these 'temporary equilibria'.[5]

Thus, Hicks's approach to the theoretical core of the *Treatise* anticipates very clearly the analytical viewpoint from which he reviewed the *General Theory* in 1936 and gave a 'potted version' (1967, p. VII) of it in his famous 1937 'Mr. Keynes's and the "Classics"'. In particular, the basic logic according to which dropping an equation or another to determine the rate of interest 'is purely a question of convenience' (1936, p. 246), and that, in the *General Theory*, 'it is the liquidity preference doctrine which is vital' (1937, p. 133) *is already there in this 1935 paper*. Of course, the income-adjustment process is still absent; but the conceptual framework of that 1935 article is unmistakably ready to include it without any major theoretical difficulty.

8.3 PRINCIPAL CONCLUSIONS

It is now possible to put together some of the conclusions reached so far.

First, and most important, in the *Treatise*, Keynes definitively solved the 'threefold-margin' issue which had marred the Cambridge monetary theory for more than sixty years. Based on a strict use of marginal utility analysis Keynes's portfolio analysis gave at last a proper theoretical framework to the speculative demand for money and cut through the irritating stock–flow, wealth–income confusion held so long by quantity theorists.

Second, this liquidity-preference analysis of the demand for money implies that there is a direct influence of this demand on the rate of interest; i.e. that, to the long-recognised *wealth-effect* of money-changes is added a portfolio adjustment *substitution-effect* (or, alternatively, that a change in the composition of portfolio assets can alter the rate of interest without any money-change having to take place).

Third, Keynes's novel analysis of the speculative demand for money has several important consequences on the traditional theory of interest. The supply-and-demand for money previously listed as mere components of the supply-and-demand for loanable funds take, with the substitution-effect, the full meaning they never had in previous Cambridge formulation of the theory of interest. Hence, liquidity preference is *not* in contradiction either with Marshall's 'real' theory in terms of productivity and thrift (or supply-and-demand of capital as a flow, or investment and saving) or with the theory accepted at least since Marshall as the standard explanation of the short-run interest-rate in a monetary economy. Quite the contrary: a loanable-funds theory of interest *without* a proper explanation of its liquidity-preference component would be as *incomplete* as the Cambridge version was until the *Treatise*.

Since the 'liquidity-preference' doctrine was already part and parcel of the *Treatise*, if not the core of its conceptual framework, it can no longer be one of the two main novelties of the *General Theory* (the other being the multiplier). Despite the weakness of Keynes's critical argument in chapter 14 of the *General Theory*, this implies that the thrust of Keynes's critique of the orthodox theory of interest could *not* be aimed at its alleged neglect of the monetary factors. Moreover, since Keynes held in the *Treatise* a loanable-funds theory of interest *including* liquidity preference, it was a false issue to offer him as an alternative to his admittedly weak liquidity-preference-interest theory the very argument he had specifically rejected as a 'non-sense theory' (see below, Chapter 9).

Lastly, it seems reasonable to conclude that the dominant interest theory held in the early 1930s by Keynes and Hicks anticipated the post-*General Theory* loanable-funds theory popularised by Hicks

(1939) and Robertson (1940).[6] For a large variety of short-lived elements including liquidity preference, the market-rate of interest may diverge from the long-run full-employment 'natural' rate of interest. Such divergences open a gap between saving and investment. However, as on any other market, and thanks to the investment-demand function elastic with respect to the rate of interest, changes in the market-rate of interest will take place as long as the gap between saving and investment is not bridged; viz. as long as the market-rate is not equal to the 'normal' rate determined by the dominant forces of productivity and thrift.

8.4 THE *TREATISE* AND QUANTITY ADJUSTMENTS

As a complement to Chapter 8 the irritating question of output and income variations in the *Treatise* and post-*Treatise* literature has to be briefly discussed now. On the one hand, two examples drawn respectively from Keynes's Harris Foundation Lecture (1931) and Joan Robinson's 'Theory of Money and the Analysis of Output' (1933) show with great clarity that output variations as an adjusting mechanism between saving and investment are, on Keynes's own hypothesis, strictly *incompatible* with the analytical framework of the *Treatise*. On the other, despite Kahn's departure from the fixed-output assumption of the *Treatise*, his 1931 multiplier article is no more than an unsuccessful attempt to introduce quantity adjustments in the fundamental equations framework; or, put in a slightly different way, that there is *no* logical equivalence between the multiplier and the principle of effective demand.

Shortly before the publication of the *Treatise* Hawtrey had already made a penetrating remark on one particular aspect of the basic analytical framework underpinning the fundamental equations:[7]

> [your] formula only takes account of the reduction of prices in relation to costs, and does not recognise *the possibility of a reduction of output* being caused directly by a contraction of demand without an intervening fall of price. (JMK, xiii, p. 152; italic added).

Similarly the entire argument contained in the *Manifesto* submitted to Keynes by Joan and Austin Robinson and Richard Kahn is also centred on the lack of reference to output variations in the *Treatise*.[8]

This same line of criticism was eventually reworked by Joan Robinson in her 1933 article: since the adjustment between saving and investment is achieved through price variations only, there must be an implicit assumption of a fixed output (1933b, pp. 17–18).

Writing to Joan Robinson about her article, Keynes answered her main argument with characteristic good faith:

> I think you are a little hard on me as regards the assumption of constant output. [It] is quite true that I have not followed out the consequences of changes in output in the earlier theoretical part [i.e. Books III and IV]. I admit that this wants doing, and I shall be doing it in my lectures; though that does not absolve me from being criticized for not having done it in my *Treatise*. But in my *Treatise* itself, I have long discussion with [of?] the effects of changes in output; it is only at a particular point in the preliminary theoretical argument that I assume constant output, and I am at pains to make this absolutely clear. (JMK, xiii, p. 270)

As a matter of fact, Keynes had rightly dismissed Hawtrey's argument on the ground that he was 'not dealing with the complete set of causes which determine volume of output. For this would have led me an endlessly long journey into the theory of short-period supply. . . .' (JMK, xiii, pp. 145–6). Hawtrey's argument brings in variations of output in a 'non-essential' way: quantity adjustments arise only from temporary short-run rigidities; in the long run the logic of Hawtrey's cumulative process is perfectly in line with the traditional price-level argument common to Marshall and Keynes.

It may help to illustrate how Keynes handles in a 'non-essential' way variations of output in the *Treatise* itself with the 'banana parable'.

Instead of recouping their losses by curtailing their normal expenditures on consumption (leaving thus the volume of output untouched) like in the 'Danaid jar' case (JMK, v, p. 125), in the 'banana parable', entrepreneurs recoup their losses by reducing employment and/or wages. Hence the aggregate expenditures and eventually the volume of output are reduced accordingly, leaving unchanged the gap between saving and investment.

As a matter of fact the sudden 'thrift campaign' in a fully employed Eden economy (in a saving-investment equilibrium) generates losses against which entrepreneurs try to protect themselves by laying-off workers and/or reducing wages. Such reductions in the aggregate costs of production simply cause 'the spending power of the public' (JMK, v, p. 160) – and hence consumption expenditures – to 'be reduced just as much' leaving *unchanged* the gap between saving and investment. In terms of the first fundamental equations:

$$P = \frac{E}{O} + \frac{I' - S}{R}$$

The 'thrift campaign' generates a contraction of E (the equivalent of income in the *Treatise*) and hence of output, *without* having the slightest influence on the excess of S over I'. Once again this argument shows very clearly that the second term of the right-hand side of both fundamental equations is strictly linked with variations of the rate of interest *only*. It is only when the market-rate is back in equality with the 'normal' rate that the equilibrium between I' and S will be re-established.

The absence of a functional relationship between saving and income is, of course, another way to show that before the discovery of the 'fundamental psychological law' (which expresses the crucial fact that the marginal propensity to spend is less than unity) output variations were dealt with in a 'non-essential' way. As long as saving is not made a function of income Keynes had to fall back on the rate of interest to adjust saving to investment. In his June 1931 Harris Foundation Lecture Keynes made another attempt to deal more explicitly than in the *Treatise* with output variations. This time an excess of saving over investment generates a fall in output which leads to what seems to be 'an equilibrium at less than full employment' (JMK, xiii, p. 343).

However this so-called 'spurious equilibrium' (JMK, xiii, p. 356, see also JMK, xx, pp. 58, 63–4, 68 and 71) has nothing in common with the unemployment equilibrium of the *General Theory*. In the context of the *Treatise* in which Keynes is still conducting his analysis, this equilibrium is no more than the transitory point at the bottom of a cycle; there the excess of saving over investment which has generated the slump, is suddenly replaced by an excess of investment over saving which generates recovery. This transitory 'spurious equilibrium' simply marks the upturn of the cycle and has nothing to do with a *continuing* state of unemployment equilibrium at which saving *is equal* to investment for an indeterminate period of time. In fact there is not, strictly speaking, an equilibrium (even short-lived) between saving and investment, because, on the basis of the *Treatise* definiions, this is only possible at full employment and this inflexion-point s characterised by an instantaneous switch from one *disequilibrium* $S > I$) to another $(I > S)$. Moreover, as in the *Treatise*, the entire argument explaining why the economy is pushed towards that 'spurious equilibrium' is conducted in terms of changes in *investment* and not, in a *General Theory* fashion, in terms of changes in savings through variations of income.

Finally, in his third lecture, Keynes makes amply clear that 'the problem of recovery . . . is . . . a problem of re-establishing the volume of investment *[by means of]* a fall in the long-term rate of *[interest]*' (JMK, xiii, p. 358). Indeed, nothing could be more in line with orthodox thinking than a lowering of the interest-rate to bring investment back into equality with saving.

Despite the first apparition in writing of the idea of a change in employment (and hence in output) as a force connecting variations of saving to variations of investment, Kahn's famous *multiplier article* follows exactly the same logic.[9] As is well known, the crux of this article was twofold. First, Kahn wanted to dispose once and for all of the 'Treasury View'.[10] Second, and more constructively, he intended not so much to point out that an increase in government investment would generate 'secondary employments', a fact well known at least since Keynes's 1929 'Can Lloyd George do it?' (JMK, ix, pp. 104–7), but to give a precise estimate of that magnitude; namely, to explain why the multiplier is not infinite, or alternatively, where the leakages are.

In the course of his discussion Kahn makes a digression in order to connect his analysis with the fundamental equations of the *Treatise* (1931, pp. 8–10). It is in this revealing passage that Kahn shows with the utmost clarity that, despite his recognising that an increase in investment is matched in certain circumstances by an equal increase in saving, he had not grasped the vital importance of that analysis.

The starting-point of Kahn's argument is a slump-situation displaying unused capacities and substantial unemployment. According to the first fundamental equation Kahn is explicitly referring to (1931, p. 10), in such a situation the cost of new investment-goods exceeds savings $(I' > S)$ and the supply of consumption-goods is perfectly elastic. What is then 'the net effect on the difference between savings and investment . . . of the building of roads' (1931, p. 8)?

The first thing to be noted is that – applying to that case his basic relation between government investment and output (and consequently employment) – Kahn explicitly establishes a connection between an increase in investment and an increase in saving: an increase in public investment generates an increase in the volume of saving *through* an increase in the level of output (income).[11]

However, three crucial restrictions built into the *Treatise* framework in which Kahn is conducting his analysis reduce the apparent novelty of this equilibrating effect of changes in output to very little.

First, as in the *Treatise*, Kahn implicitly assumes that the marginal propensity to spend is unity. An exogenous increase in output through government investments does not affect the discrepancy between saving and investment; or, for that matter, between I' and S:

> when [the supply of consumption-goods] is perfectly elastic . . .[t]he price-level of consumption-goods is then constant, and, however great may be the cost of the investment that is taking place in road-building, the secondary employment will be such that the total alleviation . . . *keeps the difference between total savings and total investment at a total amount* (or, more accurately, at an amount that varies in direct proportion with the output of consumption-goods). (1931, p. 10; italic added)

In simpler terms changes in the level of output *can not* close the gap between saving and investment.

Second, if Kahn is able to conclude that an increment of investment ($\Delta I'$) will be matched by an *equal* increment of saving (ΔS) so that the gap between them is constant, he clearly does *not* apply this piece of analysis to the *original* discrepancy between I' and S. Should he have done so he would have been led to Keynes's central idea that there can be an equilibrium between S and I' at less than full employment; namely, he would have discovered the principle of effective demand.

Third, and in addition to the two previous hefty arguments against an equivalence between Kahn's multiplier and the principle of effective demand, it is possible to quote passages from the same paper where Kahn displays strong belief in favour of the orthodox saving-investment technique of analysis. On the one hand, and in a pure *Treatise*-like fashion, Kahn has to admit that the equality between saving and investment is possible in one case only: 'this is the case to which Mr. Keynes' equations apply in their full simplicity. It occurs *when the whole of the factors of production are employed* . . .'.(1931, p. 10; italic added) On the other hand, to attain such a full-employment equilibrium where saving is equal to investment, there exists 'a more natural route' (1931, p. 6) than public works; namely, variations of the rate of interest. As Kahn puts it:

> But . . . it must not be forgotten that the whole point of a policy of public works is that it enables an increase in the rate of home investment to take place without that *fall* in the rate of interest that would be necessary if we were relying on private enterprise. (1931, p. 26; see also p. 10)

In her 1933 paper Joan Robinson gives her version of the connection between an 'increase in output [which] must bring about an increase in savings equal to the original increase in investment' (1933b, p. 18). However, despite the fact that her paper is viewed by Klein 'as one of the first expositions . . . of the really essential parts of the *General Theory*' (1968, p. 39), and for basically the same reason than for Kahn's, it did not quite escape from the *Treatise* theoretical framework.

Instead of working with the first fundamental equation as Kahn does, Joan Robinson approaches the problem through the second fundamental equation (price-level of output as a whole). Her starting-point is a case where $I = S$ *and* where the supply of output as a whole is perfectly *elastic*:

> The price level will only be in equilibrium when savings are equal to investment [i.e. at full-employment equilibrium implying a perfectly *in*elastic supply of output]. Well and good. But suppose that over a certain range the supply of goods is perfectly elastic? Then, whatever happens, prices cannot rise or fall. Since Mr. Keynes' truisms must be true, a rise or fall in demand for goods, which will be met by an increase or decrease of output without any change in prices, *must necessarily be accompanied by changes in savings and investment which keep the two in equality.* (1933b, p. 18; italic added).

It is quite clear that, in terms of the definitions of the *Treatise*, such a piece of analysis, and the resulting fact that 'output may be in equilibrium at any number of different levels' (1933b, p. 17), is impossible. Joan Robinson simply violates the logic of the second fundamental equation in postulating $I = S$ at less than full employment.[12] (Kahn, on the contrary, was at pains to emphasise that his starting-point involved $I' > S$, which in turn implies the necessary elasticity of the supply of consumption-goods). Such an approach amounts to nothing else but begging the whole question: it is evident that if one *postulates* that an underemployment equilibrium exists (i.e. that $I = S$ at less than full employment) it is then very easy to demonstrate that an increase in investment is necessarily accompanied by changes in output and savings which *keep S and I in* equality. Unfortunately it does not explain why I was equal to S in the first place.

These three examples drawn from Keynes's, Kahn's and Joan Robinson's writings between 1930 and 1932 show how crucial was the discovery of what Keynes called later the 'fundamental psychological law' in the elaboration of the fundamentals of the principle of effective demand. Put in the perspective of this lengthy and uncertain groping process of the early 1930s, Keynes's famous 1937 letter to Harrod takes a sharper signification:

> One of the most important transitions for me, after my *Treatise on Money* had been published, was suddenly realising . . . the complete disappearance of the theory of the demand and supply for output as a whole, i.e. the theory of employment. . . . It only came after I had enunciated to myself the psychological law that, when income increases, the gap between income and consumption will increase, - a conclusion of vast importance to my own thinking but not apparently, expressed just like this, to anyone else's. (JMK, xiv, p. 85)

The first indications that Keynes was heading towards an understanding of the equilibrating role of changes in output appear in a letter to Kahn dated 20 September 1931. In that letter (JMK), xiii, pp. 373–5) Keynes hints for the first time at the idea of a savings function. The marginal propensity to consume is no longer equal to one so that 'each level of aggregate output has an appropriate proportion of saving to incomes attached to it'. In other words, changes in the level of output *can* act to close the gap between saving and investment and push the economy towards a position of zero profit 'before O reaches maximum'; this is, accordingly, and in Keynes's own words a position of '"long-period unemployment"'; i.e. an equilibrium short of full employment' (JMK, xiii, p. 374).

9 The *General Theory* and the Principle of Effective Demand

When it comes to the *General Theory*, and whatever position one might adopt, one is inevitably condemned to be alternately torn between Scylla and Charybdis. On the one hand, there is today no accepted view of what it was exactly that Keynes actually accomplished (be it at the purely theoretical level or even what his Schumpeterian 'vision' was). Practically every economist is keen to offer his own idiosyncratic interpretation of Keynes's *magnum opus*, differing of course sometimes more than on some find analytical points from the other '4,827' reinterpretations currently available (Weintraub, 1979, p. 38). On the other hand, the ever-rising tide of articles and books devoted to explorations of the remotest corners of Keynes's analytical framework leaves very little room – if any – for major improvements. Furthermore the relationship between saving and investment is geometrically in the very eye of the maelstrom Keynes started with his principle of effective demand.

Accordingly, the tone as well as the style of this chapter is inevitably different from all what has come before. Condemned to make the reader's blood-pressure rise either by offering yet another re-interpretation of the *General Theory* or by reusing yet again the same set of quotations/arguments the present author feels bound, already at that stage, to lay his cards on the table. Though fully aware of the weakness of many elements of Keynes's argument he nevertheless strongly believes in the validity of the *General Theory*'s fundamental theoretical insights into the instability of decentralised economies: there is no obvious mechanism by which intertemporal decisions can be co-ordinated. In particular Keynes especially disliked the simplification according to which the rate of interest is determined by savings and investment. Or, to use the traditional Marshallian terminology, real variables cannot only deviate from their 'natural' values, but there is also no built-in mechanism which ensures – even in the long run – a return of such a full-employment equilibrium. In short, in the *General Theory*, Keynes gives strong arguments why he does not believe the invisible hand to be performing as well as Marshall,

Hawtrey, Robertson and Hayek thought it was.[1] However, it will also be made abundantly clear that Keynes's theoretical framework is not capable of bearing the weight he clearly assigned to it.

The aim of this chapter will therefore be twofold: on the one hand to show first and foremost that the principle of effective demand was clearly seen by Keynes not only as his fundamental theoretical novelty, but also as the piece of analysis solving at last the saving-investment riddle dating back to Marshall. On the other, to determine exactly what were the remnants of 'the habitual modes of thought and expression' (JMK, vii, p. xxiii) Keynes did not manage to escape from, opening thus wide the door to the neo-classical synthesis. By so doing it will eventually be possible to suggest that the recent general dissatisfaction with such a theoretical framework (which has led to the monetarist and rational expectations counter-revolutions) has emphasised once again the need for a 'theory of effective demand' which breaks definitively with the traditional view of how markets work.

9.1 THE PRINCIPLE OF EFFECTIVE DEMAND AS A DIRECT CHALLENGE TO THE 'FORCED SAVING' DOCTRINE

The first fully fledged formulation of the principle of effective demand appears in the concluding section of chapter 7 of the *General Theory*:

> The reconciliation of the identity between saving and investment with the apparent 'free-will' of the individual to save what he chooses irrespective of what he or others may be investing, essentially depends on saving being, like spending, a two-sided affair. For although the amount of his own saving is unlikely to have any significant influence on his own income, the reactions of the amount of his consumption on the income of others makes it impossible for all individuals simultaneously to save any given sums. Every such attempt to save more by reducing consumption will so affect incomes that the attempt necessarily defeats itself. It is, of course, just as impossible for the community as a whole to save *less* than the amount of current investment, since the attempt to do so will necessarily raise incomes to a level at which the sums which individuals choose to save add up to a figure exactly equal to the amount of investment. (JMK vii, p. 84)

This central analytical argument of the *General Theory* cuts through several Gordian knots of the pre-1936 trade-cycle theory. It is sufficient at the stage to simply formulate its two main and well-known corollaries. On the one hand, if the principle of effective demand guarantees that the equality between planned saving and planned investment will be achieved through variations in the level of aggregate output and employment, there is no longer any built-in mechanism to guarantee that this equality will coincide with a full utilisation of productive capacity.[2] In short, the possibility of 'unemployment equilibria' is thus asserted.

On the other hand, the explanation of the determination of the interest-rate through liquidity preference is thus logically *independent* from this new adjusting mechanism between saving and investment.

This first formulation[3] appears in the last section of the chapter devoted by Keynes to a step-by-step critique of previously held concepts of saving and investment.

In fact, in this crucial chapter 7, the thrust of Keynes's argument is not so much directed at the traditional adjustment mechanism itself, but at the premises underlying the concept of saving behind that mechanism. It is only after the muddle surrounding saving as 'a one sided-affair' (JMK vii, p. 81) had been cleared up that Keynes was in a position to formulate the principle of effective demand. Hence, the crucial importance of his radical critique of the orthodox concept of saving made up of a *stock* of *ex ante* saving (the 'lump-of-saving' idea) to which is added (or substracted) a *flow* of 'forced' ('abortive') savings resulting from temporary phenomena, of mainly monetary origin. Probing the solidity of the 'real' theoretical infrastructure on which Robertson's 'forced-saving' doctrine is built, Keynes is 'simply' arguing that *the level of investment is no longer determined by the community's decision to save.*

His argument is in four points. Starting from his static definitions reached in chapter 6 according to which '*saving* and *investment* . . . are [*ex definitione*] necessarily equal in amount' (JMK, vii, p. 74) he argues that to assert the contrary is 'due to a special definition of income and hence of the excess of income over consumption' (ibid. p. 77). The analytical models of Hawtrey, Keynes's *Treatise* and Robertson are then successively examined with this problem of definition in mind. However, once Keynes reaches 'the much vaguer ideas associated with the phrase "forced saving"' (ibid. p. 79) his critique takes a much more fundamental turn. And an extension of the one-sided-transaction argument leads him ultimately to the first statement of the principle of effective demand, quoted above.

In the last section of his chapter 6 Keynes lays down the fundamentals behind 'The definition of income, saving and investment' (ibid. pp. 61–5). Far from being a tautology as it is sometimes argued,[4] the argument which leads Keynes to assert a definitional equality between saving and investment is a first preliminary step to prepare the ground for a more general formulation of the principle of effective demand. As a matter of fact Keynes's analysis 'in terms of the instantaneous multiplier' (Pasinetti, 1974, p. 45) allows him to discuss the new relationship between saving and the *causal* process linking, via output, investment to saving without having to introduce the lagged multiplier involving the long series of successive steps during which decisions to save are adapted to investment through variations of output.

Keynes's entire demonstration relies on the functional relationship between income and saving resulting from his discovery of the 'fundamental psychological law'. Since *the marginal propensity to consume is no longer equal to unity*, variations in the level of income induced by variations in the level of investment foster variations in the volume of saving. Hence, unlike in the orthodox approach, the act of saving is no longer a one-sided transaction depending exclusively on the will of the individual saver. Quite the contrary. As Keynes puts it:

A decision to consume or not to consume truly lies within the power of the individual; so does a decision to invest or not to invest. The amounts of aggregate income and of aggregate saving are the *results* of the free choices of individuals whether or not to consume or whether or not to invest; but they are neither of them capable of assuming an independent value resulting from a separate set of decisions taken irrespective of the decision concerning consumption and investment. (JMK, vii, p. 65)

Clearly saving is a *residual* magnitude resulting from the investment process and no longer determining it.[5] Accordingly in the adjustment process between investment and saving the Marshallian propensity to save linked to the rate of interest is replaced by the propensity to consume.

The final static equivalence between these two magnitudes eventually emerges 'from the *bilateral* character of the transactions between the producer on the one hand, and, on the other hand, the consumer or purchaser of capital equipment' (ibid. p. 63). Since all incomes are derived either from producing consumption-goods or saved, the income derived from producing consumption-goods is equal to what is spent on them. Hence, the excess of income over consumption – namely, saving – is equal to the addition to the capital equipment – namely, investment. Or, alternatively the amount saved is equal to the income derived from the production of investment-goods (ibid. p. 63).

Hence, without any reference to the multiplier mechanism, without formally introducing variations of income as the adjusting mechanism, without relying on any definitional subtlety, without even alluding to the rate of interest and without, of course, introducing money factors, Keynes is able to break up completely the symmetry of the traditional approach to saving and investment. From its central role as the pre-existing magnitude without which the investment process cannot take place and to which the volume of investment has eventually to adjust in the long run, the concept of saving is reduced to a mere residual unable to assume any value independently of investment and income.

As James Meade has summarised it in a splendid aphorism:

> Keynes's intellectual revolution was to shift economists from thinking normally in terms of a model of reality in which a dog called *savings* wagged his tail labelled *investment* to thinking in terms of a model in which a dog called *investment* wagged his tail labelled *savings*. (1975, p. 82)

In the first three sections of chapter 7 Keynes makes then heroic (and charitable) attempts to accomodate Hawtrey's, Robertson's and his own *Treatise* formulations with his new version of the relation between saving and investment. Considering that everyone agrees on the meaning of saving as the excess of income over consumption, Keynes rightly argues that problems arise 'either out of the definition of *investment* or out of that of *income*' (ibid. p. 74).

The problem linked with definitions is very easily solved and does not raise any important issue. Hawtrey is Keynes's main target on that question. Repeating an argument already put forward in the *Treatise* (JMK, v, pp. 173–4) Keynes simply rejects Hawtrey's idea of excluding from the definition of investment unforeseen variations in the stocks of unsold goods. Such an approach, dating back to *Good and Bad Trade*, clearly implies an inequality between saving and investment.[6] Keynes, however, dismisses Hawtrey's case on the grounds that he sees no point in laying stress on stock variations, at the expense of other factors (as, for example, variations of unused capacities) as the only determinant of the entrepreneurs' scale of output (ibid. p. 76). In other words, there is no reason in discriminating in favour of one type of investment only. Investment has to include not only liquid (or working) capital, but also fixed capital (much more important by its sheer size).

The build-up to the formulation of the principle of effective demand actually starts with Keynes's discussion of his *Treatise* version of the saving-investment riddle. In the critique of his former approach, as well as in the following half-page devoted to Robertson's 1933 model, Keynes rightly focuses his attention on the *peculiarity* of the definition of *income* used in both formulations (ibid. p. 77). By realising that, in the *Treatise*, the notion of 'normal profit' is linked with a 'normal' volume of output and income, Keynes starts in earnest his devastating critique against central orthodox idea that saving is equal to investment at a full-employment level of income only. The fact that, in the *Treatise*, saving could exceed investment, was the indication, says Keynes, 'that a decline was taking place in the actual profits, so that they would be under a motive to contract output' (ibid. p. 77). Then Keynes makes a rather daring suggestion in order to show that 'the new argument . . . is essentially a development of the old' (ibid. p. 78). In the *Treatise* it is the *current* change in the excess of investment over saving which governs changes in the volume of output; in the *General Theory* it is 'the expectation of an increased excess of investment over saving, given the former volume of output and employment [which] induce[s] entrepreneurs to increase the volume of employment and output' (ibid. p. 78).

Such a desperate attempt to reconcile the irreconcilable calls for two remarks. On the one hand, and as in his preface (ibid. p. xxii), Keynes is clearly yielding to the temptation to rewrite the *Treatise* in order to convince the reader of the existence of an element of continuity between his two big books. Bearing in mind his failure to deal with the effects of changes in output in the *Treatise* it is ironic (to say the least) that, in the *General Theory*, Keynes should visualise a divergence between saving and investment (as defined in the *Treatise*) as 'the motive force governing changes in the volume of output' *without even mentioning changes in the price-level*! On the other hand, and given the set of definitions arrived at in the *General Theory*, it is simply impossible to conceive of a situation in which saving would not tend to be equal to investment: there cannot be an 'expectation of an *increased excess* of investment over saving' as an inducement to raise the level of output since the actual level of output already guarantees the equality between saving and investment in the first place.

The same misunderstanding arises in connection with Robertson's set of definitions of his 1933 and 1934 articles. It comes close to begging the whole question to argue that 'when Mr. Robertson says that there is an excess of saving over investment, he means literally the same thing as I mean when I say that income is falling, and the excess of saving in his sense is exactly equal to the decline of income in my sense' (ibid. p. 78). Leaving aside the fact that Robertson's paper is couched even more dramatically than the *Treatise* in terms of price (not output) variations, Keynes is here once again trying to mix oil with water. Since Robertson's result ($S > I$) can only be made congruent with Keynes's argument by postulating that the marginal propensity to spend is unity (or alternatively that variations of output do *not* act as an equilibrating force), and since the core of Keynes's argument precisely relies on the expression of the 'fundamental psychological law', it is hard to see how 'Robertson's method might be regarded as an alternative attempt' (ibid. p. 78) to Keynes's. Fortunately the impression left by this dubious exercise is quickly dispelled when Keynes turns to a critique of the idea of 'forced saving'.

In the *Treatise* Keynes attacked Robertson (and Hayek) for viewing 'forced saving' as a phenomenon resulting from *and* measured by changes in the quantity of money or credit.[7] The main novelty of the *Treatise* framework was to deny that approach on the grounds of the influence of the speculative demand for money on the rate of interest.

In the *General Theory* the attack is much more fundamental. Since the idea of 'forced saving' only makes sense with reference to a 'normal' volume of savings, and hence to a 'normal' rate of interest, Keynes's violent critique of this concept which 'has no defined meaning' (JMK, xiii, p. 479) is in fact a frontal attack, the first of its kind, against the traditional intertemporal adjusting properties of the rate of interest. Moreover, this critique naturally leads Keynes to discuss changes in the volume of savings and hence variations in the volume of investment and income. Quite clearly, through a critical review of this concept of 'forced saving', Keynes is moving towards his first statement of the principle of effective demand.

Keynes does not argue that a change in the volume of money/credit has no influence on the volume of savings. Quite the contrary. As will be discussed later (Section 9.3), changes in the quantity of money, *through their effect on the rate of interest*, do involve, via changes in the volume and the distribution of income, a change in the amount of saving. But, and it is at that crucial point that Keynes is parting company with the orthodox approach (including the *Treatise*):

> such changes in the amounts saved are no more 'forced savings' than any other changes in the amounts saved due to a change in circumstances; and there is no means of distinguishing between one case and another, *unless we specify the amount saved in certain given conditions as our norm or standard.* (JMK, vii, p. 80; italic added)

And Keynes to add:

> 'forced saving' has no meaning until we have specified some standard rate of saving. If we select (as might be reasonable) the rate of saving which corresponds to an established state of full employment, the above definition would become: 'Forced saving is the excess of actual saving over what would be saved if there were full employment in a period *of long-period equilibrium*'. (ibid; italic added)

Two main comments stem immediately from this clean breakaway from earlier approaches. *First, whatever* the origin (monetary or not) of an increase in investment may be, there will always be a corresponding increase in the volume of saving via variations in the level of output which will in turn keep saving equal to investment. The fixed investment-constant output hypothesis used previously by Keynes is thus removed. Such an increase in the volume of savings is 'forced' on nobody except in a situation of full employment in which a rising price-level takes the place of variations of output as the adjusting mechanism between saving and investment. In short, the equality between saving and investment is no longer an exclusive characteristic of a long-run full-employment equilibrium. Moreover, this traditional centre of gravity – one among an infinite number of situations in which saving is equal to investment – is only hit by chance if the economic system is left to its own device. Hence, concludes Keynes, 'a forced excess of saving would be a very rare and a very unstable phenomenon, and a forced *deficiency* of saving the usual state of affairs' (ibid. p. 80).

Second, in this analysis, the rate of interest, quite remarkably, does *not* appear. The reason is very simple. In the principle of effective demand the rate of interest has *no part whatsoever* to play in closing a gap which . . . no longer exists. Furthermore, the concept of a 'natural', 'normal' or equilibrium rate of interest is as meaningless as its twin idea of a long-run full-employment level of income. Hence, all the sophisticated trade-cycle theory built with great care from Marshall to Robertson on the idea of divergences between the natural and market-rates of interest goes overboard.

In this second line of attack on Robertson's 'forced saving' doctrine, Keynes clearly re-asserts that 'there is no special virtue in the pre-existing rate of interest' (ibid. p. 328) as far as the equality between investment and saving is concerned.[8] Similarly, in the chapter on 'The Essential Properties of Interest and Money' he couches a similar argument in much stronger terms (ibid. pp. 242–3). Later, in his lengthy discussion of the concept of finance, Keynes makes equally clear that 'the rate of interest . . . has nothing whatever to do with current saving or new investment' (JMK, xiv, p. 213) or, in a letter to Myrdal 'that it is not the rate of interest which makes saving and investment equal, since they are equal *ex definitione* whatever the rate of interest' (JMK, xxix, pp. 262–3).

Finally before reaching the first fully fledged positive statement of his principle of effective demand Keynes uses the concept of saving as a residual and secondary line of attack against the idea of 'forced saving'. This time the 'optical illusion' due to regarding saving as a one-sided transaction is directly connected with Robertson's and Pigou's concepts of 'saving created by the banking system' or 'saving running to waste in the banking system' (JMK, vii, pp. 81–2).

In the case of 'abortive saving', the so-called savings 'lost in the banking system' are in fact not 'lost' at all, rather they have simply *failed to come into existence* for the obvious reason that as fast as an individual (or group of individuals) increases his savings by reducing his expenditures, other individuals' incomes fall off and they save less as much as he saves more.

Similarly, the idea of 'forced saving' as a result of a credit expansion which allows investment to take place without a corresponding amount of 'genuine saving' is also the result of focusing one's attention on one aspect only of an increase of bank credit to entrepreneurs. Clearly, at less than full employment, any increase in bank credit fosters a corresponding excess of income over expenditure on consumption (ibid. pp. 82–3).

Everything is thus ready for Keynes to formulate the first general statement of the principle of effective demand quoted earlier. In the last analysis, if the fundamental psychological law and the marginal propensity to consume have an important part to play in the working of the principle of effective demand, they are ultimately consequences of the fundamentally new proposition that, unlike at the individual level, changes in investment, consumption and saving *do* affect aggregate income.

9.2   THE SCOPE OF VALIDITY OF THE PRINCIPLE OF EFFECTIVE DEMAND

It has been shown so far how, for Keynes, savings always tend to be equal to investment through variations of the level of income and how the operation of the principle of effective demand determines a level of output and income which is only accidentally that which generates full employment. It remains, of course, to face the important question as to the scope of validity of Keynes's novel principle. In particular, is this validity confined to the short-period or, could it, suitably amended, also provide a long-period theory of output and employment?

If the principle of effective demand is robust enough to support a long-run theory of output and employment, it is obvious that the traditional tendency towards full employment underlying the whole Marshallian approach would go overboard. Conversely, to confine the validity of the principle of effective demand to short periods (either in the neo-classical synthesis or in the intertemporal equilibrium fashion) would either leave intact the long-run orthodox theory of a self-adjusting economy, or herald the abandonment of the traditional long-period method of analysis itself. This theoretical problem is well outside the scope of this study. However, without venturing further on these controversial grounds, it is of the utmost importance for the present argument to consider what Keynes's *own* opinion about the long-run validity of the principle of effective demand was.

In a full-employment situation, characterised by an inelastic supply of output as a whole,[9] Keynes readily admits that the principle of effective demand is replaced by the traditional inflation-cum-'forced-saving' process. Prices and money-wages, and hence the nominal value of national income and the transactions demand for money, will increase until they cause a rise in the rate of interest large enough to close the gap between saving and investment (ibid. p. 202). Indeed, in this marginal case, Keynes appears to be back into the Marshallian orthodox framework, which he, after all, repeatedly considers as compatible with a full-employment (or given) level of income (ibid. p. 378).

However, this dual analysis of the saving-investment equality does not mean that, for him, the principle of effective demand is a 'special' short-run case and the full-employment interest-rate adjustment the general long-term adjusting mechanism. Since this principle postulates that, if left to its own devices, the economic system has no built-in mechanism ensuring a tendency towards full employment, it is only in the accidental event of a full-employment level of income that the orthodox explanation would take over from Keynes's income-adjustment process. Moreover, since no mechanism ensures that the economic system would remain at a full-employment level of income, the validity of the traditional mechanism would be reduced to very particular, unusual and short-lived situations. Clearly, for Keynes, the principle of effective demand *is* the long-run 'natural' (or 'normal') explanation of the relation between saving and investment.

Keynes's analysis of the process of capital formation is a good example of his attempt to extend the validity of the principle of effective demand into the longer run. By sticking firmly to the idea that the rate of interest can adequately be explained by liquidity preference, and without inquiring how liquidity preference is determined, Keynes denies in the long run any influence of the propensity to save on the rate of interest. Thus, even if he does not offer any new argument against the traditional theory of capital accumulation (capital as a stock) than he had previously offered against the traditional investment theory (capital as a flow), many a statement in this chapter clearly demonstrate that the mechanisms of the principle of effective demand are seen by Keynes as relevant to an analysis of capital accumulation as they are to the understanding of the short-run equality between saving and investment:

> An act of individual saving means – so to speak – decision not to have dinner to-day. But it does not necessitate a decision to have dinner or to buy a pair of boots a week hence or a year hence *or to consume any specified thing at any specified date*. Thus it depresses the business of preparing today's dinner without stimulating the business of making ready for some future act of consumption. *It is*

*not a substitution of future consumption-demand for present
consumption-demand*, – it is a net diminution of such demand.
(ibid. p. 210; italic added)

Keynes's attack against the productivity theory of capital in favour of
a rather dubious scarcity theory (ibid. pp. 213–17)[10] is another
attempt to disconnect the rate of interest from the productivity of
capital and the 'price of waiting'. By dismissing (a bit lightly)
Marshall's terminology Keynes is also clearly trying to deny the rate
of interest any co-ordinating, or adjusting influence in the long-run
process of capital accumulation between the supply-and-demand for
capital as a stock.

However Keynes's clearest (and most celebrated) application of
his principle to a long-run argument takes also place in this same
chapter. Discussing the case of community 'so well equipped with
capital that its marginal efficiency is zero' Keynes argues that

> the stock of capital and the level of employment will have to shrink
> until the community becomes so impoverished that the aggregate
> of saving has become zero. . . . Thus for [such a] society, . . . the
> position of equilibrium, under conditions of *laissez-faire*, will be
> one in which employment is low enough and the standard of life
> sufficiently miserable to bring savings to zero. *More probably there
> will be a general movement round this equilibrium position*' (ibid.
> pp. 217–18; italic added)

Clearly, in the long run, and thanks to the principle of effective
demand, saving is always equal to investment; the equilibrium position around which the system oscillates allows for a substantial and
permanent volume of structural unemployment and the rate of interest does not adjust investment to full-employment saving. Keynes
considers that, if left to its own devices:

> [the economic system] seems capable of remaining in a chronic
> condition of sub-normal activity for a considerable period without
> any marked tendency either towards recovery or towards complete
> collapse. Moreover, the evidence indicates that full, or even ap-
> proximately full, employment is of rare and short lived occurrence.
> (ibid. pp. 249–50; see also p. 204)

Finally, in his 1939 preface to the French edition of the *General
Theory*, immediately after having dismissed 'the rate of interest [as]

the equilibrating price-factor determined by the point of intersection of the supply curve of savings and the demand curve for investment', Keynes reasserts with utmost clarity that 'aggregate saving is necessarily *and in all circumstances* exactly equal to aggregate investment' (ibid. p. xxxiv; italic added).

Even the very terminology used by Keynes is reminiscent of Marshall's long-period dominant forces which, however slowly, tend in the long run to push the economic system towards a centre of gravity. This position has however nothing to do with the 'spurious equilibrium' (JMK, xiii, p. 536) discussed earlier in connection with the *Treatise*. Quite the contrary. Since the rate of interest no longer plays its adjusting part, this centre of gravity does not coincide with a full-employment level of output; it is indeed an 'equilibrium position short of full employment' (JMK, xiii, p. 374): 'we oscillate . . . round an intermediate position appreciably *below full employment* . . . [and this] mean position [is] determined by *'natural' tendencies which are likely to persist'* (ibid. p. 254; italic added).

From all this evidence it appears clearly that Keynes was fully convinced that his principle of effective demand was providing an explanation of the determination of a long-period 'normal' level of output and employment; or, put in other words, that, in the long run, and at the exclusion of all influence of the rate of interest, the equality between savings and investment would be guaranteed by variations in the level of income only.

Unfortunately it is not enough to assert the principle of effective demand as the new adjusting mechanism between saving and investment to be in a position to dispose altogether of the traditional role attributed to the rate of interest by the entire Cambridge School. This long-run validity Keynes seems to have attributed to the principle of effective demand can only be secured if, simultaneously, a plausible alternative to *and* a solid critique of the orthodox theory of interest are offered. Unfortunately, in the *General Theory*, both arguments are very weak indeed.

This fact, coupled with Keynes's simultaneous adoption of the concept of marginal efficiency of capital, opened wide the door to the various neo-classical rehabilitations of the traditional long-run self-adjusting approach. To understand how Keynes failed to give strong theoretical bases to his insights into the long-run working of the principle of effective demand, it is to a discussion of both his liquidity-preference theory and his marginal efficiency of capital that we now turn.

9.3　LIQUIDITY PREFERENCE AS AN 'ALTERNATIVE' THEORY OF INTEREST

Once Keynes had rejected the traditional idea that 'the rate of interest . . . depends on the interaction of the schedule of marginal efficiency of capital with the psychological propensity to save' (JMK, vii, p. 165) he was left with the question of *how* it is determined. His solution is well known:

> The rate of interest is not the 'price' which brings into equilibrium the demand for resources to invest with the readiness to abstain from present consumption. It is the 'price' which equilibrates the desire to hold wealth in the form of cash with the available quantity of cash. (ibid. p. 167)

It is important at the outset of this discussion to note that the adoption of this particular 'alternative' theory of interest was not for Keynes the result of carefully planned and carried-out research. Quite the contrary. Since his central idea was to offer an interest theory free from any influence of productivity and thrift (and since he assumed that liquidity preference is free from such influences), it is more for this reason than for the strength of liquidity preference itself that he made this choice. Hence, he 'shopped around' until he found what he thought would be a suitable substitute for Marshall's theory:

> the initial novelty [of my *General Theory*] lies in my maintaining that it is not the rate of interest, but the level of incomes which ensures equality between saving and investment. *The arguments which lead up to this initial conclusion are independent of my subsequent theory of the rate of interest*, and in fact I reached it before I had reached the latter theory. But the result of it was to leave the rate of interest in the air. If the rate of interest is not determined by saving and investment in the same way in which price is determined by supply and demand, how is it determined? One naturally began by supposing that the rate of interest must be determined in some sense by productivity – that it was, perhaps, simply the monetary equivalent of the marginal efficiency of capital, the latter being independently fixed by physical and technical considerations in conjunction with the expected demand. It was only when this line of approach led repeatedly to what seemed to be circular reasoning, that I hit on what I now think to be the true

explanation. The resulting theory, *whether right or wrong*, is exceedingly simple – namely that the rate of interest on a loan of given quality and maturity has to be established at the level which, in the opinion of those who have the opportunity of choice – i.e. of wealth-holders – equalises the attractions of holding idle cash and of holding the loan. *It would be true to say that this by itself does not carry us very far*. But it gives us firm and intelligible ground from which to proceed. (JMK xiv, pp. 212–13; italic added)

The last two italicised passages are very revealing. Keynes is not sure indeed of the robustness of his 'alternative' theory. But in order to close his system he had to offer 'something' of an explanation of the determinants of the rate of interest. Once again the 'separability' argument comes into the picture: Keynes is convinced of the validity of his novel explanation of the adjusting mechanism between saving and investment and does not realise that the weakness of his 'alternative' liquidity-preference theory might well (and in fact did) undermine the long-run validity of the principle of effective demand. In other words, even if he explicitly acknowledges the fact that his 'alternative' theory may be 'wrong' or 'does not carry us very far', Keynes is clearly not aware of the self-defeating influence it could have (and actually had at the hands of the neo-classical synthesis) on the positive argument of the *General Theory*.[11]

However, before probing the solidity of this liquidity-preference theory, two remarks on Keynes's skeletal critique of the Marshallian theory of interest are in order.

First, the only attack against the *internal logic* of this interest theory (a critique Keynes kept repeating in the post-*General Theory* debate) is no more than an updated version of Marshall's earlier doubts about the marginalist theory of interest. And, since the 1920s and 1930s saw an orgy of debates on capital theory there is nothing original in that. As Keynes argues:

an attempt to derive the rate of interest from the marginal efficiency of capital involves a logical error . . . [because] the marginal efficiency of capital partly depends on the scale of current investment, and we must already know the rate of interest before we can calculate what this scale will be. (JMK, xiv, p. 477, and vii, p. 184)

But instead of taking that promising line further[12] Keynes switched to a much weaker *indeterminacy* argument (JMK, vii, pp. 179–82).[13]

As is well known, Keynes argues that the intersection of the investment-demand saving-supply curves cannot determine the rate of interest because the position of the saving schedule will vary with the level of real income. Thus, one cannot know what the rate of interest will be unless one already knows the level of income. And, similarly, one cannot know the level of income without already knowing the rate of interest, since a lower interest-rate means a larger volume of investment, and, hence, a higher level of income. Hence, given the marginal-efficiency-of-capital schedule, there are therefore not one but many rates of interest at which planned investment and planned saving are equal – in fact one for each level of real income (JMK, vii, p. 181, and xiii, p. 559).

Like practically all the founding fathers of marginalism, Marshall had already drawn such a clear, if somewhat incomplete, functional relationship between the level of income and the volume of saving (see above, pp. 16–17). However, he did nothing with such a critical relationship. In particular he was unable to draw a saving-supply curve relating directly – and under all circumstances – the volume of saving to the rate of interest. Finally it was however possible to conclude that the full-employment schedule of savings is in the long run the only one to which Marshall needed to refer in order to determine his equilibrium rate of interest. Hence, it is rather surprising to find Keynes (and Harrod) unaware of this standard Marshallian assumption (also used by Cassel; see JMK, vii, p. 182): in the long run, the saving-supply curve shifts to the right as a result of the increase in output to come to rest in a position in which it is identical with the full-employment schedule of saving. Nothing is thus 'indeterminate' in such a theoretical framework.

There is no transition between Keynes's first and second strand of his critique. In the course of his discussion of Harrod's diagram (JMK, vii, p. 180) Keynes is led to the conclusion that the only way to dispose of the 'indeterminacy' of the Marshallian theory is to introduce into the picture liquidity preference and the quantity of money. Or, put the other way round, the traditional interest theory is indeterminate because in its analytical framework, 'money [is] used solely for transactions and never as a store of value' (JMK, vii, p. 182).

Since Keynes was, with Robertson, the leading authority who had been endeavouring ever since 1911 to complete Marshall's unfinished loanable-funds theory of interest (a task he eventually fulfilled himself in the *Treatise*) how could he accuse the received Cambridge orthodoxy of having neglected altogether before 1936 the influence of money on the rate of interest?

In fact Keynes is launching his attack against the wrong target. If Marshall's interest theory may be found guilty of neglecting the influence of the demand for money on the rate of interest it is certainly not the case of its numerous offsprings at Cambridge. After all, the main body of the present book is entirely devoted to a lengthy discussion of the (eventually successful) pre-1936 attempts to provide a theoretical basis for the influence of the speculative demand for money on the rate of interest. It is this loanable-funds version of the Marshallian interest theory brought to fruition in the *Treatise* that Keynes should have tackled and not Marshall's version, which in 1936 had been superseded for a good many years. Thus, blunt assertions according to which, since the rate of interest cannot be the reward of waiting, it has to be the reward for not hoarding (JMK, vii, p. 182) or that 'the attempt to build a bridge [between value and monetary theories] on the part of the neo-classical school [namely, post-Marshallian economists including himself] has led to the worse muddles of all' (ibid. p. 183) fail completely to take into account the sophisticated stage the loanable-funds theory of interest reached before 1936, notably in the *Treatise*. Both components of Keynes's critique appear thus hardly satisfactory. No wonder Robertson accused Keynes of 'shying at a "composite Aunt Sally of uncertain age"' (JMK, xiv, p. 215, and Robertson, 1937, p. 436). This lack of a sound critique of the Marshallian interest theory eventually forced Keynes to rest his case for less-than-full-employment equilibria on the strength of his 'alternative' theory of interest alone.

Since the fundamentals of the liquidity theory have already been examined apropos the *Treatise* it suffices here to examine the particularity of the 1936 version, leaving aside for later (Section 9.4), the problem of the connection between the liquidity-preference and the loanable-funds theories of interest.

First, Keynes is very careful not to use the term 'saving' in connection with the first set of decisions an individual is faced with when deciding on his optimum portfolio. While in the *Treatise* 'a man is deciding . . . between present consumption . . . and *saving*' (JMK, v, p. 127; italic added), in the *General Theory* the individual has characteristically to determine 'how much of his income he will consume and how much he will reserve in *some* form of *command over future consumption*' (JMK, vii, p. 166; italic added). Since the concept of *ex ante* saving is meaningless for Keynes (above, p. 159

and also JMK, xiv, pp. 216–22, 323, and xxix, p. 276) he is clearly
bound to abandon the 'threefold-margin' argument of the *Treatise*.

The fact that the individual has only a choice between two alternatives, from which saving is excluded, is even made in the concluding
section of chapter 13, 'The General Theory of Interest':

> the decision to hoard [i.e. a first approximation to the concept of
> liquidity preference] is not taken absolutely or without regard to
> the advantages offered for parting with liquidity; – it results from a
> balancing of advantages, and we have to know what lies in the
> other scale. (ibid. p. 174)

Clearly there are only two scales in Keynes's balance: one contain-
ing various assets and the other cash. In the *General Theory* the
choice at the margin is between holding money and holding assets
(bonds or equities) only. The rate of interest does not measure either
the individual's time-preference (choice between present or future
consumption; namely, savings) or the marginal productivity of capital. Accordingly the rate of interest is neither the reward of not-
spending nor the profitability of capital. Thus, for Keynes, the rate of
interest has no influence on the volume of consumption (or marginal
propensity to consume) or, directly[14] on the marginal efficiency of
capital: it is the price that has to be paid to borrow money, or,
alternatively, the cost of holding money.

Compared with his earlier loanable-funds approach (see, e.g., JMK,
xx, p. 84), in his liquidity-preference theory, Keynes simply discards the
supply of 'credit' (or saving) and the demand for 'credit' (or investment). Hence, bearing in mind that the decision to hold money is not
taken regardless of the reward for not hoarding, the rate of interest has
to be determined by the intersection of the supply-and-demand curves
for money. Graphically speaking this amounts to reversing the ordering
on Lerner's famous diagram (1938b, p. 281). Instead of visualising
Keynes's theory as adding to the saving-investment curves the supply-
and-demand for money-schedules, this approach visualises the *General
Theory* as trying to dispose of the saving-investment curves of the
Treatise, leaving the supply-and-demand curves for money as the only
determinants of the interest-rate (see Leijonhufvud, 1981, pp. 169–70
for a similar argument). Ultimately, this rate of interest influences only
the individual's decisions of how his 'command over future consumption' is allocated between alternative assets and has nothing to do with
the volume of saving.

Second, the portfolio-choice model of the *General Theory* introduces an additional and third component to those used in the *Treatise*. In this latter book there are only two assets from which to choose: money and equity securities. In contrast the corresponding model of the *General Theory* is developed with much more rigour and precision. It includes three alternative assets: money, bonds and capital assets. In Keynes's words, 'liquidity-preference due to the speculative-motive . . . the functional relationship between the rate of interest (or price of debts) and the quantity of money' (ibid. p. 173). This three-asset model is also a two-stage one. In the first stage the individual compares the marginal efficiency of capital with the current market-rate of interest; he then chooses between holding physical capital (or equities); namely, investing, and holding other assets.[15] In the second stage, and on the basis of a comparison between the current market-rate of interest and his own 'expectations as to the future of [this] rate of interest' (ibid. p. 170), this individual chooses between holding these assets in the form of long-term bonds or in the form of cash.

Third, the demand for money may then be split between M_1 and M_2, where M_1 corresponds to the precautionary and transactions demands taken together, and M_2 to the speculative demand for money. The former varies in a fairly stable way with changes in income (Y), the latter depends upon the reward for not-hoarding, i.e. the rate of interest. In short, and to use Keynes's equation: $M = M_1 + M_2 = L_1(Y) + L_2(r)$. In conjunction with the supply of money (JMK, vii, p. 205) the rate of interest is determined on the money-market only by the function $M_2(r)$. However, and this is a point that subsequently revealed itself to be crucial for the long-run validity of Keynes's 'alternative' theory of interest, 'what matters is not the *absolute* level of r but the degree of its divergence from what is considered a fairly *safe* level of r' (ibid. p. 201).

Although Keynes considers $M_2(r)$ as a stable and well-behaved function (ibid. 201–2), *it leaves totally unexplained what Keynes is in fact trying to explain: how is the long-run 'natural' rate of interest determined?* Or, as Robertson subsequently put it:

the trouble about this theory is that while it tells us something about what determines the divergence between the actual and the normal rates, it tells us nothing whatever about what determines the normal rate and therefore, given the degree of divergence, the actual rate. (1959, pp. 65; see also 1940, p. 25)

In fact, to consider that the current rate of interest is what it is because it is expected by individuals to become other than it actually is can hardly be seen as a satisfactory explanation of the dominant forces which, in the long run, ultimately determine the 'normal' rate of interest. Or, put in other words, despite Keynes's assertion to the contrary, the rejection of the 'threefold-margin' argument which is implied by the rejection of the concepts of productivity and thrift does leave interest theory in the air.

Fourth, the validity of Keynes's liquidity-preference theory clearly rests on the (doubtful) assumption of a large degree of stability of the wealth-owners' expectations concerning the rate of interest. Should it not be the case, nothing would be left of Keynes's *rationale* for the speculative demand for money and hence of his interest theory. It is only because wealth-owners have fairly stable views about what constitutes a 'normal' rate of interest that the interest-elasticity of the speculative demand for money makes sense. If one were to assume, for example, that the gap between the actual and expected rates is fairly *stable*; namely, that the expected rate tends (given a suitable time-lag) to move in parallel with the actual rate, the argument underlying Keynes's speculative demand for money would collapse. It is only because there are unexpected divergences between the expected and the current rate that wealth-owners alter their speculative demand for money.

Following Marshall, Keynes argues (ibid. p. 201) that the rate of long-term loans is a good proxy for the long-run 'normal' rate of interest; or, in other words, that this interest-rate is largely determined by wealth-owners' views about the 'normal' rate of interest. However, and once again, the trouble in Keynes's theory is that (unlike in Marshall's) *the way these views are formed is simply left unexplained*. In the terminology used time and again from Marshall onward, Keynes's liquidity-preference theory simply pretends to explain how the market-rate of interest fluctuates around a long-run 'normal' rate which the theory does not explain. It is hardly a sound logical procedure to describe the fluctuations of a magnitude without defining that magnitude in the first place. And it leaves the door widely open to a rehabilitation of the traditional interest theory.[16] Keynes would not have long to wait for Robertson to point out – even *before* the publication of the *General Theory* (JMK, xiii, pp. 499, 509) – that the only sound explanation of how these expectations are formed is given, on average and over the long period, by . . . 'none other than our old friends productivity and thrift' (1959, p. 72; see also 1940, p. 9). In short, Keynes's missing explanation about the determination of the long-run 'normal' rate could easily be provided by a rehabilitation, in a suitable form, of the orthodox interest theory.

Hence, together with the marginal-efficiency-of-capital schedule (or more properly, as a result of the adoption of such a curve; see below, Section 9.4), the short-run character of Keynes's liquidity-preference theory provide a very clear starting-point for a direct defence of the Marshallian interest-rate theory. Such a rehabilitation confines in turn the relevance of the principle of effective demand to the analysis of short-period disequilibria in which the 'psychological factors' already discussed by Marshall constitute an obstacle which can prevent a return to the full employment of factors (even for indefinite periods of time) but do not alter the essence of the theory.

In February 1935, commenting on a draft of the first eighteen chapters of the *General Theory*, Robertson fired the first salvo in the 'loanable-funds versus liquidity-preference' debate.

> I feel I should like to add that in the long run and in most communities the most important force modifying the average liquidity function for the whole community is a change in the propensity to spend [i.e. thrift] on the part of the ordinary population. (JMK, xiii, p. 499; see also p. 509)

From that early statement to the last flare-up of the debate in the early 1960s in terms of the more general problem of stock – flow analysis, the question as to the equivalence of the two theories has been ceaselessly filling the columns of all major periodicals.[17] However, one central idea on which all economists seem to agree (may be at the exception of J. Robinson, 1951, and Kahn, 1954) is that Keynes was wrong when he argued in his famous 'Alternative Theories of the Rate of Interest' that these 'theories are, I believe, radically opposed to one another' (JMK, xiv, p. 202).

Robertson's demonstration (1936, pp. 175–91; 1937, pp. 429–35; 1940, pp. 16–17; 1959, pp. 60–75) is the natural and ultimate extension of Marshall's original argument. His critique of Keynes's liquidity preference is based on the short-run restrictive approach that Keynes gives to the 'speculative demand' for money and its exclusive influence on the rate of interest (1940, p. 25). For Robertson, in line with the Cambridge equation, there is no point, in the long run, in setting the rate of interest in a direct functional relation with the

speculative demand for money only. Clearly, in the terminology used
earlier, it leaves the determinants of the wealth-owners' *stable expectations* in the air. For what Robertson calls the 'neo-Marshallian' (i.e.
mainly himself), the whole of the demand for money ($M_1 + M_2$) has
to be included in the analysis in order to extend Keynes's theory to
the long run. For obvious reason the fact that Keynes unduly neglects
the demand for money for 'precautionary' and 'transaction' purposes; namely, that his procedure lumps together 'in the same port-
manteau those who desire to *hold* more money and those who desire
to *use* it' (1936, p. 177) is seen by Robertson as 'the canker at the
heart of the Keynesian theory of interest' (1959, p. 64). By including
the demand for money M_1, and, thus, the factors which determine
this magnitude, Robertson can logically reintroduce 'the fundamental phenomena of Productivity and Thrift' (1940, p. 25) Keynes
desperately tried to keep out of the picture. Thus, by considering the
total demand for money (active and speculative), Robertson can take
into account the two possible causes which tend, for example, to raise
the rate of interest; namely, 'an increase in economic activity [and] a
movement of confidence . . . leading people to desire to hold more
money idle at any given rate of interest' (1959, p. 62). Thus, Robertson has operated a full circle.

Indeed, this 'long-period demand for money' is nothing else but
the Marshallian k, namely the proportion of resources (income and
wealth) over which people wish to keep command in monetary
form.[18] Hence, through the long-run satisfaction derived at the
margin by wealth-owners from holding money, Robertson is back,
thanks to the 'threefold-margin' argument, not only to an explanation of the stability of the wealth-owners' expectations as to the
future rate of interest in terms of productivity and thrift, but also to
the loanable-funds theory of interest. Keynes's liquidity-preference
theory can thus be reduced to 'a theory of the influences limiting
speculative movements in the rate' in the short period (1959, p. 66).

Thus, through a theoretically sound and legitimate addition of the
active demand for money to the speculative demand for money,
Robertson is able to 'peg' Keynes's short-run liquidity-preference
interest-theory and to fill the lacuna left in the *General Theory*, but,
at the cost of reducing to short periods only the validity of the
principle of effective demand. With the exception of the liquidity trap
that Pigou describes as Keynes's 'Day of Judgement' (1936, p. 129)
the rate of interest operates simultaneously on the 'threefold-margin'
of time-preference (consumption decisions), marginal productivity of

capital (investment decisions) and liquidity preference (decisions as to the relative sizes of bond and money holdings). Hence, besides the level of income, saving does *also* depend on the rate of interest and 'the proposition that the marginal convenience of holding money is equated with the rate of interest [does not] exclude and invalidate the proposition that the marginal inconvenience of refraining from consumption is equated with the rate of interest' (1940, p. 16).

If such an interpretation of Keynes's liquidity-preference theory as the one implied here is accepted (namely, liquidity-preference as a mere component, though vital, of a more general loanable-funds theory) it is easy to deduce the formal equivalence between both theories. In fact Robertson's procedure corresponds to a type of proof already pointed at in the *Treatise* and in his own 1933 'Saving and Hoarding'. For the market of loanable funds to be in equilibrium (i.e. for the rate of interest, income, saving and investment to be unchanged over a succession of short periods, or, alternatively for the value of the interest-rate to be at its 'normal' level) two requirements must be simultaneously fulfilled: saving must be equal to investment; and the demand for money must be equal to its supply.

Hence it is clear, as Johnson puts it, that the 'choice between the two theories is a matter of judgement as to which emphasis is more realistic' (1951–2, p. 92). Hicks provides a similar proof of equivalence between these two theories, though in a much simple and straightforward way. Using the general equilibrium framework built for his 1935 'Suggestion for Simplifying the Theory of Money' Hicks gives three successive demonstrations of the formal identity of the liquidity-preference and loanable-funds theories of interest (1936, pp. 245–7; 1937, pp. 138–41 and 1946, pp. 153–62).

Along the same line than Robertson, he points out easily the fundamental lacuna of Keynes's theory when applied to the long period: 'to say that the rate of interest on perfectly safe securities is determined by nothing else but uncertainty of future interest rates seems to leave interest hanging by its own bootstraps' (1946, p. 164). Hicks can then safely argue that the choice between one or the other 'is purely a question of convenience' (1936, p. 246). Indeed, thanks to the freedom given by Walras's law to 'drop' one of the market excess-demand equations, if one 'drops' the money equation, we end up with a loanable-funds theory; and if one 'drops, the bond equation, we end up with a liquidity-preference theory.[19] Hence, by turning the causal system of the *General Theory* into a system of simultaneous equations in order to fill the lacuna left by Keynes in his interest theory, Hicks, like Robertson, clearly demonstrates that, except for the 'liquidity-trap' case, the rate of interest is determined *in the long run* by the 'real' factors productivity and thrift. This result is obviously identical to that obtained by Marshall even if, unlike in the system of the founder of the Cambridge School, the demand for money acquires a long-run respectability.

Keynes's ultimate line of defence during the 'finance' debate is nothing more than a repetition, in an even more obscure and protracted form, of all the main arguments and criticisms raised in favour and against the liquidity-preference theory of interest. And the result is exactly the same: the addition of a 'finance' motive as yet another determinant of the demand for money does not fill in any way the gaping hole left by Keynes in his theory.

Under the joint pressure of Ohlin, Hicks and Robertson, Keynes was led in his 1937 'Alternative Theories' paper to take into account in his theoretical structure the problem of financing investment. In his relentless attack against Keynes's dictum that, even in the long run, the rate of interest has nothing to do with saving, Robertson argues that, like the 'transactions' and 'precautionary' demand for money, the demand for 'finance' in order to bridge 'the interregnum between the intentions to invest and its achievement' (JMK, xiv, p. 219)[20] is altered by changes in the volume of investment. Obviously such variations in the demand for 'finance' do influence the rate of interest if they are not matched by a corresponding variation in the money-supply.

In Keynes's own words:

> If investment is proceeding at a steady rate, the finance . . . can be supplied from a revolving fund of a more or less constant amount. . . . But if decisions to invest are (e.g.) increasing, the extra finance involved will constitute an additional demand for money.
>
> Now a pressure to secure more finance than usual may easily affect the rate of interest through its influence on the demand for money; and unless the banking system is prepared to augment the supply of money, lack of finance may prove an important obstacle to more than a certain amount of investment decisions being on the tapis at the same time.

And, anticipating the obvious and expected objection by his opponents, Keynes immediately adds: 'But "finance" has nothing to do with saving (ibid. p. 209). To such a statement, Robertson (1938, p. 317), Ohlin (1937a, p. 114), and Shaw (1938, p. 838) could only answer in a small voice: but, *how* is this demand for 'finance' determined? Clearly this is yet another aspect of the fundamental long-run flaw of Keynes's liquidity-preference theory. By arguing on very strong logical grounds that the demand for 'finance' cannot but be related to the marginal efficiency of investment, Keynes's opponents safely reintroduce in the picture the concept of productivity (see, for example, Robertson, 1940, pp. 12–13). Moreover, and despite Keynes's claim that 'finance' 'is the parent, not the twin of increased saving' (ibid. p. 281), the size of this revolving fund is also necessarily linked in the long run with savings, and, hence, in yet another way with the rate of interest (Robertson, 1938, pp. 317–8, 555–6). Thus, like the other components of the demand for money, 'finance' needs to be 'pegged' to long-run determinants which – as Keynes's critiques readily suggested – are none other by productivity and thrift.

9.4 THE MARGINAL EFFICIENCY OF CAPITAL

A discussion of Keynes's investment theory is the complementary element necessary to understand not only the general structure of the *General Theory*, but also the reasons why Keynes's opponents were so successful in their rehabilitation of the traditional long-run adjusting mechanism between saving and investment. Or, put in other words, why Keynes's insight into the instability of decentralised economies got so easily lost in the neo-classical synthesis.

Despite his claim that '*no* theory of interest can be derived from marginal efficiency' (JMK, xiii, p. 631) Keynes adopts part and parcel Marshall's interest-elastic investment-demand curve as the main component of his investment theory. The adoption of such a theory is, of course, hardly compatible with the idea that the equality between saving and investment has 'nothing' to do with the rate of interest.

Robertson was among the first, even before the publication of the *General Theory*, to react against Keynes's assertions that, in the long run, an increase in the productivity of investment (i.e. a shift of the marginal-efficiency-of-capital schedule) cannot increase the rate of interest, and that an increase in thrift cannot lower the rate of interest (JMK, xiii, pp. 499, 509, 521). Harrod (ibid. pp. 545–6, 554) and Hawtrey (ibid. pp. 590–1), while recognising Keynes's attempts to get rid of Marshall's interest theory also adopted the point of view that, in the end, Keynes's assertion was valid in the short run only.[21]

It is equally easy to quote from Keynes's own writings many examples of explicit denials of the influence of these two factors on the rate of interest. Or, put in a different way, that the very concepts of investment-demand and saving-supply curves elastic with respect to the rate of interest are non sequitur.

Besides general statements according to which 'a decrease in spending will [not] tend to lower the rate of interest and an increase in investment to raise it' (JMK, viii, p. 185), or that '[I] can discover no simple or direct relationship such as has been commonly supposed to relate the productivity of capital to the rate of interest' (JMK, xiv, p. 12), Keynes can be much more precise in his attacks against Marshall's curves. For example, when Robertson suggests that any rightward movement in the expected marginal-productivity-of-loanable-funds curve would tend to increase the rate of interest, Keynes replies that, within the *General Theory*, 'it is precisely this proposition which I am denying' (JMK, xiii, p. 523). Similarly, answering a letter from Hawtrey, he writes back:

> When the schedule of the marginal efficiency of capital rises the rate of investment is pushed up so as to keep the actual marginal efficiency of capital in equilibrium with the conventional [i.e. separately determined] rate of interest. (JMK, xiv, p. 12; see also pp. 15–16)

And, on the influence of saving, he answers a letter from Robertson in the following terms:

> one of my main points is precisely that changes in the propensity to spend are in themselves . . . wholly and of logical necessity[22] irrelevant to liquidity preference [i.e. to the rate of interest]. (JMK, xiii, p. 515)

Eventually a passage from a letter, part of the 1935 exchange with Harrod, gives at its best the full flavour of Keynes's wrath against the very idea of interest-elastic supply-and-demand curves for 'free'capital: 'In truth there are no such things as these schedules. *They are completely bogus*' (JMK, xiii, p. 551; italic added). After such scathing attacks on the downward-sloping investment-demand curve, any reader of the *General Theory* is genuinely surprised, to say the least, by the discovery that Keynes's investment theory *precisely* rests on such a marginal productivity of capital function: 'the schedule of the marginal efficiency of capital tells us . . . what . . . the output of new investment will be . . . [at any] given . . . rate of interest' (JMK, viii, p. 184).

An increase in investment in any given type of capital goods would diminish the marginal efficiency of that type of capital, partly because its prospective yield would fall and partly because its supply-price (or cost of production) would rise. For Keynes the latter is 'the more important in producing equilibrium in the short run' (ibid. p. 136), the influence of the former taking place over longer periods of time. And he concludes his analysis by aggregating the decreasing curves of marginal efficiency of each type of capital-good 'so as to provide a schedule relating the rate of aggregate investment to the corresponding marginal efficiency of capital in general' (ibid. p. 136).

In the last analysis it is this schedule which, under the assumption that investment is pushed to the point where there is no longer any class of capital assets the marginal efficiency of which exceeds the current rate of interest, becomes – on Keynes's own definition – 'the investment-demand schedule' (ibid. p. 137). Clearly, and given Marshall's *ceteris paribus* clause, this schedule is interest-elastic in the sense that the demand for investment is inversely related to the rate of interest.

Despite various additions to Marshall's original analysis (in particular the entire chapter 12 devoted to the influence of long-term expectations on investment decisions) there is no substantial difference between Keynes and his mentor on the circumstances which determine not only the inverse relation between investment and the rate of interest, but also the slope of this investment-demand function.[23]

Finally Keynes goes even as far as to admit that there is no 'material difference . . . between my schedule of the marginal efficiency of capital or investment-demand schedule and the demand curve for capital contemplated by some of the classical [i.e. marginalist] writers who have been quoted above' (ibid. p. 178).[24]

As a consequence the role played by this function in the traditional Marshallian theory of interest is also played in Keynes's analysis. Indeed the adoption of this curve implies not only the existence of a unique 'natural' full-employment rate of interest, but also the fact that full employment can always be reached through successive reductions of the rate of interest.

Of course, as soon had he adopted this investment-demand curve,

Keynes had only one way left to rescue the validity of the principle of effective demand: to supply reasons why the rate of interest will not tend towards its full-employment 'natural' level. By adopting such an approach he was bound to relapse into the dominant 'trade-cycle' theory he had done so much to improve in the *Treatise*. Moreover, such an escape route was also prone to provide a solid rationale for these interpretations of the *General Theory* (heralded by Robertson and Hicks) that deny the long-period validity of the principle of effective demand and to reassert the Marshallian concept of a 'natural' rate of interest as the centre of gravity towards which the market-rate is tending.

As shown earlier the liquidity-preference theory is the short-run device Keynes proposed to escape from the paradox his marginal efficiency of capital had led his analysis into. The rate of interest would be determined in the money market, i.e. independently of both the equality between saving and investment and the marginal efficiency of capital. Indeed this distinction between the rate of interest and the marginal efficiency of capital is crucial for Keynes. Well aware that it is the only way to avoid an explicit return to the rate of interest as the adjusting mechanism between saving and investment, he went on repeating over and over again that 'the marginal efficiency of capital is, in itself, a different thing from the ruling rate of interest' (ibid. p. 165).

However, Keynes himself cannot eventually escape the fact that it is the *monetary* character of the rate of interest which prevents its attaining its full-employment value:

> Thus in the absence of money and in the absence – we must, of course, also suppose – of any other commodity with the assumed characteristics of money, the rates of interest would only reach equilibrium when there is full employment. (ibid. p. 235)

However, such a device can hardly be seen as having a long-run theoretical validity.

Once again, if Keynes wanted to prove that in the long run, the economic system tends to a less-than-full-employment level of output, he would have had to *demonstrate*, and not only to assert, that a unique 'natural' rate of interest does not exist. The adoption of a schedule of marginal efficiency of capital can hardly be seen as having helped Keynes in placing the weight he so obviously wished to put on the long-run validity of the principle of effective demand. In other words Keynes's adoption of the first fundamental proposition of Marshall's interest theory (interest-elastic investment-demand curve) leaves him with a critique of the second proposition (sensitivity of the rate of interest to a gap between investment and full-employment saving) as the only way to support the long-run validity of his new relationship between saving and investment. But clearly such a method is not only logically weak (you cannot dismiss an existence theorem simply on the grounds of difficulties in the stability analysis), but also displays strong and unmistakable similarities with the then dominant trade-cycle approach to economic fluctuations.

9.5 CONCLUDING REMARKS

Throughout Chapter 9 it has been argued that, in the *General Theory*, Keynes's theoretical framework is not capable of bearing the weight clearly assigned to it. In other words, if Keynes's insights into the pathologies of decentralised economies seem to this author to be correct, his attempts to forge these insights into a coherent theory seem to have failed. Or, as Hahn put it recently: 'I consider that Keynes . . . left many gaping holes in his theory; I none the less hold that his insights were several orders more profound and realistic than those of his recent critics' (1982, pp. x–xi). By resting his case on the terrain of monetary theory only, Keynes decisively undermined the conclusions he was pointing at with his principle of effective demand. As a matter of fact, trapped by the logic of his investment/interest theory, he was ultimately forced to defend the long-run validity of this principle on the weaker grounds that the effects of uncertainty linked with monetary factors inhibit (or even prohibit) the tendency to the full-employment level.

Even before 1936 Robertson had already expressed with great insight the theoretical limits of what Keynes could claim within the analytical framework of the *General Theory*. Considering Keynes's scepticism about 'how far management of the rate of interest is capable of continuously stimulating the appropriate volume of investment' (JMK, vii, p. 164) – namely, Keynes's justification by means of *monetary* factors of 'conditions [of] chronic and endemic [unemployment]' (JMK, xiii, p. 500) – Robertson wrote:

I take this proposition to be the real *differentia* of the book, marking it off from your own *Treatise* as well as from most of the other literature of disequilibrium, which runs, as the *Treatise* did, *in terms of fluctuations around a norm and not of chronic failure to get up to a norm.* (ibid. p. 500; italic added)

Clearly, and despite Keynes's claims to the contrary, all what the theoretical model of the *General Theory* can safely offer is an explanation of why the system can be stuck practically for ever in an underemployment disequilibrium; what it can certainly not do is to demonstrate the existence of a long-run unemployment equilibrium. To put the same argument in yet another slightly different way, the analytical framework of the *General Theory* cannot secure the long-run validity of the principle of effective demand. More generally it does not support Keynes's assertion that the marginalist theoretical representation of a decentralised economy is either inconsistent or unstable. Interestingly enough, during the 'finance debate', alerted by Keynes's insistence about the long-run validity of the principle of effective demand, Ohlin had already outlined with surprising lucidity the preliminary conditions to start a reconstruction of economic theory if Keynes's principle were to be saved: 'Anyone who refuses to accept this analysis of the pricing of claims [i.e. the loanable-funds theory of interest] must, I think, refute also the Marshallian supply and demand curve analysis *in toto*' (1937b, p. 426).

In 1934 Keynes had already outlined himself the absolute necessity of an all-out theoretical attack against the 'citadel of the nineteenth-century self-adjusting school' if his new relationship between saving and investment were to be given a 'general case' status:

On the one side are those who believe that the existing economic system is, in the long run, a self-adjusting system, though with creaks and groans and jerks, and interrupted by time lags, outside interference and mistakes. These authorities do not, of course, believe that the system is automatically or immediately self-adjusting. But they do believe that it has an inherent tendency towards self-adjustment, if it is not interfered with and if the action of change and chance is not too rapid.

On the other side of the gulf are those who reject the idea that the existing economic system is, in any significant sense, self-adjusting. They believe that the failure of effective demand to reach the full potentialities of supply . . . is due to much more fundamental causes. . . .

The strength of the self-adjustment school depends on its having behind it almost the whole body or organised economic thinking and doctrine of the last hundred years. This is a formidable power. . . .

Now *I* range myself with the heretics. I believe their flair and their instinct move them towards the right conclusion. But I was brought up in the citadel and I recognise its power and might. A large part of the established body of economic doctrine I cannot but accept as broadly correct. I do not doubt it. For me, therefore, it is impossible to rest satisfied until I can put my finger on the flaw in that part of the orthodox reasoning which leads to the conclusions which for various reasons seem to me to be inacceptable. I believe that I am on my way to do so. *There is, I am convinced, a fatal flaw in that part of the orthodox reasoning which deals with the theory of what determines the level of effective demand and the volume of aggregate employment; the flaw being largely due to the failure of the classical doctrine to develop a satisfactory theory of the rate of interest. . . .*

Now the school which believes in self-adjustment is, in fact, assuming that the rate of interest adjusts itself more or less automatically, so as to encourage just the right amount of production of capital goods to keep our incomes at the maximum level which our energies and our organisation and our knowledge of how to produce efficiently are capable of providing. This is, however, pure assumption. There is no theoretical reason for believing it to be true. (JMK, xiii, pp. 486–90; italic added)

Nothing could be clearer. However, even by Keynes's standard, this was a very tall order. Despite decisively cutting through the saving-investment Gordian knot, Keynes failed to bring down the Marshallian 'citadel' and, hence, did not manage to turn his principle of effective demand into a long-run theory of production. It is nevertheless of prime importance to realise that it is through this very – if incomplete – novel solution to the saving-investment relationships that Keynes introduced into economic theory a fundamental insight on the instability of the private sector which is still today at the heart of the theoretical debate.

Conclusion

The foregoing argument and analysis have demonstrated that, from the turn of the century to the early 1940s, the analysis in terms of saving and investment was one of the central issues discussed by all leading economists; and not only in Cambridge. Whatever their respective positions about what the relationships between these 'formidable concepts' (Robertson, 1915, p. xii) were, there is no doubt that all of of them considered that issue as central to the whole body of economic theory.

By concentrating their theoretical effort on the relationships between investment, saving, the rate of interest and, later the level of income and employment, Marshall's pupils were in fact reviving in a very different theoretical set-up the famous debate which had taken place a century earlier between some of the Classical economists in term of Say's law. However, this time, and in opposition with the Classical (and in particular Ricardian) framework, the Marshallian long-run model did include in the most basic postulate of its capital and interest theory the fundamental marginalist idea that the economic system displays a tendency towards the full utilisation of productive capacity. During nearly thirty years of 'high theory', the entire debate that took place between Pigou, Keynes, Robertson, Hawtrey and Lavington centred not on the validity of this basic concept of an interest-elastic investment-demand curve, but on the ability of the rate of interest to adjust investment decisions to full-employment saving. Or, put in other words, it focused on the analysis of various short-run forces (e.g. the uncertainty linked with monetary factors) that inhibit, or even prohibit, the rate of interest to attain its 'natural' (i.e. full-employment, or equilibrium) level.

In 1936, breaking completely with this line of argument, Keynes visualised his principle of effective demand as a new long-run adjustment process between saving and investment. For the author of the *General Theory*, investment is no longer dependent on savings decisions, the rate of interest has no part to play in the adjustment process between these two magnitudes and, even in the long run and in 'normal' situations, the tendency to full utilisation of productive capacity is no longer a characteristic of decentralised economies. Put in a slightly different way the possibility of persistent unemployment is asserted. However, it was rapidly shown that the analytical frame-

work of the *General Theory* was not capable of bearing the weight
Keynes clearly assigned to the principle of effective demand.

Hence, when definitions of saving and investment along Robertsonian and Hicksian lines reached a general acceptance in the profession and despite some rear-guard skirmishes around liquidity
preference and loanable funds, this central issue – 'which dominated
the [macroeconomic] field in this century' (Leijonhufvud, 1981,
p. 132) – completely disappeared from the theoretical agenda. Simultaneously the development of Solovian in place of Harrodian dynamics
strengthened this return to standard neo-classical economics. In the
traditional English economic terminology, and in sharp contrast with
Keynes's principle of effective demand, the Leda of investment again
yielded to the Swan of savings.

The growing dissatisfaction with the dichotomy between a rigorous
price-theory and the 'ad-hocery' of so-called 'Keynesian' macroeconomic theory – followed hard on heels by Friedman's revival of the
quantity theory of money – buried what little was left of Keynes's
insights as suggested by the principle of effective demand. The
subsequent advent of the adaptive and then rational-expectations
schools relying on Walrasian general equilibrium techniques in which
current prices always clear current markets 'have loaded the dice by
proposing a model where no *raison d'être* for macropolicy of the
Keynesian type exists' (Hahn, 1984, p. 287). In particular, and by
definition, there is no room in these models for involuntary unemployment. As rational expectations theorists readily admit, by using
this approach, they explicitly connect their line of research with
'interwar business cycle theorists . . . [who sought] the incorporation
of cyclical phenomena into the system of economic equilibrium
theory' (Lucas, 1981, p. 215). The cart of economic theory has thus
neatly come full circle to end even one step further back than
Keynes's pre-1936 starting-point. Indeed the core of the present
essay has shown that the whole pre-*General Theory* trade-cycle
theory was clearly concerned with the problem of pushing the economy to its natural rate and not to describe, like rational expectation
theorists, an economy that is there already.

In the *General Theory*, one of Keynes's sharpest rebukes to his
fellow economists was already to accuse them of discussing economic
fluctuations in terms of a model that allowed no place to involuntary
unemployment. He attempted to provide a theory that would remedy
this shortcoming. With the principle of effective demand, he thought
to have found a simple answer. Unfortunately it was soon made clear

that Keynes's alternative theory of the adjusting mechanism between saving and investment could not bear, in the long run, the weight he assigned to it. However, after some thirty years of theoretical eclipse, Keynes's pregnant insights are back at the centre of the theoretical debate. Since the late 1960s the necessity to formulate a meaningful theory of effective demand has even been paradoxically sharpened by the theoretical challenge of these various schools of thought that consider Keynes's vision of decentralised economies as an old canard (McCallum, 1980, p. 299).

From very different angles, with diametrically opposed time-spans in mind, and with a widely different support within the profession, two streams of economic theorising have taken up that challenge. Though with very different objectives in mind, both the powerful modern non-Walrasian temporary equilibrium approach and the neo-Ricardian School are sharing Keynes's doubts in the stability of decentralised economies. In particular they both consider that there is no obvious mechanism by which intertemporal decisions can be co-ordinated.

The former – dropping the traditional short-run/long-run method – attempts to analyse *short-period* positions of a decentralised economy *in sequence over time*; the time-honoured idea of a centre of gravity around which the system is seen to oscillate disappears completely from this analytical picture. The latter – rejecting the entire marginalist framework on the grounds of the inconsistencies revealed by the capital debate of the 1960s – attempts to graft Keynes's principle of effective demand (his theory of production) on to a Ricardian–Sraffian theory of value and distribution. In other words these authors try to co-ordinate a long-run surplus theory of value and distribution with Keynes's insights into the theory of output. Both approaches are still in their infancies. But this should not be too worrisome. As Hahn remarked at the Keynes Centenary Conference:

> It took us almost two hundred years to translate Adam Smith's vision into something sufficiently precise to allow us to argue about it. It will certainly take a long time to accomplish the same task for Keynes. (1983, p. 74)

The central aim of this essay was to put in its proper historical and theoretical perspectives Keynes's particular aversion to the simplification according to which the rate of interest is determined by savings and investment. Or, to use the traditional Marshallian terminology, why there is no obvious built-in mechanism which ensures – even in the long run – a full-employment equilibrium.

The present author leaves it to his readers to decide whether he has made his case in this book, but at any rate, the wish to make that case has been the principal motive for writing it.

Notes and References

1. Introduction

1. Recently revived by Garegnani (1978–9), Leijonhufvud (1981) and Milgate (1982).
2. In 1968 Blaug was already complaining about this lack of systematic studies in that area (1968, p. 664). Although it is true that Eshag (1963) covers the same terrains, he only alludes very briefly to the saving-investment technique of analysis (pp. 58–62) in his general study of the Cambridge monetary theory. The present study intends precisely to highlight the fundamental importance of this technique of analysis by approaching it from a very different perspective leading eventually to very different conclusions. Furthermore, in history-of-analysis terms this study roughly takes up the story where Corry (1962) left it with his contribution on saving and investment in English economics between 1800 and 1850.
3. Indeed, Marshall's theory is nothing but an application to the determination of the interest-rate of the traditional distinction (dating back at least to Smith and Turgot) between 'natural' and market prices. The former reflect the long-run dominant forces at work in an economy; the latter incorporate the short-lived phenomena which make the actual market values oscillate around the centre of gravity determined by the 'natural' ('normal' or equilibrium) magnitude. For recent discussions of that type of analysis at the root of Marshall's *Principles* see Garegnani (1976), Bharadwaj (1978) and (1983).

2. Supply and Demand for 'Free' Capital and the Rate of Interest

1. Since Marshall and all his pupils at Cambridge (including Keynes) assumed that full utilisation of the existing capital equipment would allow for the employment of the entire labour force, we will always refer to that particular definition of productive capacity. See, however, Chapter 9 of this text, in which Keynes's idea of unemployment equilibrium is linked with a long-run below capacity utilisation of equipment generating itself – 'structural unemployment'. In that case the equipment of capital goods in existence, together with only that part of the total labour force required for its full employment will coincide with a more general definition of productive capacity.
2. This uniform rate of profit earned on each and every capital good will – in the aggregate – determine the share of the national product allocated to the owners of such goods. This arises from the most crucial characteristic of the marginal theory according to which distribution is determined by a pricing process within the sphere of market exchange.

3. Robertson was the first in Cambridge to work out thoroughly that distinction with respect to wages in his celebrated 'Wage-Grumbles' 'wages tend to measure [and not to determine] the marginal productivity of labour . . .'. (1931a, p. 42).
4. Eleven years before the first edition of the *Principles*, Marshall was already convinced of 'this fundamental unity' (1961, p. viii, n. 1). See in his and his wife's *Economics of Industry* (1879), the chapter on distribution (BK II, chap. vi, pp. 94–100), particularly p. 96:

> We have then to seek for the laws which determine in the long-run . . . interest . . . and . . . earnings. This inquiry has two sides, that of Supply and Demand.

5. For exact references to Wicksell (1893), Edgeworth (1889), Wicksteed (1894), Flux (1894), Marshall (1879, 1890), Walras (1896) and Pareto (1897) on the marginal productivity theory of distribution and Euler's theorem see Stigler, 1941, pp. 320–87.
6. As Keynes put it clearly much later: 'The quasi-rent of an asset in any period is the money value of the service it renders, or money income derived from it, in that period . . . .[I]f, as Marshall rightly does, we calculate the value of capital asset by capitalising its quasi-rent on terms supplied by the loan-rate of interest, then, by virtue of the circularity of the procedure, the quasi-rent of an asset reckoned as a percentage of its capital value is necessarily the same thing as the loan-rate of interest . . .'. (JMK, xxix, pp. 111 and 119; see also JMK, vii, p. 184).
7. See Robertson's ironic remarks in his *Lectures* (1958, p. 70) on the 'odd sort of superstition floating about that [the] dependence of saving on income is a new discovery . . .'. For a good example of that 'superstition' see Dillard, 1948, pp. 189–93.
8. In Cassel's words: 'The principal tendency on the supply side, in fact the only one which has more than a very limited range, is the growth of social productivity *and the consequent growth of the capacity for saving*' (1903, p. 154). Keynes himself readily admits in the *General Theory* that his saving function is not new; when he comes to discuss it he refers to Cassel's more complete treatment instead of quoting Marshall's brief discussion (JMK, vii, pp. 182–4; Cassel, 1903, pp. 154–7). Simultaneously Keynes was obviously keen on showing that 'the traditional analysis has been aware that saving depends on income but it has overlooked the fact that income depends on investment . . .'. (JMK, vii, p. 184).
9. In that respect a little-quoted passage which appeared in the first edition of the *Principles* (1890) only is worth reproducing:

> while market prices oscillate about a position of market equilibrium, which perhaps oscillates about a position of short-period normal equilibrium, that position in its turn may not remain stationary, but may move onwards in one direction, or may oscillate more slowly round a position of long-period normal equilibrium; and that again in its turn may itself be liable to slow changes, possibly having

an oscillatory movement, the period of which ranges over many generations or even centuries. (1961, ii, p. 395).

10. These curves are also called 'schedules of the marginal efficiency of investment' (*MEI*) by Lerner (1944, p. 334). Keynes called 'marginal efficiency of capital' this very schedule of *MEI* (JMK, vii, p. 136). Lerner suggests it is because 'any point on the schedule represents a situation in which both the *social* marginal efficiency of *investment* and the *private* marginal productivity of *capital* are equal to the rate of interest. [Keynes's] terminology fails to distinguish clearly between these two fundamentally different concepts'. (1944, p. 334 n.)

11. None other but Pigou (1949a, pp. 99–102 and 1953, pp. 27–8) misinterpreted Marshall and accused him of saying stock when he meant flow of savings. See, however, Marshall's clear-cut stock-flow argument (1961, p. 534) and Lerner's critique of Pigou's *Employment and Equilibrium* (1942, pp. 250–1).

12. As Keynes puts it in his critique of Marshall's theory of interest (JMK, vii, p. 175; see also pp. 93, 165 and 175–80).

3. Marshall's Monetary Theory

1. For more details on the 'oral tradition' that grew up in Cambridge in monetary theory until the early 1920s see Keynes's obituary of Marshall (JMK, x, p. 189).

2. This approach is in fact the very classical doctrine inherited from J. S. Mill and Ricardo (and criticised by Tooke). Marshall and Wicksell are both keen on emphasising the continuity between their and the classical approach as far as the quantity theory is concerned, while they are perfectly aware at the same time of the fundamental antagonism between their respective theories of value. On the connection between Mill's and Marshall's versions of the quantity theory see Kahn, 1984, pp. 39–40.

3. By 'stability analysis' we mean the usual Walrasian tâtonnement process through which the market 'by the mechanism of free competition' will itself reach the equilibrium given by the system of excess-demand equations (Walras, 1954, pp. 242–3). Clearly, in the 'real world', such an adjustment process (following, for example, a once and for all departure from equilibrium) is not instantaneous and may be indeed a long-drawn-out and cumulative one (see also Patinkin, 1965, pp. 162–7, 604–5 and 707, for a similar use of this expression sometimes identified with dynamic analysis).

4. Wicksell's cumulative process relies exactly on the same monetary system than Marshall's. The system is *not* unstable (i.e. explosive): after an initial disturbance, it is not going to move indefinitely away from any equilibrium position (see 1935, p. 189; 1936, p. 135). The internal drain on bank reserves will, sooner or later, grind the cumulative process to a halt by forcing banks to raise their rate of interest to a level compatible with the level of their reserves (on various interpretations of the 'stability' of

Wicksell's cumulative process see Patinkin, 1965, pp. 587–97).

5. This was in fact brought to fruition by Keynes himself in the *Treatise*.

6. Under such conditions, and under such conditions only, '*other things being equal*, prices rise or fall proportionately to every increase or diminution [of the volume of money] used as the standard of value' (1926, p. 21).

7. Despite the time-honoured and misleading formal setting given by Pigou to the Cambridge equation in which wealth is not clearly separated from income. See his definition of R in $M = kR/P$ (1917, p. 180). See also Kahn, 1984, pp. 29, 42–3 and 48.

8. It must be noted incidentally that this diagrammatic exposition is the only really *new* element in *Money, Credit and Commerce*. It can, however, be found in an earlier and until recently unpublished essay on 'Money' written between *c.* 1867 and 1872 (see Whitaker, 1975, ii, p. 278). Marshall's diagram can thus probably be seen as reflecting the state of the art at Cambridge at the beginning of the 1920s. It is certainly not in contradiction either with Pigou's slightly earlier exposition (1917) or with the version worked out by Keynes the same year in the *Tract on Monetary Reform*.

9. In his 1917 essay Pigou had made a very strong point as well of the fact that 'when k and R are taken as constant, $[P = kR/M]$ . . . is, of course, the equation of a rectangular hyperbola' (1917, p. 177).

10. For once, Marshall's claim that his line of inquiry is nothing but an extension of the English Classical Economists' approach is perfectly justified.

11. Wicksell is, of course, the only one to have come close to a full understanding of the part played by the real-balance effect in the monetary stability analysis (1936, pp. 29–40), even if he did not draw all the conclusions he could have reached with the analytical devices he had ready at hand.

12. We will stick to this Marshallian terminology throughout. In order to avoid confusions we use the term 'real' rate of interest (on the market for 'free' capital) as opposed to the rate of discount (loan market). As a matter of fact Marshall also uses the term 'rate of interest' for long-term *loans*. Put in a nutshell, and using Marshall's terminology, the 'mean' rate of discount (short-run) is a function of the 'mean' rate of interest (long-run) which is in turn a function of the 'real' rate of interest (1926, p. 51). Marshall is not always very consistent with this set of definitions. He notably fails to make clear that in a situation of equilibrium, when the two rates are equal, what he calls the 'interest rate' (1926, p. 130) can be seen as determined either on the market for loans or on the market for 'free' capital.

13. The same reasoning would obviously apply in the case of a fall in the rate of discount following a drop in the demand for loans.

14. This clear-cut distinction between interest on money and interest on 'real' capital is not new. However, when it comes to applying this distinction to an analytical purpose, Marshall is among the first (before Wicksell) to escape from what J. S. Mill calls 'the most inextricable confusion [between] these two subjects' (1909, p. 637).

15. Keynes had already noticed Marshall's perplexity as to the causal sequence linking higher prices and higher discount rates (JMK, v, p. 172 n. 1). There appears to be a confusion between the idea of higher prices increasing discount (1926, p. 271) and the idea – relevant to a subsequent period – of an increased demand of capital due to the *expectation* of higher prices which, in turn, raises prices.

16. In fact Keynes's 'Gibson paradox' had already been discussed *and* solved in 1927 by Pigou in his *Industrial Fluctuations* (1929, p. 277).

17. Since Marshall gives later two excellent descriptions of the connections between the rate of discount and the fluctuations of the gold reserves (1926, pp. 126–7 and 158) it is very surprising that in the case we are interested in, he does not carry out his analysis to its logical end. The description given on p. 158 would have required very few amendments to be perfectly adapted to the 'cumulative process', the stability of which entirely relies on the bankers' intention to keep a given relationship between their reserves in gold and their supply for credit.

18. See, however, his allusion to what could be dubbed the 'Cantillon effect'. Asked by a member of the Indian Currency Committee if he 'would regard the rate of discount as affected not so much by the total value as by the distribution of the currency – the hands in which it stands?' – Marshall answered – 'I should think that that was largely true' (1926, p. 307). Being perfectly aware of the different impact of an increase of the money-supply according to the benefit of which people it is granted, it is surprising that Marshall did not carry out this line of analysis to its logical end.

19. As Patinkin puts it: 'The distinction between the short-run variability of interest in the face of monetary increase and its long-run invariability . . . represents . . . the well-reasoned conclusion of the analysis . . . which takes account of the effect of a rising price-level in the commodity market on the rate of interest.' (1965, p. 369)

20. Marshall actually does not make use of the term 'loanable funds' which first appeared in Robertson's celebrated essay of 1939 (1940, p. 2). However, it is clear that Marshall means the same thing when he uses the expression 'market for loans'.

21. It is the nearest Marshall comes to include Keynes's speculative demand for money in his interest theory.

22. Unlike in Marshall's theory, short-run deviations *do* alter the magnitudes expressing dominant forces; or, in other words during the trade cycle *only*, implications of long-period marginalist theory are temporarily kept at bay. The 'long-run normal value' of these magnitudes is 'a norm around which actual value oscillates, as a pendulum does about a vertical line, or a 'sine curve' about a horizontal one, so that . . . whenever it diverges from it a force, which will ultimately be victorious, is at work, tending to bring it back again' (Robertson, 1957, p. 95). It is because this traditional method makes a clear distinction between the *object* of its analytical inquiry (the long-run dominant forces) and the *theory* which is to explain the state or magnitude of this object (the classical or marginalist theory of value) that the explanation of oscillations around the centre of gravity is separate from the theory which defines this very expression of dominant forces.

In the same vein Hayek argues that 'the incorporation of cyclical phenomena into the system of economic equilibrium theory, with which they are in apparent contradiction, remains the crucial problem of Trade Cycle theory' (1933, p. 33 n.).

Interestingly enough, some forty-five years later, one of the leaders of the Rational Expectation School is still able to quote approvingly Hayek's methodological dictum (Lucas, 1981, p. 215). Though in somewhat different a disguise, this shows the continuity existing between the 1930s and today's market-clearing sequential-stability analysis. Furthermore, both Hayek and Lucas display the same (unproven) faith not only in the stability of the economic system, but also in the uniqueness of both the long-run equilibrium and the stability path leading to it. (On the origin of the notion of 'intertemporal equilibrium', see Hicks, 1965, chap. vi and Milgate, 1982, chap. viii).

Similarly Keynes had also fully understood by the late 1920s the necessity to bridge the gap between value and trade-cycle theory with some sort of sequential analysis. Despite this substantial departure from Marshall's strict dichotomy, Keynes was still able, some fifty years later, to connect his own research with Marshall's original suggestion:

> Marshall, in his anxiety to push economic theory on to the point where it regains contact with the real world, was a little disposed sometimes to camouflage the essentially static character of his equilibrium theory with many wise and penetrating *obiter dicta* on dynamical problems. The distinction between the long period and the short period is a first step towards the theory of a moving system. But now at last, we are . . . on the eve of a new step forward, which, if it is made successfully, will enormously increase the applicability of theory to practice – namely, an advance to an understanding of the detailed behaviour of an economic system which is not in static equilibrium. (JMK, vi, p. 365)

4. Early Contributions I

1. 'for use in the payment of wages and for retail purchases' (1911, p. 395)
2. More precisely Tooke's original idea had not yet been rescued from oblivion. See below, Section 4.3, the crucial contribution by Hawtrey to that rehabilitation of the income approach to the quantity theory.
3. This will eventually become an important stepping-stone in our demonstration that – in the *General Theory* – it is the principle of effective demand and not the liquidity-preference doctrine which is crucial. Or, in other words, that Keynes could hardly have claimed to have 'largely revolutionised . . . the way the world thinks about economic problems' (JMK, xiii, p. 492) if his only contribution to economic theory amounted to emphasise the influence of the speculative demand for money on the rate of interest.

4. Tooke, 1844, p. 123. Including Wicksell, whose monetary theory is a systematic extension of Tooke's '13th thesis' (1935, p. 202; 1936, p. 99), all the other main pre-1918 'income-approach' theorists are Continental: Wagner (1909), Wieser (1909), von Mises (1912) and Schumpeter (1917) being the most prominent. For an history of the 'income approach', together with an exhaustive bibliography, see Marget, 1938, p. 302–43.

5. Hawtrey himself explicitly considers his version of the 'income approach' as 'a form of the quantity theory' (1923, p. 60).

6. In view of the major theoretical developments which took place in Cambridge during the 1920s, it is essential to stress the importance of *Currency and Credit* as *the* standard textbook on money and banking on the Cambridge Economics Tripos Reading Lists together with Fisher's *Purchasing Power of Money* (see E.A.G. Robinson quoted by Hicks, E.A.G 1969, p. 118, Howson, 1978, p. 506, and Davis, 1981, p. 204). On the more specific influence of Hawtrey on Keynes in the early 1920s, Harrod writes that Keynes 'was close in accord . . . with Mr. R. G. Hawtrey on the subject of banking policy and owed much to his writing' (1972, p. 420). In a footnote 14 appended to that quotation, Harrod adds: 'In the autumn of 1922, [Keynes] held Mr. Hawtrey up to me as the best writer on currency and credit.' (See also, for a similar remark, p. 414.) Eventually Keynes himself, in an enthusiastic review of the 1919 edition of *Currency and Credit*, goes as far as to write:

> This is one of the most original and profound treatises on the Theory of money which has appeared for many years. . . .It is a book with some fundamental thought in it, and likely, in my judgement, to exercise a significant influence on future expositions of monetary theory. (1920, p. 362)

Though not strictly speaking a member of the Cambridge School, Hawtrey's lifelong close connection with it and his early widespread influence on its teaching clearly allow us – following Eshag (1963, p. 97) – to consider him as one of the main initiators of the Cambridge saving-investment research programme.

7. Schumpeter goes as far as to link Hawtrey's analysis with the doctrine preached by the all-too-numerous 'monetary' cranks' of the 1920s and 1930s. See Schumpeter, 1927, p. 42 where Hawtrey is put in the same bag as Bellerby (1924); see also Pigou, 1913b, p. 582, and Saulnier, 1938, pp. 21–2, for similar reactions.

8. And that, at least until the publication of Pigou's 1943 'The Classical Stationary State'. See, however, below, n. 10, ch. 8.

9. See Hicks, 1969, pp. 119–20 and Howson, 1978, p. 505.

10. Though less sharply, the effects of a sudden increase of the stock of money are analysed by Hawtrey in precisely the same manner as those of a diminution (1913, pp. 49–50; see also 1926a, p. 422, for stage three).

11. $r_p = r_n$ multiplied by variations of the price-level; or, as Hawtrey puts it himself as late as 1967, in *Incomes and Money*: 'The "natural rate" is the rate of interest that would prevail under stable conditions. The "profit rate" is the natural rate modified to allow for changes in the price-level, that is, the "real rate"' (1967, p. xii).

12. In a slightly different way – the drop in consumers' outlay is no longer due to the introduction of a new government tax, but to an increased propensity to save – the same argument is put forward to Keynes by Hawtrey during their pre-*Treatise* exchange to show that quantity adjustments come before price-adjustments (JMK, xiii, pp. 152–3).

13. Seventeen years later Hawtrey was to criticise Keynes along the same line for the latter's concentration on price-changes only in the *Treatise* framework of analysis (JMK, xiii, pp. 150–1, 165 and 166–7).

14. Hawtrey adopts in fact exactly the same argument as Wicksell (of which he once again knew nothing). The 'cumulative process' is *not* an unstable explosive process (1938, pp. 205–6): the expansion of bank loans ultimately brings about an internal drain in the banking system, which, in turn, forces the banks to raise their rate (Wicksell, 1935, p. 201; 1936, p. 136). On this cash-drain stabilising mechanism in Hawtrey's framework see also Saulnier, 1938, pp. 74–7 and 83, and Davis, 1981, p. 210.

15. There are some analogies between the so-called 'liquidity trap' case Keynes is alluding to in the *General Theory* (JMK, vii, p. 172) and Hawtrey's 'special case'. Both of them depend on *expectations*: high rate of deflation for Hawtrey and low rate of interest for Keynes. Similarly the idea that, in a credit deadlock, traders may use part of their idle balances to buy securities thus adding to the resources of the investment market and lowering further the interest rates somewhat anticipates the 'buckets-in-a-well' argument of Keynes's *Treatise* (below, Chapter 4, Section 4.2).

16. For a detailed technical discussion of Hawtrey's 'incentive theory of Bank rate' see Cramp, 1962, pp. 47–50.

17. Once again, it may not be out of place to recall here that for marginalist economists the notion of *temporary* deviations refers to the nature of the forces at work and *not* to a definite period of calendar time.

18. In the closing chapter of *Good and Bad Trade*, Hawtrey outlines for the first time what became to be known in the 1920s as the *Treasury View*:

> The . . . principle that the Government should add to the effective demand for labour at the time when effective demand of private traders falls off . . . overlook[s] the fact that the Government by the very fact of borrowing for his expenditure is withdrawing from the investment market savings which would otherwise be applied to the creation of capital. (1913, p. 260; see also 1925, p. 104, for a slightly different wording)

The adoption of this position is nothing else but a by-product of Hawtrey's interest theory, and, hence, of his conception of a 'lump-of-saving' pre-existing the investment process. As in Marshall, the causality firmly runs from saving to investment. Thus, and it seems very logical, Hawtrey asserts that any public work undertaken by the Government would simply reduce the size of the 'lump-of-saving' available for private investment. In his 1925 'Public Expenditure and the Demand for Labour', Hawtrey took account of some of the remarks levelled at his 1913 formulation of the 'Treasury View' by Robertson and others. He understood the important 'exception' that a public expenditure policy could work to the extent that people can be induced to shift out of *idle* money-balances into securities (1925, pp. 109–11). But this 'could only occur in exceptional circumstances' (1925, p. 110). However, if in this exceptional case 'additional public expenditure can . . . give additional employment if it increases the rapidity of circulation of money' (1925, p. 111), *the general case still holds good:*

> expenditure on public works, if accompanied by a creation of credit, will give employment. But . . . a creation of credit unaccompanied by any expenditure on public works *would be equally effective in giving employment.* (1925, p. 112, italic added)

Put in a nutshell, public expenditures are not justified because –*given the elasticity of the investment demand curve* – a proper interest/credit policy would be equally effective in raising the level of employment. In other words the whole argument relies entirely on the idea that – barring a 'credit deadlock' which might justify government interventions (1937a, pp. 124–5) – a low bank-rate is all what is needed to revive business investment. What separates Hawtrey's from Robertson's analysis is not Marshall's investment-demand function but the degree of elasticity each of them attributes to that crucial relationship.

19. In various places, but less clearly than Marshall, Hawtrey views the rate of interest as being not only the reward for waiting, but also the measure of the 'loss on idle balances' (1913, p. 12; 1919, pp. 37–8, 40, 110, 188, 217).

20. Another proof that Hawtrey held a primitive version of the loanable funds theory of interest is offered by Robertson. In his 1937 Reply to Keynes's 'Alternative Theories of Interest', the latter points out that his own theory, 'a common sense account of events in terms of supply and demand for loanable funds', is nothing else but an attempt 'to give a rather pedantic precision to the ordinary view enshrined in such well-known studies of the capital and credit markets as those of *Lavington* and *Hawtrey* . . .'. (1937, p. 428; italic added)

21. For a similar argument see Kaldor, 1938, pp. 78–9.

22. In the 'inflationary case' Hawtrey is well aware of the fundamentally different consequences of a drop in interest-rate on an economy with or without unused capacity. When the economy is working at full, or near-full capacity, an increase in the credit supply will raise the *price-level*; if there are unused capacity, similar measures would increase the *volume of output and employment* (1913, pp. 49–50; 1926c, p. 428; compare with Keynes's well-known statement in JMK, vii, p. 296).

23. 'I have adhered consistently to my fundamental ideas since 1913. . . . I do not think this conservatism is a merit; indeed I should rather like to go in for something novel and extravagant if only I could be convinced of it.' (Hawtrey to Keynes, 1937; JMK, xiv, p. 55)

24. The fact that quantity adjustments are present in Hawtrey's stability process does not mean that he can be heralded as a 'neglected precursor' of Keynes's principle of effective demand. This ludicrous claim (see

Davis, 1981, p. 217) probably rests on a confusion between short-run quantity adjustments that are perfectly plausible within the Marshallian interest-theory – trade-cycle framework and changes in output which bring about equality between savings and investment (i.e. Keynes's principle of effective demand). Indeed, it is precisely the distinction made by Keynes around 1932 between these two types of adjustment that marks the crucial turning-point in the whole saving-investment story. But much more about that distinction in Chapter 4 below.

25. Letter from Pigou to Robertson 'dated 1913', quoted by Presley (1979a) p. 10. See also Robertson (1915) p. 212.

26. In the same way the upturn is stimulated by an increase in the marginal utility of capital goods. This characteristic of the upturn therefore guarantees the *inevitability* of the downturn, and vice versa.

27. In that respect Robertson is very close to Schumpeter's 1912 *Theory of Economic Development*, which explains booms and depressions in terms of 'changes in methods of production and transportation, or in changes in industrial organisation, or in the production of new article, or in the opening up of new markets or of new sources of material. *The recurring periods of prosperity of the cyclical movement are the form progress takes in capitalistic society.*' (1927, p. 30)

28. Many other illustrations of the inelasticity of the investment-demand curve can be found in *Industrial Fluctuation*; see, e.g., pp. 60, 211 n. 1, 218, 221, 228, 239.

29. Such a statement echoes that made by Hayek (quoted above, ch. 3, n. 22) on the necessity of using equilibrium analysis to deal with trade-cycle theory.

30. It is no surprise that Robertson's argument displays a somewhat Hayekian flavour. Both Robertson (1915, pp. 4 n. 1 and 171 n. 2) and Hayek (e.g. 1933, pp. 79–80 and 90) refer to Spiethoff and while they were to criticise the latter's so-called non-monetary theory of the cycle, they took over from him the all-important notion of 'shortage of saving'.

31. In a sense, Robertson's interest theory in *Industrial Fluctuation* is exclusively 'real', i.e. is not of the loanable-funds type like in Marshall. Investment *stricto sensu* is adjusted to saving *stricto sensu* via changes in the rate of interest ; or, alternatively, the productivity and thrift factors are the only elements taken into account in the determination of the rate of interest.

32. In 1924 Keynes also held a lump-of-savings theory (Harrod, 1972, pp. 414–15) when he gave for the first time his support to a programme of public works without, however, formally offering a theoretical refutation of the 'Treasury View'. His main idea was in fact 'to bring in the state' to divert from foreign to home investment the exported part of that lump-of-savings badly needed to stimulate the domestic capital market and the level of employment (see below, Section 5.1). It is in 1929 only that he rejected the 'Treasury View' along exactly the *same* line as Robertson did as early as 1915.

33. If it does not, a lowering of the rate of discount is powerless to alter the underlying real forces at work in the economy.

34. Or, alternatively, 'intertemporal equilibrium' understood as an analysis of short-period positions of a market economy *in sequence over time.* Hicks (1946, p. 257 n. 2; 1964, pp. 311–12, and 1965, p. 58) and Hahn (1984, p. 178) are both considering Robertson as their most notable English predecessor in the theory of 'temporary equilibrium'.

35. A similar presentation can be found in Presley (1979a, pp. 102–5). However, the emphasis put on the various steps is different from ours. For an earlier and somewhat different discussion see also Saulnier, 1938, pp. 134–72.

36. It is in *Banking Policy* (chapter v and and its appendix) that Robertson tackled for the first time the fundamental link between money and price theory which is, after all, at the root of the 'forced-saving' process (see below, Section 6.2). The lag of consumers' income behind prices – another way to express 'forced saving' – may be aggravated by wage rigidities for which Robertson gives due acknowledgement to Hawtrey (1913, p. 163, and 1915, p. 218 n. 2).

5. Early Contributions II

1. See JMK, xiii, pp. 2–3 and Robertson, 1915, p. 218. In many respects Fisher appears to be a kind of scapegoat for Robertson and Keynes, who dared not attack Marshall head-on.

2. Incidentally it is interesting to note that Pigou, Robertson and Hawtrey were among the participants at the Political Economy Club meeting at which Keynes read his paper (see *Centenary Volume*, vol. *VI*, 1921, p. 174). Even if the detailed minutes of evidence might reveal a remark from one of them hinting at the idea of forced saving, it would not change the basic fact that the first version of the forced-saving process was to wait another eight years to eventually surface in the first edition of Robertson's *Money* (1922).

3. This ranges from a nearly total absence of reference to wealth (Pigou, Lavington) to an explicit inclusion of this variable in the formal analysis (Marshall, 1923, pp. 44–5; Robertson, 1926, p. 46; Keynes, JMK, iv, p. 64 without, however, understanding the theoretical implications of such an addition to the traditional income determinant of the Cambridge k (see Patinkin, 1974, p. 13). See, however, Kahn's argument (1984, p. 48), according to which Robertson's inclusion of the wealth variable appears only in the second (1928) edition of *Money* and was made under Keynes's influence. If Kahn may be right as far as the first edition of *Money* is concerned, he has, however, neglected the reference given above to *Banking Policy*.

4. An increase in wealth fosters increased holdings of all assets including money, whereas an increased income raises the demand for money only (transaction demand) at the expense of other assets.

5. As E.A.G. Robinson put it in his 1946 Obituary of Keynes:

> In the twenties . . . his pupils . . . thought of him, indeed I suspect that he thought of himself, primarily as one who had in unusual degree the capacity to apply to the economic problems of the day the *corpus* of economic thinking which he had inherited from Marshall. (1946, p. 50)

On the idea that Keynes's policy proposals were often ahead of their theoretical formulations see also E. A. G. Robinson, 1983, pp. 256–7, and Kahn, 1984, pp. 77.

6. Robertson comments rightly on this passage that 'Lavington had better . . . have written "measured by"' (1940, p. 17).

7. According to Wright (1927, p. 504) it was Lavington who coined the saying: 'It's all in Marshall, if you'll only take the trouble to dig it out.' See also Schumpeter's appreciation of Lavington's contribution as 'unconditionally Marshallian' (1954, p. 1084). In his *English Capital Market* Lavington expresses himself in the following way:

> The occasional acknowledgments made . . . to Dr. Marshall and Professor Pigou are a very imperfect recognition of the extent to which I am in their debt. From their writings and teaching are derived most of the general conceptions in the book which are tolerably certain of acceptance. (1921, p. 283).

See also the Preface to *The Trade Cycle* in which Robertson is added to Marshall and Pigou as members 'of a comparatively small group of economists whose interpretations of the very complicated phenomena of cyclical fluctuations seem to me to be most acceptable'. (1922, p. 7)

8. Or what Lavington calls 'the differences in the rates at which waiting and investment proceed' (1921, p. 70). Among other causes for these two rates to differ, Lavington extensively discusses the supply side of the capital market: *risk* (1921, chap. 13), *imperfect knowledge* (1921, chap. 14), the immobility of invested resources (1921, chap. 15). Eventually, the supply price of capital is composed of the 'net rate of interest' (waiting), 'the price of risk-bearing' plus the cost of 'services involved in carrying capital between the two parties concerned' (1921, p. 101).

9. 'The primary influence affecting the annual volume of the stream of investment are evidently those which govern the power and the will to save. . . '. (1921, p. 69).

10. The supply of 'Command over Capital' is made up of 'the quantity of real resources which the public are prepared to transfer to the control of the banks' (i.e. savings *stricto sensu*) and of variations of the money-supply, and particularly bank loans. Clearly, and once again, we have here a loanable-funds theory of interest.

11. Hayek (1935, p. 25 n. 1) is the only theorist of the 1930s to refer to this essay and to appreciate its novelty insofar as Cambridge in the 1920s is concerned.

12. It may be worth underlining once again the fact that the essence of any trade-cycle theory – and Pigou's is no exception – is to deal with

variations of output and employment and not only with price-adjustments (1924, p. 93). However, it must equally be clear that, in this framework economic agents respond to *price* signals only; hence, variations of output and employment can only result from lags, rigidities, inelasticities and other imperfections of the market mechanisms.

13. However, Pigou is careful to make clear that the amount of forced saving extracted from owners of fixed incomes is *less* than proportionate than the volume of additional purchasing power thrown on to the market by businessmen. As a matter of fact the rise in the price-level induces owners of fixed income to reduce *first* their voluntary savings *before* reducing their consumption (1924, p. 111).

14. In fact this piece of analysis is very much reminiscent of Hawtrey's *credit deadlock*. With Hawtrey's wage-rigidity case discussed earlier and this interest-inelastic investment-demand function, we already have in *1924* two (out of three) elements of the 'traditional' neo-classical synthesis of the *General Theory* as epitomised by the *IS–LM* curves.

6. *Banking Policy and the Price Level* and the 'Kinds of Savings'

1. Apart from Moggridge's editorial comments in JMK, xiii, xiv and xxix, see Samuelson, 1963, pp. 519–21; Hicks, 1964, pp. 308–12; Patinkin, 1976, pp. 30–1, 61–3; Presley, 1979a, pp. 75–84 and 216–21; Presley, 1981, pp. 175–6; and Kahn, 1984, pp. 115–16 and 185–8.

2. As Harrod remarked in his biography: 'They had many a long talk, chasing the truth.' (1972, p. 436) Moggridge, in his editorial comments to the Keynes–Robertson correspondence, adds: 'We will never know the full extent of this collaboration, if only because so much was oral and because early drafts do not survive.' (JMK, xiii, p. 29)

3. See, however, Presley, 1979a, pp. 79–81 and 115–16, for a detailed discussion of this early (namely, pre-1930) disagreement between the two men. For a brief comment in the same vein see also Samuelson, 1963, p. 520.

4. 'It was Keynes who *made me* introduce "Induced Lacking"' (letter from Robertson to T. Wilson, 31 Oct 1953, quoted by Presley, 1979a, p. 286 n. 75).

5. Keynes refers only accidentally to induced lacking in the *Treatise* (JMK, v, pp. 154 n., 268–71) after having given it a much more prominent part to play in earlier drafts (see JMK, xiii, pp. 105–6).

6. See, however, Presley, 1979a, pp. 232–35 (and particularly the footnote 58) for a letter by Robertson to Patinkin arguing that some passages of *Banking Policy and the Price Level* (1926, p. 49, and appendix to chapter v) and 'Saving and Hoarding' (1933a, p. 78) 'might have been accounted to me' as performing stability analysis (Robertson quoted in Presley, 1979a, p. 234). Judging from the second edition of *Money, Interest and Prices* (1965, pp. 604–5) Patinkin was not convinced by Robertson's claims.

7. For Keynes's ultimate dismissal of induced lacking as 'too precarious a

source of additional savings to deserve separate notice' see*Treatise* (JMK, v, p. 269).

8. $kY - akY$ = proportion of kY devoted to non-circulating capital purposes, e.g. instrumental capital, government debts, etc. . . .

   $C - bC$ = proportion of circulating capital built up with voluntary savings or self-investment.

9. For a detailed discussion of these two versions of the 'forced-saving' process in the evolution of economic analysis, together with all the relevant bibliographical references see Hayek, 1932c, pp. 183–97; 1935, pp. 1–31; and Viner, 1937, pp. 185–200.

10. At least up until and including the second edition (1935) of *Prices and Production*. Hayek was to recant his position in 1939 in a way making it much similar to Robertson's. The entire discussion of the 'Ricardo Effect' is an attempt to explain crisis by means of a rise in the rate of return on consumer-goods industries relative to capital-goods industries. The result is a theory very close to the Robertsonian concept of the inevitability of crises fostered by recurrent revisions 'of the marginal utility of acquiring capital goods by entrepreneurs'.

11. The part played by *stocks* in Robertson's analysis of the 'forced-saving' process is very small (1926, pp. 82–3). He clearly sees them as acting only as buffers between variations of consumption demand and changes in the level of production. However, the best part of Hawtrey's review article on *Banking Policy* (1926c, pp. 417–23) is a vigorous denial of Robertson's central thesis on the ground of stock availability. In fact, if Hawtrey may be justified to find Robertson's analysis of the role played by stocks insufficient, he is wrong on the analytical issue. If it is true that an increased demand following a rise in the supply of bank-loans may initially reduce stocks rather than raise prices, sooner or later, prices will have to rise to ration out commodities, performing thus 'forced saving'. As a matter of fact the subsequent replenishment of stocks by dealers can only be realised through a rise of the prices charged to, that is by a transfer of real purchasing power from consumers to dealers and ultimately to producers. Clearly this mechanism is nothing else but a more complicated way of stating Robertson's forced-saving argument (see Hawtrey, 1926c, p. 427, and 1928, pp. 128–9). Despite Hawtrey's rather explicit recognition of the validity of Robertson's thesis, he kept repeating over and over again that 'there is no such thing as forced saving' (1937a, p. 253). As late as 1937, and still on the ground of the availability of stocks, he launched exactly the same attack this time in his review of Hayek's version of the 'forced-saving' process (1937a, pp. 251–3).

12. Before 1930 Pigou provided the clearest formulation of the *interest theory* underlying the 'forced saving' process. (In his review of *Banking Policy*, besides a hopeless attempt to actually *measure* the exact amount of 'forced-saving' yielded during a given period (1926, pp. 216–21; 1929, pp. 152–8), Pigou adopted part-and-parcel Robertson's analysis, though with very different aims in mind). Pigou's interest theory calls for three comments. First, it is clear that his version of the loanable-funds theory of interest examines the *flow* of loanable funds made available/asked for

during a given time-period (or Robertson's day). On the supply side this flow is, of course, made up of voluntary savings, net dishoarding and newly created bank-loans (1929, p. 275). Second, 'adjustments in the prices of securities . . . and in the prices of commodities' (1929, p. 276) are the self-defeating consequences of any discrepancy between these two rates (1929, p. 277). Third, and this appears to be the first clear statement of this fact in Cambridge, Pigou explicitly demonstrates that the logical consequence of the 'forced-saving' process is the recognition that changes in the market-rate of interest *do* influence the 'normal' rate of interest and, hence, the rate of accumulation:

> *it is not true that t[he] real rate is determined by conditions wholly outside bankers' control.* (1929, p. 277; italic added)

Clearly 'real' equilibrium magnitudes, unlike in Marshall, can be altered by monetary forces.

7. Saving, Investment and the Theoretical Framework of the Treatise (1930)

1. See JMK, v, pp. 269–70; thus Moggridge appears to be wrong when he argues in his editor's notes that 'Chapter 23 disappeared in late revisions' (JMK, xiii, p. 83).
2. However, and as for Hawtrey, this functional relationship between S and Y does *not* mean in any way whatsoever that Keynes had, in the *Treatise*, grown aware of the theoretical consequences of such an embryonic saving-function.
3. What could be a better anticipation of the liquidity-preference equation of the *General Theory* (JMK, vii, p. 199):

$$`M = M_1 + M_2 = L_1 (Y) + L_2 (r)`?$$

4. In fact this idea is nothing else but what Keynes considered before the *Treatise* as Robertson's and Pigou's 'obstinate misunderstanding' (see above, Section I, and again in JMK, xiii, pp. 225–6). See also Hahn, 1984, p. 295 for a recent reference – though in a slightly different context – to Robertson's 'buckets'.
5. In that respect Durbin is very clear when, in his discussion of the 'Dynamics of Industrial and Financial Circulations', he argues along similar lines:

> The fact is that the Rate of Interest may not be so quantitatively important in the *short-run* as the 'delicate apparatus of marginal analysis' might lead us to suppose. [However], what I am trying to say is perfectly consistent with a normal supply and demand analysis of the capital market; it is not the least inconoclastic. All that I am doing is to give reasons for believing that the market Demand Curve for capital . . . is very inelastic. (1935, pp. 83–4)

6. Hayek rightly complained in his two-part review of the *Treatise* that Keynes's contribution is not 'based on a clear and definite theory of capital and saving' (1931b, p. 278). For a similar and more recent argument see Leijonhufvud, 1981, p. 173. It is true that Keynes's definition of the natural rate of interest is, to say the least, rather cavalier:

> At the equilibrium level [of interest] the demand for savings is equal to the supply and there is no unemployment. (JMK, xx, p. 353; see also pp. 457 and 477–8, and JMK, xiii, p. 254)

To this charge, Keynes no less rightly answered that if he agreed 'with him [i.e. Hayek] that a clear account of the factors determining the natural rate of interest ought to have a place in a completed *Treatise on Money* . . . [his] own ideas about it were still too much in embryo to deserve publication'. (JMK, xiii, p. 253)

In other words Keynes simply tries to convey the fact that: (1) capital theory has not really its place in a narrowly defined treatise on money as his own, and (2) Marshall's capital theory (the only one he knew) underlies implicitly his monetary theory.

7. See, for example, the reference to an 'indefinite prolongation of chronic unemployment' in the chapter on the bank-rate (JMK, v, p. 186) and to the 'chronic unemployment' already alluded to (see JMK, xx, pp. 47, 50, 56–7, 75, 379 and 480).

8. This explanation has been raised for the first time in Milgate, 1982, pp. 167–71.

8. Further Reflections on the Rate of Interest (1930–5)

1. Once again it is important to underline that Keynes's argument does not rest on an assumption about mistaken banking policy. Moreover, it is quite clear that Keynes had at that time no idea about a saving-function; or, more properly speaking this banana-grower parable assumes that the marginal propensity to spend is equal to one so that a decline in output and income cannot reduce the excess of saving over investment.

2. Another way of visualising Robertson's approach would be to consider his idea of quasi-natural rate of interest in terms of the 'length of the short period' already used in our discussion of Keynes's *Treatise*. Even if 'disequilibrium situations' in Keynes's framework, or quasi-natural rates in Robertson's terminology, could drag on for substantial periods of time, the dominant forces at work in the economy guarantee a *tendency* towards a full-employment equilibrium.

3. This difference is simply explained by the absence of a saving-function.

4. A notion which is the cornerstone on which the whole modern non-Walrasian temporary equilibrium theory is built.

5. It may be worth recalling here that such a temporary equilibrium – as opposed to the Marshallian 'normal' long-run position expressed by the

first term of Keynes's fundamental equations – is associated with a stock of capital *not* yielding a uniform return on its supply price.

6. Put in another way, to introduce variations of income as a *co-determinant with the rate of interest* of the saving-function.

7. These remarks made on the *Treatise* galley-proofs eventually appeared in the most elaborate review of these two volumes, included as the sixth chapter of Hawtrey's *Art of Central Banking* (1932, pp. 336–8). In these pages Hawtrey attacks Keynes for his neglect of output variations along the lines he had himself followed as early as 1913 (see above, Chapter 3, Section 2, II).

8. Though less emphatically, Pigou also shared this point of view. See his letter to Keynes in the autumn of 1929 (JMK, xxix, p. 5).

9. In his *Capital and Employment* (1982, pp. 79–81), Milgate looks at Kahn's article from a slightly different angle, but reaches a very similar conclusion.

10. See the letter from Kahn to Patinkin in Patinkin and Leith (eds), 1977, p. 147. See also Patinkin, 1982, pp. 29–30 and 197–99.

11. Incidentally a reduction of the interest-rate and public works are two ways to use 'in times of depression savings [which] are *not* otherwise so applied' (Robertson, 1915, p. 253 n. 1). Thus there is nothing contradictory between the multiplier analysis and the orthodox relationship between saving and investment (see in his 1926, pp. 95–6, Robertson's suggestion of public works as a remedy to an inelastic-investment-demand curve).

12. For a more detailed discussion of that argument see Milgate, 1982, p. 81.

9. The *General Theory* and the Principle of Effective Demand

1. And, unfortunately as well as Friedman, Lucas, Barro, Brunner *et al.* think it is.

2. Which corresponds, as in Marshall's model, to full employment of the labour force.

3. For other formulations of the principle of effective demand see JMK, xxix, p. 106, JMK vii, pp. xxiii, 31, 63–4, 84, 111, 117, 178, 183–4, 339, 375, JMK, xiv, pp. 210, 212, 222, JMK, xiii, p. 550, and JMK, xiv, p. 281.

4. See, e.g., Lerner, 1936, pp. 210–11 and 1938a, pp. 297–305; Ohlin, 1937a, p. 96; Robertson, 1940, pp. 5–6; Wilson, 1949, p. 36. For a contrasted approach see Pasinetti, 1974, p. 45. This interpretation results from a widespread confusion between an *ex-post* identity necessarily true and the hypothesis of constant output (implying a constant volume of investment and a constant marginal prospensity to consume) made by Keynes for expositional reasons (ibid. p. 64).

5. Pasinetti formulates this major characteristic of Keynes's analysis in the following way: 'Total savings are, so to speak, an entirely passive variable, which always turns out to be equal to total investments, whatever the decisions to save may be.' (1974, p. 45) See also Leijonhufvud's discussion of saving as a 'passive variable' (1981, p. 175).

6. For example, an undesigned increment of the stock of unsold goods would correspond to an excess of saving over investment. Ohlin's *ex-post/ex-ante* approach relies on a very similar argument (1937a, p. 101). See JMK, xiii, pp. 599, 604, 611–12, 616, 624 for the passages relevant to Hawtrey's definition of investment in the course of an exchange of letters with Keynes in the autumn of 1935.

7. Conversely, that the excess of saving over investment is measured by an increase of inactive deposits (JMK, xiii, p. 246).

8. Keynes dubbed *neutral* the 'natural' rate of interest which would accidentally 'prevail when output and employment are such that the elasticity of employment as a whole is zero' (ibid. p. 243).

9. See Keynes's references to that characteristic of full employment in the *General Theory* itself (JMK, vii, p. 283); see also JMK, xiv, pp. 58, 71, 104.

10. Scarcity has little meaning in economic theory except in so far as it determines the 'actual' point on the marginal-efficiency-of-capital schedule. However, in that case, Keynes's sentence according to which 'if capital becomes less scarce, the excess yield will diminish' (JMK, vii, p. 213) simply expresses what Keynes tries to refute; namely, that capital has become less *productive*.

11. Moreover, the fact that liquidity preference was *the* foremost theoretical novelty of the *Treatise* excludes its being at the same time the original contribution of the *General Theory* to economic theory. See, however, Hicks, 1937, p. 133, and Patinkin, 1965, p. 374, for two opposite views which clearly reflect the short-run neo-classical approach to the principle of effective demand.

12. On Harrod's being instrumental in deflecting Keynes from more fundamental criticisms of the internal logic of the traditional interest theory see Milgate, 1977, and 1982, pp. 113–22. After reading the Keynes–Harrod correspondence on this question, one cannot escape the feeling that Keynes gave up rather easily to Harrod's argument that 'to convict the classical economists of confusion or circularity within the limitation of their own premises . . . is not essential for your purpose. . . . Such a criticism is bound to seem unfair and I believe it is unfair.' (JMK, xii, p. 546).

13. In fact Milgate has shown quite clearly that more than 60 per cent of the draft chapter 14 of the *General Theory* – and precisely the section devoted to the internal logic of Marshall's interest theory – are absent from the published version. Moreover, Keynes never came back on this line of argument.

14. The rate of marginal efficiency of capital and the rate of interest are not the same thing, though they tend to be equal simply because, when they differ, it pays entrepreneurs to rise/lower the level of activity. (i.e. the volume of investment) in such a way which makes these two rates equal.

15. It is at this point that the liquidity-preference theory of interest reveals most clearly its main weakness. In the long run, since the effects of short-run monetary factors on the rate of interest can be safely ignored, the marginal efficiency of capital will step in again as a determinant of the rate of interest.

16. A slightly different interpretation of liquidity preference due to Hicks (1937, p. 137), Modigliani (1944, p. 193) and brought to a very sophisticated stage by Tobin (1958, pp. 65 and 84) puts forward that the demand for money is not dominated by uncertainties concerning deviations of the actual rates from the conventional rate, but is instead derived from the relative convenience and risk involved in holding wealth in money form. However, the outcome of the approach is very similar to the one discussed in the text. In the longer run the effects which uncertainty and instability might have in the short run are considerably reduced and, without having recourse to the stability of views about a 'normal' rate of interest, this interpretation of liquidity preference attributes a sufficient stability to the demand for money and, hence, to the rate of interest. With such a long-run stable demand for money-function, one may, of course, readily conclude that – barring the 'liquidity trap' case (Mr Keynes's 'special case') in which the demand for money is infinitely elastic with respect to the interest-rate – a fall in money-wages or an increase in the quantity of money will lead to a fall in the rate of interest and foster a tendency of investment to equate full-employment savings (see Robertson, 1940, pp. 25–6, for an earlier discussion of these two interpretations of liquidity preference; see also Kahn, 1954, pp. 72–3).

17. See, *inter alia*, Haley, 1948, pp. 39–44; Shackle, 1961, pp. 222–35, and the whole of chapter 13 in Lutz, 1967, pp. 165–85.

18. It may well be to point here that such an approach is made in terms of *stocks*.

19. For the same argument see Ohlin, 1937b, p. 425.

20. Alternatively 'before the corresponding saving has taken place' (JMK, xiv, p. 207).

21. Most modern commentators would probably agree with that dichotomy between Keynes's claims and what his theory can actually bear (see, e.g., Garegnani, 1978–9, pp. 72–3 and 75–9; Hahn, 1982, pp. x–xi: Johnson, 1961, p. 14; Leijonhufvud, 1981, pp. 169–73; Patinkin, 1976, pp. 99 and 114; Presley, 1979a, p. 183).

22. A clear reference indeed to the 'separability argument'.

23. In other words it means that Keynes's conclusion that the state of long-term expectations is generally steady (ibid. p. 162) is extremely similar, though more detailed with its understanding of the working of the financial markets, to Marshall's treatment of expectations (see above, Chapter 3, Section 4).

24. The writers in question – Marshall, Cassel, Carver, Flux, Taussig and Walras – can hardly be considered as 'classical' economists in the sense usually given today to the Smith–Say–Ricardo–Malthus school. The term 'neo-classical' or better 'marginalist' is clearly more appropriate. Once again (see, e.g., ibid. p. 3 n. 1) Keynes seems to have been victim of his unfortunate habit of bundling up indiscriminately together schools of thought which would mix as well as oil would with water.

Bibliography

AFTALION, A. (1927) *Monnaie, prix et change* (Paris, Sirey).

ARMSTRONG, W. E. (1936) *Saving and Investment* (London, G. Routledge).

ASIMAKOPULOS, A. (1982) 'Keynes' Theory of Effective Demand Revisited', *Australian Economic Papers*, **21**, pp. 18–36.

BAGEHOT, W. (1883) *Lombard Street* (London, Kegan Paul) (1st edn, 1873).

BELLERBY, J. R. (1924) *Control of Credit as a Remedy for Unemployment* (London, P. S. King).

BENASSY, J.-P. (1976) 'Théorie du déséquilibre et fondements micro-économiques de la macroéconomie', *Revue Économique*, **27**, pp. 755–804.

BHARADWAJ, K. (1978) 'The Subversion of Classical Analysis: Alfred Marshall's Early Writing on Value', *Cambridge Journal of Economics*, **2**, pp. 253–71.

— (1983) 'On Effective Demand: Certain Recent Critiques', in Kregel (ed.) (1983) pp. 3–27.

BLAUG, M. (1968) *Economic Theory in Retrospect*, 2nd edn (London, Heinemann (1st edn, 1962).

BLISS, C. (1982) 'Two Views of Macroeconomics', *Oxford Economic Papers*, **34**, pp. 1–12.

CANTILLON, R. (1952) *Essai sur la nature du commerce en général* (1755) (Paris, INED).

CASSEL, G. (1903) *The Nature and Necessity of Interest* (London, Macmillan).

— (1923) *The Theory of Social Economy* (New York, Harcourt & Brace).

CLEMENCE, R. V. (1951) *Essays of J. A. Schumpeter* (Cambridge, Mass., Addison-Wesley).

COLLARD, D. (1981) 'A. C. Pigou, 1877–1959' in O'Brien and Presley (eds) (1981) pp. 105–39.

CORRY, B. A. (1962) *Money, Saving and Investment in English Economics, 1800–1850* (London, Macmillan).

CRAMP, A. B. (1962) *Opinion on Bank Rate, 1822–1860* (London, LSE – G. Bell & Sons).

DAVENPORT, H. J. (1935) *The Economics of Alfred Marshall* (Cornell, Cornell U.P.).

DAVIS, E. G. (1981) 'R. G. Hawtrey, 1879–1975, in O'Brien and Presley (eds) (1981) pp. 203–233.

DESAI, M. (1982) 'The Task of Monetary Theory: The Hayek–Sraffa Debate in a Modern Perspective', in Baranzini, M. (ed.) (1982) *Advances in Economic Theory* (Oxford, Blackwell) pp. 149–70.

DILLARD, D. (1948) *The Economics of John Maynard Keynes* (New York, Prentice-Hall).

DOBB, M. (1937) *Political Economy and Capitalism* (London, Routledge & Kegan Paul).

DURBIN, E. F. M. (1935) *The Problem of Credit Policy* (London, Chapman & Hall).

EATWELL, J. (1979) 'Theories of Value, Output and Employment', in Eatwell and Milgate (eds) (1983) pp. 93–128.

EATWELL, J. and MILGATE M. (eds.) (1983) *Keynes's Economics and the Theory of Value and Distribution* (London, Duckworth).

ELLIS, H. S. (1934) *German Monetary Theory (1905–1933)* (Cambridge, Mass., Harvard U.P.).

ESHAG, E. (1963) *From Marshall to Keynes* (Oxford, Blackwell).

FENDER, J. (1981) *Understanding Keynes. An Analysis of the General Theory* (London, Wheatsheaf Books).

FISHER, I. (1907) *The Rate of Interest* (New York, The Macmillan Co.).

__ (1911) *The Purchasing Power of Money* (New York, The Macmillan Co.).

FOURAKER, L. E. (1958) 'The Cambridge Didactic Style', *Journal of Political Economy*, **66**, pp. 65–73.

GAREGNANI, P. (1970) 'Heterogeneous Capital, the Production Function and the Theory of Distribution', *Review of Economic Studies*, **37**, pp. 407–36.

__ (1976) 'On a Change in the Notion of Equilibrium in recent Work on Value', in M. Brown *et al.*, *Essays in Modern Capital Theory* (Amsterdam, North-Holland, 1976) pp. 25–45.

__ (1978–9). 'Notes on Consumption, Investment and Effective Demand' (1964–5), trans. J. Kregel and I. Steedman, *Cambridge Journal of Economics*, **2**, pp. 335–53, **3**, pp. 63–82.

__ (1979) 'Notes on Consumption, Investment and Effective Demand: A Reply to Joan Robinson', *Cambridge Journal of Economics*, **3**, pp. 181–7.

__ (1983) 'Two Routes to Effective Demand', in Kregel (ed.) (1983) pp. 69–80.

GERBIER, B. (1976) *Alfred Marshall. Théoricien de l'action efficace et critique radical de l'économie pure* (Grenoble, Université des Sciences Sociales).

GRANDMONT, J. M. (1983) *Money and Value. A Reconsideration of Classical and Neoclassical Monetary Theories* (Cambridge/Paris, Cambridge U.P./Maison des Sciences de l'Homme).

HABERLER, G. (1952) *Prosperity and Depression*, 3rd edn (1st edn, 1937) (New York, United Nations).

HAHN, F. H. (1965) 'On some problems of proving the existence of an equilibrium in a monetary economy', as in *Monetary Theory* (R. W. Clower, ed.), (Harmondsworth, Penguin Books, 1969) pp. 191–201.

__ (1982). *Money and Inflation* (Oxford, Blackwell).

__ (1983). 'Comment on Meltzer', in Worswick and Trevithick (eds) (1983) pp. 72–4.

__ (1984) *Equilibrium and Macroeconomics* (Oxford, Blackwell).

HAHN, F. H. and BRECHLING, F. P. R. (1965) *The Theory of Interest Rates* (London, Macmillan).

HALEY, B. F. (1948) 'Value and Distribution', in H. S. Ellis (ed.) *A Survey*

of Contemporary Economics, vol. I (Philadelphia, Blakiston, 1948) pp.
1–48.

HANSEN, A. H. (1953) *A Guide to Keynes* (New York, McGraw-Hill).

HANSSON, B. A. (1982) *The Stockholm School and the Development of
Dynamic Method* (London, Croom Helm).

HARCOURT, G. C. (1972) *Some Cambridge Controversies in the Theory of
Capital* (Cambridge, Cambridge U.P.).

HARROD, R. F. (1972) *The Life of John Maynard Keynes* (1951) (London,
Penguin Books).

HAWTREY, R. G. (1913) *Good and Bad Trade* (London, Longmans).

— (1919) *Currency and Credit* (London, Longmans, Green & Co.).

— (1923) *Currency and Credit*, 2nd edn (London, Longmans, Green & Co.).

— (1925)'Public Expenditure and the Demand for Labour', *Economic
Journal*, **35**, as in Hawtrey (1928) pp. 104–18.

— (1926a) *The Economic Problem* (London, Longmans, Green & Co.).

— (1926b) *Monetary Reconstruction* 2nd edn (1st edn, 1922) (London,
Longmans, Green & Co.).

— (1926c) 'Mr. Robertson on Banking Policy', *Economic Journal*, **36**, pp.
417–33.

— (1928) *Trade and Credit* (London, Longmans).

— (1932) *The Art of Central Banking* (London, Longmans, Green & Co.).

— (1933a) *Trade Depression and the Way Out* (1931) (London, Longmans).

— (1933b) 'Mr. Robertson on "Saving and Hoarding"', *Economic Journal*,
43, pp. 701–8.

— (1935) 'Review of *The Theory of Money and Credit* by L. von Mises',
Economic Journal, **45**, pp. 509–18.

— (1937a) *Capital and Employment* (New York, Longmans, Green & Co.).

— (1937b) 'Alternative Theories of the Rate of Interest. Rejoinder', *Economic Journal*, **47**, pp. 436–43.

— (1938) *A Century of Bank Rate* (London, Longmans, Green & Co.).

— (1967) *Incomes and Money* (London, Longmans).

HAYEK, F. A. (1931a) 'The "Paradox" of Saving' (1929) trans. N. Kaldor
and G. Tugendhat, *Economica*, **11**, as in Hayek (1939) pp. 199–263.

— (1931b and 1932a) 'Reflections on the Pure Theory of Money of Mr. J. M.
Keynes', *Economica*, **11**, pp. 270–95, and **12**, pp. 22–44.

— (1931c) 'A Rejoinder to Mr. Keynes', *Economica*, **11**, pp. 398–403.

— (1932b) 'Money and Capital: A Reply', *Economic Journal*, **42**, pp.
237–49.

— (1932c) 'A Note on the Development of the Doctrine of Forced Saving',
Quarterly Journal of Economics, **47**, as in Hayek (1939) pp. 183–97.

— (1933) *Monetary Theory and the Trade Cycle* (1929) trans. N. Kaldor and
H. M. Crome (London, Cape).

— (1935) *Prices and Production*, 2nd edn (1st edn, 1931) (London, Routledge & Kegan Paul).

— (1939) *Profits, Interest and Investment* (London, Routledge).

HENDERSON, H. D. (1922) *Supply and Demand* (Cambridge, Nisbet and
Cambridge U.P.).

HICKS, J. R. (1935) 'A Suggestion for Simplifying the Theory of Money',
Economica, **2**, as in Hicks (1967) pp. 61–82.

__ (1936) 'Mr. Keynes' Theory of Employment', *Economic Journal*, **46**, pp. 238–53.

__ (1937) 'Mr. Keynes and the Classics: A Suggested Interpretation', *Econometrica*, **5**, as in Hicks (1967) pp. 126–42.

__ (1939) 'Mr Hawtrey on Bank Rate and the Long-term Rate of Interest', *Manchester School*, **10**, pp. 21–37.

__ (1942) 'The Monetary Theory of D. H. Robertson', *Economica*, **9**, pp. 53–7.

__ (1946) *Value and Capital*, 2nd edn (1st edn, 1939) (Oxford, Clarendon Press).

__ (1964) 'Dennis Holme Robertson. 1890–1963', in *Proceedings of the British Academy*, **50**, pp. 305–16.

__ (1965) *Capital and Growth* (Oxford, Clarendon Press).

__ (1967) *Critical Essays in Monetary Theory* (Oxford, Clarendon Press).

__ (1969) 'Hawtrey', *Journal of Money, Credit and Banking*, **1**, as in Hicks (1977) pp. 118–33.

__ (1973) 'Recollections and Documents', *Economica*, **39**, as in Hicks (1977) pp. 134–48.

__ (1977) *Economic Perspectives* (Oxford, Clarendon Press).

HOWSON, S. (1978) 'Monetary Theory and Policy in the 20th Century: the Career of R. G. Hawtrey', *Proceedings of the Seventh International Economic History Congress* (M. Flinn, ed.) (Edinburgh, Edinburgh, U.P., 1978) vol. 2, pp. 505–11.

HUME, D. (1742) 'Of Money', in *Writings in Economics* (London, Nelson) pp. 33–46.

JOHNSON, E. S. and JOHNSON, H. G. (1978) *The Shadow of Keynes. Understanding Keynes, Cambridge and Keynesian Economics* (Oxford, Blackwell).

JOHNSON, H. G. (1951–2) 'Some Cambridge Controversies in Monetary Theory', *Review of Economic Studies*, **19**, pp. 90–104.

__ (1961) 'The General Theory after Twenty-five Years', *American Economic Review*, **51**, pp. 1–17.

JOHNSON, H. G. and NORBAY, A. R. (eds) (1974) *Issues in Monetary Economics* (Oxford, Oxford U.P.).

KAHN, R. F. (1931) 'The Relation of Home Investment to Unemployment', *Economic Journal*, **41**, as in Kahn (1972) pp. 1–7.

__ (1954) 'Some Notes on Liquidity Preference', *Manchester School*, **8**, as in Kahn (1972) pp. 72–96.

__ (1972) *Selected Essays on Employment and Growth* (Cambridge, Cambridge U.P.).

__ (1974) *On Re-Reading Keynes* (London, Oxford U.P.).

__ (1984) *The Making of Keynes' General Theory* (Cambridge, Cambridge U.P.).

KALDOR, N. (1938) 'Hawtrey on Short- and Long-term Investment', *Economica*, **18**, as in Kaldor (1960b) pp. 75–82.

__ (1955–6) 'Alternative Theories of Distribution', *Review of Economic Studies*, **28**, as in Kaldor (1960) pp. 209–36.

__ (1960a) *Essays on Economic Stability and Growth* (London, Duckworth).

__ (1960b) *Essays in Value and Distribution* (London, Duckworth).

KEYNES, J. M. (1911) 'Review of *The Purchasing Power of Money: It*
Determination and Relation to Credit, Interest and Crisis, by I. Fisher'
Economic Journal, **21**, pp. 393–8.
— (1914) 'Review of *Theorie des Geldes und der Umlaufsmittel*, by L. voi
Mises, and of *Geld und Kapital*, by F. Bendixen', *Economic Journal*, **24**
pp. 417–20.
— (1920) 'Review of *Currency and Credit*, by R. G. Hawtrey', *Economi*
Journal, **30**, pp. 362–5.
— (1923) 'Bank Rate and Stability of Prices – A Reply to Critics', *The Natior*
& The Athenaeum, **33**, p. 530.
— (1924a) 'Does Unemployment Need a Drastic Remedy?', *The Nation &*
The Athanaeum, **35**, pp. 235–6.
— (1924b) 'A Drastic Remedy for Unemployment: Reply to Critics', *Th*
Nation & The Athenaeum, **35**, pp. 311–12.
— (1973 – to date) *The Collected Writings of John Maynard Keynes* (London
Macmillan). Abbreviated throughout this study as JMK.
KLEIN, L. R. (1968) *The Keynesian Revolution*, 2nd edn (1st edn, 1954
(London, Macmillan).
KREGEL, J. A. (ed.) (1983) *Distribution, Effective Demand and Interna*
tional Economic Relations (London, Macmillan).
LAVINGTON, F. (1921) *The English Capital Market* (London, Methuen)
— (1922) *The Trade Cycle* (London, P. S. King).
LEIJONHUFVUD, A. (1968) *On Keynesian Economics and the Economic:*
of Keynes (London, Oxford U.P.).
— (1981) *Information and Coordination* (Oxford, Oxford U.P.).
LEKACHMAN, R. (ed.) (1964) *Keynes' General Theory. Report of Three*
Decades (London, Macmillan).
LERNER, A. (1936) 'Mr. Keynes' "General Theory of Employment"', *Inter*
national Labour Review, **34**, as in Lekachman (ed.) (1964) pp. 203–22.
— (1937) 'Capital, Investment and Interest', *Proceedings of the Manchester*
Statistical Society, as in Lerner (1953a) pp. 347–53.
— (1938a) 'Saving equals Investment', *Quarterly Journal of Economics*, **52**
pp. 297–309.
— (1938b) 'Alternative Formulations of the Theory of Interest', *Economic*
Journal, **48**, as in Lerner (1953a) pp. 277–304.
— (1942) 'Employment and Equilibrium: a Review of Professor Pigou':
Book', *Review of Economic Statistics*, **24**, as in Lerner (1953a) pp. 242–59.
— (1944) *The Economics of Control* (New York, The Macmillan Co.).
— (1953a) *Essays in Economic Analysis* (London, Macmillan).
— (1953b) 'On the Marginal Product of Capital and the Marginal Efficiency
of Investment', *Journal of Political Economy*, **61**, pp.1–14.
LESCURE, J. (1913) *Des crises générales et périodiques de surproductior*
(Paris, Rivière).
LUCAS, R. E. (1981) *Studies in Business-cycle Theory* (Cambridge, Mass.
MIT Press).
LUNDBERG, E. (1937) *Studies in the Theory of Economic Expansion* (Nev
York, Kelley reprint, 1955).
LUTZ, F. A. (1967) *The Theory of Interest* (1956), trans. C. Wittich (Chi-
cago, Aldine Publ. Co.).

MCCALLUM, B. T. (1980) 'Hahn's Theoretical Viewpoint on Unemployment: A Comment', *Economica*, **47**, pp. 299–303.
MACFIE, A. L. (1934) *Theories of the Trade Cycle* (London, Macmillan).
MARGET, A. (1938–42) *The Theory of Prices*, in 2 vols (New York, Kelley reprint, 1966).
MARSHALL, A. (1867) 'Money', as in Whitaker (ed.) (1975) vol. 2, pp. 277–8.
__ ('about 1871') 'Essay on Money' as in Whitaker (ed.) (1975) vol. 1, pp. 164–76.
__ (1923) *Money, Credit and Commerce* (London, Macmillan).
__ (1926) *Official Papers*, ed. J. M. Keynes (London, Macmillan).
__ (1961) *The Principles of Economics*, 9th (variorum) edn, ed. C. W. Guillebaud in 2 vols (London, Macmillan) (1st edn, 1890). Unless otherwise stated, all reference are to vol. I: *Text*.
MARSHALL, A. and PALEY, MARY (1879) *The Economics of Industry* (London, Macmillan).
MEADE, J. (1975) 'The Keynesian Revolution', in M. Keynes (ed.) *Essays on John Maynard Keynes* (Cambridge, Cambridge U.P., 1975) pp. 82–8.
MEHTA, G. (1977) *The Structure of the Keynesian Revolution* (London, Macmillan).
MELTZER, A. H. (1981) 'On Keynes's *General Theory*', *Journal of Economic Literature*, **19**, pp. 34–64.
MILGATE, M. (1977) 'Keynes on the "Classical" Theory of Interest', *Cambridge Journal of Economics*, **1**, pp. 307–15.
__ (1979a) 'On the Origin of the Notion of "Intertemporal Equilibrium"', *Economica*, **46**, pp. 1–10.
__ (1982) *Capital and Employment* (London, Academic Press).
__ (1983) 'Keynes and Pigou on the Gold Standard and Monetary Theory', *Contributions to Political Economy*, **2**, pp. 39–48.
MILL, J. S. (1874) *Essays on Some Unsettled Questions of Political Economy*, 2nd edn (1st edn. 1844) (London, Longmans & Green).
__(1909) *Principles of Political Economy*, W. Ashly edn (London, Longmans & Green) (1st edn, 1848).
MINSKY, H. P. (1983) 'Notes on Effective Demand', in Kregel (1983) pp. 43–49.
MISES, L. VON (1934) *The Theory of Money and Credit* (1912), trans. H. E. Batson (London, Routledge & Kegan Paul).
MODIGLIANI, F. (1944) 'Liquidity Preference and the Theory of Interest and Money', *Econometrica*, **12**, as in F. A. Lutz and L. W. Mints (eds) *Readings in Monetary Theory* (London, Allen & Unwin, 1952) pp. 186–239.
MOGGRIDGE, D. E. (1973) 'From the *Treatise* to the *General Theory*: An Exercise in Chronology', *History of Political Economy*, **5**, pp. 72–88.
__ (1976) *Keynes* (London, Fontana Collins).
MYRDAL, G. (1939) *Monetary Equilibrium* (1929) (London, Hodge).
O'BRIEN, D. P. (1981) 'A. Marshall, 1842–1924', in O'Brien and Presley (eds) (1981) pp. 36–71.
O'BRIEN, D. P. and PRESLEY, J. R. (eds) (1981) *Pioneers of Modern Economics in Britain* (London, Macmillan).

OHLIN, B. (1937a) 'Some Notes on the Stockholm Theory of Savings and Investment', *Economic Journal*, **47**, as in G. Haberler (ed.) *Readings in Business Cycle Theory* (Philadelphia, Blakiston, 1944) pp. 87–130.
___ (1937b) 'Alternative Theories of the Rate of Interest. Rejoinder', *Economic Journal*, **47**, pp. 424–7.
OVERSTONE, LORD (1837) *Reflections suggested by a Perusal of Mr. J. Horsley Palmer's Pamphlet on the Causes and Consequences of the Pressure on the Money Market* (London, Richardson).
PARETO, V. (1896–7) *Cours d'économie politique*, in 2 vols (Lausanne, Corbaz).
PASINETTI, L. L. (1974) *Growth and Income Distribution* (Cambridge, Cambridge U.P.).
PATINKIN, D. (1948) 'Price Flexibility and Full Employment', *American Economic Review*, **38**, as in F. A. Lutz and L. W. Mints (eds) *Readings in Monetary Theory* (Philadelphia, Blakiston, 1951) pp. 252–83.
___ (1965) *Money, Interest and Prices*, 2nd edn (New York, Harper & Row) (1st edn, 1956).
___ (1974) 'Keynesian Monetary Theory and the Cambridge School', in H. G. Johnson and A. R. Norbay (1974) pp. 3–30.
___ (1976) *Keynes' Monetary Thought. A Study of its Development* (Durham, N. C. Duke University Press).
___ (1980) 'New Materials on the Development of Keynes' Monetary Thought', *History of Political Economy*, **12**, pp. 1–28.
___ (1982) *Anticipations of the 'General Theory'? and other essays on Keynes* (Chicago, Chicago U.P.).
PATINKIN, D., and LEITH, J. C. (eds) (1977) *Keynes, Cambridge and the General Theory* (London, Macmillan).
PIGOU, A. C. (1912) *Wealth and Welfare* (London, Macmillan).
___ (1913a) *Unemployment* (London, Williams & Norgate).
___ (1913b) 'Review of *Good and Bad Trade* by R. G. Hawtrey', *Economic Journal*, **23**, pp. 580–3.
___ (1917) 'The Exchange Value of Legal-Tender Money', *Quarterly Journal of Economics*, **32**, as in A. C. Pigou (1923) pp. 175–99.
___ (1920) *The Economics of Welfare* (London, Macmillan).
___ (1923) *Essays in Applied Economics* (London, Macmillan).
___ (1924) 'Correctives of the Trade Cycle', in *Is Unemployment Inevitable?* (W. T. Layton, ed.) (London, Macmillan) pp. 91–131.
___ (ed.) (1925) *Memorials of Alfred Marshall* (London, Macmillan).
___ (1926) 'A Contribution to the Theory of Credit', *Economic Journal*, **36**, pp. 215–27.
___ (1929) *Industrial Fluctuations*, 2nd edn (London, Macmillan) (1st edn, 1927).
___ (1933) *Theory of Unemployment* (London, Macmillan).
___ (1936) 'Mr. Keynes' General Theory of Employment, Interest and Money', *Economica*, **3**, pp. 113–32.
___ (1943) 'The Classical Stationary State', *Economic Journal*, **53**, pp. 343–51.
___ (1947) 'Economic Progress in a Stable Environment, *Economica*, **14** as in F. A. Lutz and L. W. Mints (eds) *Readings in Monetary Theory* (Philadelphia, Blakison, 1951) pp. 241–51.

__ (1949a) *Employment and Equilibrium*, 2nd edn (London, Macmillan) (1st edn, 1941).
__ (1949b) *The Veil of Money* (London, Macmillan).
__ (1950) *Keynes's General Theory* (London, Macmillan).
__ (1953) *Alfred Marshall and Current Thought* (London, Macmillan).
PIGOU, A. C. and ROBERTSON, D. H. (1931) *Economic Essays and Addresses* (London, P. S. King & Son).
POLITICAL ECONOMY CLUB (1921) *Centenary Volume* (London, Macmillan).
PRESLEY, J. R. (1979a) *Robertsonian Economics* (London, Macmillan).
__ (1979b) 'Marcel Labordère: A Neglected French Contribution to Trade Cycle Theory', *Kyklos*, **32**, pp. 802–12.
__ (1981) 'D. H. Robertson, 1869–1957', in O'Brien and Presley (1981) pp. 175–233.
PRICE, L. L. (1914) 'Review of *Les Crises périodiques de surproduction*, by A. Aftalion, *Good and Bad Trade*, by R. G. Hawtrey, *Business Cycles*, by W. Mitchell', *Journal of the Royal Statistical Society*, **76**, pp. 217–21.
RICARDO, D. (1951–73) *The Works and Correspondence of David Ricardo*, in 11 vols, ed. P. Sraffa with the collaboration of M. Dobb (Cambridge, Cambridge U.P.).
ROBERTSON, D. H. (1913) 'Review of *Good and Bad Trade*, by R. G. Hawtrey', *Cambridge Review*, **21**, pp. 162–3.
__ (1914a) 'Some Material for a Study of Trade Fluctuations', *Journal of the Royal Statistical Society*, **76**, pp. 159–78.
__ (1914b) 'Review of *Les Crises industrielles en Angleterre*, by M. Tougan-Baranowsky, and of *Les Crises périodiques de surproduction*, by A. Aftalion', *Economic Journal*, **24** pp. 81–9.
__ (1914c) 'Review of *The Cause of Business Depression*, by H. Bilgram and L. F. Levy', *Journal of the Royal Statistical Society*, **76**, pp. 878–9.
__ (1915) *A Study of Industrial Fluctuation* (London, LSE reprint, 1948) (with a new introduction).
__ (1922) *Money* (Cambridge, Nisbet and Cambridge U.P.).
__ (1926) *Banking Policy and the Price Level* (New York, Kelley reprint, 1949) (with a new introduction).
__ (1928a) 'Theories of Banking Policy', *Economica*, **8**, as in Robertson (1940) pp. 39–59.
__ (1928b) *Money*, 2nd edn (Cambridge, Nisbet and Cambridge U.P.).
__ (1931a) 'Wages-Grumbles', as in Robertson (1931c) pp. 36–47.
__ (1931b) 'Mr. Keynes' Theory of Money', *Economic Journal*, **41**, pp. 396–411.
__ (1931c) *Economic Fragments* (London, P. S. King).
__ (1931d) 'The World Slump', as in Pigou and Robertson (1931) pp. 116–38.
__ (1933a) 'Saving and Hoarding', *Economic Journal*, **43**, as in Robertson (1940) pp. 65–82.
__ (1933b) 'Mr. Robertson on "Saving and Hoarding"', *Economic Journal*, **43**, pp. 709–12.
__ (1934) 'Industrial Fluctuation and the Natural Rate of Interest', *Economic Journal*, **44**, as in Robertson (1940) pp. 83–91.
__ (1936) 'Some Notes on Mr. Keynes' General Theory of Employment', *Quarterly Journal of Economics*, **51**, pp. 168–91.

— (1937) 'Alternative Theories of the Rate of Interest. Rejoinder', *Economic Journal*, **47**, pp. 428–36.

— (1938) 'Mr. Keynes and "Finance"', *Economic Journal*, **48**, pp. 314–18 and 555–6.

— (1940) *Essays in Monetary Theory* (London, Staples Press).

— (1948) *Money*, 4th edn (Cambridge, Nisbet and Cambridge U.P.).

— (1951–2) 'Comments on Mr. Johnson's Notes', *Review of Economic Studies*, **19**, pp. 105–10.

— (1957) *Lectures on Economic Principles*, vol. 1 (London, Staples Press).

— (1958) *Lectures on Economic Principles*, vol. 2 (London, Staples Press).

— (1959) *Lectures on Economic Principles*, vol. 3 (London, Staples Press).

ROBINSON, E. A. G. (1946) 'John Maynard Keynes 1883–1946', *Economic Journal*, as in Lekachman (ed.) (1964) pp. 13–86.

— (1983) 'Impressions of Maynard Keynes', in Worswick and Trevithick (eds) (1983) pp. 255–61.

ROBINSON, J. (1933a) 'A Parable on Saving and Investment', *Economica*, **13**, pp. 75–84.

— (1933b) 'The Theory of Money and the Analysis of Output', *Review of Economic Studies*, **1**, as in Robinson (1978) pp. 14–19.

— (1937a) *Essays in the Theory of Employment* (London, Macmillan).

— (1937b) *Introduction to the Theory of Employment* (London, Macmillan).

— (1951) 'The Rate of Interest', *Econometrica*, **19**, as in Robinson (1952) pp 3–30.

— (1952) *The Rate of Interest and Other Essays* (London, Macmillan).

— (1978) *Contributions to Modern Economics* (Oxford, Blackwell).

— (1979) 'Garegnani on Effective Demand', *Cambridge Journal of Economics*, **3** pp. 179–80.

SAMUELSON, P. A. (1963) 'D. H. Robertson (1890–1963)', *Quarterly Journal of Economics*, **77**, pp. 517–36.

SAULNIER, R. (1938) *Contemporary Monetary Theory* (New York, Columbia U.P.).

SCHUMPETER, J. A. (1927) 'The Explanation of the Business Cycle', *Economica*, **7**, as in Clemence (1951) pp. 21–46.

— (1934) *The Theory of Economic Development* (1912) (Cambridge, Mass. Harvard U.P.).

— (1936) 'Review of Keynes's General Theory', *Journal of the American Statistical Association*, **31**, as in Clemence (1951) pp. 153–7.

— (1939) *Business Cycles*, in 2 vols (New York, McGraw-Hill).

— (1954) *History of Economic Analysis* (London, Oxford U.P.).

SHACKLE, G. L. S. (1961) 'Recent Theories Concerning the Nature and the Role of Interest', *Economic Journal*, **71**, pp. 209–54.

— (1967) *The Years of High Theory. Invention and Tradition in Economic Thought, 1926–1939* (Cambridge, Cambridge U.P.).

SHAW, E. S. (1938) 'False Issue in the Interest-theory Controversy', *Quarterly Journal of Economics*, **46**, pp. 838–56.

SKIDELSKY, R. (1983) *John Maynard Keynes, Hopes Betrayed 1883–1920* (London, Macmillan).

SRAFFA, P. (1932a) 'Dr. Hayek on Money and Capital', *Economic Journal*, **42**, pp. 42–53.

— (1932b) 'A Rejoinder', *Economic Journal*, **42**, pp. 249–51.

SRAFFA, P. (1960) *Production of Commodities by Means of Commodities* (Cambridge, Cambridge U.P.).

STIGLER, G. J. (1941) *Production and Distribution Theory* (New York, The Macmillan Co.).

TOBIN, J. (1958) 'Liquidity Preference as Behaviour Toward Risk', *Review of Economic Studies*, **25**, pp. 65–86.

TOOKE, T. (1844) *An Inquiry into the Currency Principle*, 2nd edn (London, Longman, Brown, Green & Longmans) (1st edn, 1844).

TOUGAN-BARANOWSKY, M. (1913) *Les Crises industrielles en Angleterre* (Paris, Giard et Brière).

TOWNSHEND, H. (1937) 'Liquidity-premium and the Theory of Value', *Economic Journal*, **47**, pp. 157–69.

VINER, J. (1937) *Studies in the Theory of International Trade* (London, Allen & Unwin).

WALRAS, L. (1954) *Elements of Pure Economics* (1874–7), trans. W. Jaffé (London, Allen & Unwin).

WEINTRAUB, E. R. (1979) *Microfoundations: The Compatibility of Microeconomics and Macroeconomics* (Cambridge, Cambridge U.P.).

WHITAKER, J. K. (ed.) (1975) *The Early Economic Writings of Alfred Marshall. 1867–1890*, in 2 vols (London, Macmillan).

WICKSELL, K. (1907) 'The Influence of the Rate of Interest on Prices', *Economic Journal* **17**, pp. 213–20.

— (1934–5) *Lectures on Political Economy* (1901–6), in 2 vols (London, Routledge & Kegan Paul).

— (1936) *Interest and Prices* (1898), trans. R. F. Kahn, (London, Macmillan).

WILSON, T. (1949) *Fluctuations in Income and Employment*, 3rd edn (London, Pitman) (1st edn, 1942).

WOLFE, J. N. (1956) 'Marshall and the Trade Cycle', *Oxford Economic Papers*, **8**, pp. 90–101.

WORSWICK, D. and TREVITHICK, J. (eds) (1983) *Keynes and the Modern World*, Proceedings of the Keynes Centenary Conference, King's College (Cambridge, Cambridge U.P.).

WRIGHT, H. (1927) 'Frederick Lavington', *Economic Journal*, **37**, pp. 503–5.

Index